ORDER AGAINST CHAOS

ORDER AGAINST CHAOS

Business Culture and Labor Ideology in America 1880-1915

Sarah Lyons Watts

Contributions in Labor Studies, Number 32

GREENWOOD PRESS
New York • Westport, Connecticut • London

305.562
W35o

Library of Congress Cataloging-in-Publication Data

Watts, Sarah Lyons.
    Order against chaos : business culture and labor ideology in
America, 1880-1915 / Sarah Lyons Watts.
        p.   cm.—(Contributions in labor studies, ISSN 0886-8239 ;
no. 32)
    Includes bibliographical references and index.
    ISBN 0-313-27588-2 (alk. paper)
    1. Working class—United States—History. 2. Corporate culture—
United States—History. I. Title. II. Series.
HD8072.W33   1991
305.5′62′0973—dc20   90-43383

British Library Cataloguing in Publication Data is available.

Library of Congress Catalog Card Number: 90-43383
ISBN: 0-313-27588-2
ISSN: 0886-8239

First published in 1991

Greenwood Press, 88 Post Road West, Westport, CT 06881
An imprint of Greenwood Publishing Group, Inc.

Printed in the United States of America

The paper used in this book complies with the
Permanent Paper Standard issued by the National
Information Standards Organization (Z39.48-1984).

10 9 8 7 6 5 4 3 2 1

for Claire

Contents

Preface

We stand not for capital against labor, but for order against chaos.
James Van Cleave, National Association of Manufacturers,
Proceedings of the Annual Convention, 1908

This book explores the U.S. business elite's cultural and ideological offensive against labor in response to the challenge of working class militancy near the turn of the century. Three case studies, the national debate during and after the Pullman strike of 1894, the labor ideology of modern, science-based management, and the National Association of Manufacturers' anti-union campaign, which began in 1903, examine transformations in the meaning of labor within industrial society in the years between 1880 and 1915. Each of these studies sheds light on a significant aspect of capital's efforts to redefine work, workers, unions, strikes, and violence along lines more conducive to the incorporation of labor into corporate society. Although these studies suggest only a small part of the story of the cultural power of corporations, together they carry important implications for the way the corporate system profoundly shaped notions about labor within industrial society. More importantly, they pose the larger question: how did advanced corporate capitalism contain the social forces it unleashed?

In declaring himself for order against chaos, James Van Cleave as president of the National Association of Manufacturers (NAM) noted a major shift taking place in the U.S. business community's view of labor-capital relations. To all observers in business and manufacturing, even the reluctant NAM, the confrontational style of labor relations was giving way to an inclusive, corporate liberal view. In its struggles against unions and its warnings of impending social warfare, capital had indeed stood against labor. The years 1877 to 1910 witnessed the

emergence of the business community's confrontational and hostile labor ideology, which emphasized the class nature of owners' attempts to fragment,
recombine, discipline, and motivate their workers. By the decade of the 1890s,
capital viewed labor as an antagonist to be met in open social and ideological
warfare. The labor ideology of American business declared the working class
different from, and opposed to, mainstream American values. It separated labor
from republican associations of prestige, value, and honor, claiming these for
itself and branding workers as villains to be coerced into rational, law-abiding
behavior.

In the late nineteenth century, changes in the organization and techniques of
industrial production had profoundly altered the context of the national discussion
concerning labor's role in industrial society. As large manufacturers came to
dominate the U.S. economy, their rationalizing needs prevailed in labor-capital
relations, providing the stimulus for creating alliances of public-labor-business
cooperation. Even as businessmen confronted labor in the workplace, the courts,
and civic arenas, they deemed their workers teachable and trainable and ultimately cognizant of the supposed commonality of their and capital's goals. In
the same logic that fostered notions of "reasonable" versus "unreasonable"
trusts, businessmen encouraged workers to forego "bad unions" for "good
unions," which would willingly comply with the social and economic objectives
of corporate capitalism. In this alleged commonality of corporate liberalism,
America's progressive and corporate-minded businessmen discovered the
grounds for labor's reincorporation into respectable society. The seeming ideological reconciliation of these forces occurred under corporate liberalism as
capital opted for responsibility and cooperation and demanded that labor, too,
forego disruption and honor its obligations to a just and orderly social whole.
Business ideology rejected labor relations that suggested a self-interested, class-
biased fray over profits and workplace control. Instead, capital set itself up as
guarantor of social order against the chaotic forces that would prevent national
progress, primarily represented by unproductive or violent labor activities within
the workplace and in the public sphere. These deliberations over the role of labor
in corporate society in three decades after 1880 represent the formation of a
crucial element of modern political discourse, the labor ideology of American
business.

The labor question emerged as part of a larger public policy debate over the
role of large corporations in national life. As Americans reflected on the impact
of industrialism on republican norms, they were compelled to reassess the responsibilities and relationship of capital and labor. To its critics, who feared the
loss of republican and small producer values in the emergence of industrialism,
the business community responded with a new worldview of corporate organization, a comprehensive liberal vision of society based on responsibility and
cooperation rather than economic chaos and class warfare. Peopled by self-reliant
workers, consumers, professionals, and small and large businessmen vying in a
democratic, meritocratic marketplace, this liberal, evolutionary political econ-

omy fulfilled the republican promise of social opportunity and egalitarianism within national progress. Appropriating the republican language of the virtuous producer, corporate liberals narrowed labor's role to a means of securing order and productivity in this new society. They redefined the moral purpose, social role, and individual obligation and reward for workers in accord with the rationalizing needs of mature industrialism and the social needs of unified corporate society. Thus, corporate liberal society overwhelmed the increasingly irretrievable dream of a broad based society of self-employed producers and proclaimed itself the twentieth-century fulfillment of the legacy of republicanism.

With the rhetoric of science-based corporate liberalism and its inclusive view of labor, businessmen drew an ideological veil over the inequities of labor-capital relations and encouraged workers to work for, not against, the system, which would, in return, fulfill for them the promise of American life. Against this highly productive, rationalized, and rational system, radical labor criticisms could only appear irrational and unpatriotic. How is this extraordinary ideological transformation to be explained? How was the business community able to shift the grounds of the debate to terms where it could more favorably argue its role in the preservation of social order? How did modern labor ideology emerge from the efforts of industrialists to contain seeming chaos in the shops and streets of America?

The emergence of Samuel Gompers and the American Federation of Labor (AFL) as the leading spokesmen for the American labor movement paved the way for the triumph of capital's new definitions of labor. The AFL defined workers in narrowly economic terms determined by their role in production rather than in broader definitions put forward by the Knights of Labor or, later, by Eugene V. Debs that workers were citizens with broad social obligations and political responsibilities. The AFL focused on institutional collective bargaining based on contracts and thus relegated itself to a functional role within the corporate structure. As the AFL position became that of American labor, craft unions accepted employers' definitions of labor, albeit for their own purposes, as a commodity within capitalist production.

Historians have long documented the changes that accompanied the rise of rationalized industrialism, including the revolutions in transportation and urbanization and the growing bureaucratization, professionalization, and secularization of modern society. In the last two decades, they have detailed the intellectual content, the social history, the institutional structure, and the rise and fall of the labor, Populist, Socialist, and reform movements that appeared in opposition to industrialism, emphasizing the relative autonomy of working class culture and its survival strategies against the dominant culture. More recently, historians of corporatism have focused on the social and cultural dimensions of the changes in techniques of industrial production in the late nineteenth century. They have described the emergence of mass society and its consolidation under the ideals and values conducive to capitalist social organization. In the last fifteen years, Alan Trachtenberg, David F. Noble, Martin Sklar, Alfred Chandler, Roland

Marchand, Peter Dobkin Hall, John Kasson, and Burton Bledstein pointed to the social, cultural, economic, structural, managerial, and technological changes after 1880 that allowed the accrual of broad social power to business elites and fostered the emergence of the triumphant business culture of the 1920s. T. J. Jackson Lears has made effective use of the concept of hegemony to analyze the process by which meaning is created and organized in society. Hegemony assumes contesting social forces and emphasizes the struggle of dominant elites and ideologies to make their social power appear necessary and legitimate. Together, these analyses of the national consolidation under capitalist social organization provide the framework for examining the labor ideology of business elites as an integral part of that consolidation.

This project was accomplished with the help of many people. I owe thanks to the librarians and archivists of the Baker Library at the Harvard Business School, the Casteñada Library at the University of Texas, Austin, the Bass Collection in Business History at the University of Oklahoma Library, the Duke University library, the libraries at the University of North Carolina at Chapel Hill, and the Crear and Regenstein Libraries at the University of Chicago. The research and loan librarians at the Wake Forest University library were extremely helpful and thorough in their efforts on my behalf. Lynn Cannon and Elizabeth Higginbotham of the Center for Research on Women at Memphis State University provided professional support and personal friendship that sustained me throughout. I am indebted to Wake Forest University for creating an atmosphere of collegiality and intellectual stimulation in which to work and for the research support and academic leave necessary to finish this project. I greatly appreciate the time many readers have spent examining all or part of the book. Among those whose criticisms have been especially incisive are David W. Noble, Eugene Genovese, T. J. Jackson Lears, Stephen Watts, Henry Reichman, Joseph Hawes, and Robert F. Donahue. In the early stages of this work, Douglas Dowd and David Milton provided crucial support and to them I owe particular thanks. From the work of Raymond Williams I received special inspiration. Most significantly, I am indebted to William K. Meyers whose critical readings and encouragement proved indispensable to the development of these ideas.

ORDER AGAINST CHAOS

Chapter 1

Introduction

Historians now mark the years between 1880 and 1915 as the beginning of mass culture in the United States and its consolidation under the ideals and values of private corporations. As capitalism evolved from its proprietary-competitive form into corporate liberalism, these years witnessed the emergence of basic institutions, the reformulation of American social thought, and the reorientation of political divisions, all part of the maturing process of corporate capitalism and the seeming triumph of commercial activity over older social forms organized around kinship, religion, and tradition. "The leaders of industry are virtually the Captains of the world," claimed National Association of Manufacturers' President David M. Parry, as industrialists extended their influence over government policy and the media, promoting self-consciously "middle class" values in work, family life, neighborhoods, schools, churches, political parties, and after 1900, trade unions. Corporations, Alan Trachtenberg has written, were not simply part of industrialization, but an immense cultural force that taught people to think and act in ways conducive to capitalist social organization.[1] Peter Dobkin Hall argued that for the remainder of the twentieth century corporations furnished the "primary instruments" for "formulating and implementing social policy, and shaping the ideological framework and intellectual instruments through which reality was defined and acted upon."[2]

This study contends that modern American attitudes toward the relationship between labor and capital as well as toward the place industrial labor was to occupy in the corporate state coalesced in the national discourses in public and professional literature spawned by industrial expansion in the decades around the turn of the century. As the nation's businessmen and manufacturers took control of formal workplace authority, they also assumed the social authority to redefine and thus create new meaning and new consciousness out of the language that described and governed the daily relations between themselves and their workers. In the "contested terrain" of national debate over the social value and function of capital and labor, they affirmed the emergence of large-scale, corporate capitalism and proposed answers to the main questions of the day: Who defines progress or the proper direction of the social order? Who defines the quality of individual contributions to it? Who defines job satisfaction or self- and social valuation?

The magnitude and significance of changes in the locus and transmission of cultural authority made the years between 1880 and 1915 critical in the evolution of industrialists' labor ideas. Recognizing new arenas of ideological conflict, manufacturers attacked workers in a battle of ideas and a struggle for public opinion. Seizing the argument over labor issues, they skillfully used the public forum to give their words didactic, coercive authority and persuasive "logic."[3] As nationwide organizations of businessmen arose to meet the charges against concentrated capital made by unionists, Populists, reformers, and socialists, they advanced arguments that asserted the moral and utilitarian value of capital and linked it to civic service, respectability, progress, national honor, and manliness. Conversely, they condemned labor's collective efforts through unions and militancy and accused them of conspiring to destroy the nation from within, thus setting a climate that helped shape public attitudes against workers. Charges and countercharges between workers and their bosses sparked an intense public debate on speakers' platforms, in the nation's press, in popular and professional journals, in schools and colleges, on city streets, and on the shop floors of factories. At stake in the capital-labor discourse were not rhetorical distinctions between selfishness and patriotism or even social conflict and social order, but, as Lawrence Goodwyn put it, "a contest over the underlying cultural values and symbols that would govern political dialogue."[4]

In the new corporate society that emerged at the end of the nineteenth century, the job of factory operative or ordinary laborer came to signify second class citizenship. This had not always been so. In the North, antebellum republicanism had revered the dignity of free labor and placed independent, self-made, property-owning yeomen, artisans, mechanics, and small businessmen at the core of a free, rational, public-spirited society. The traditional work ethic emphasized the evils of idleness and the nobility of all work, itself an obligation to society which provided individual reward and national prosperity. Even then, community leaders disdained profits derived from the "useful arts" and specified that wage work conflicted with republican values, marking, at best, a temporary status on the way to self-employment. In that proto-industrial society, social mobility for white males was realistic, the distinctions between capital and labor remained relatively blurred, and government was conducted by men of wealth, learning, and respectability. Businessmen seemed content to let ministers, jurists, educators, and moralists promote the common interests among workers and owners and espouse the republican promise.[5]

After 1877, however, the growth of industrialism and urbanization together with corporate centralization, rapid demographic expansion, international involvement, and economic instability culminated in the dramatic social reorganization of American society and the fruition of a new American culture of capitalism. While free labor, the work ethic, and the promise of rags to riches remained articles of popular faith, the factory system reduced chances for property ownership, and a more or less permanent wage-earning class emerged in the nation's largest cities and mining districts. At the same time, businessmen and managers who organized and profited from labor within the useful arts became the most admired social types. Society's conceptions about the proper relationships of labor and capital were reinterpreted to include new relations and distinctions between property ownership and the labor that made capital possible. As these distinctions increasingly appeared along class lines, Americans began to view industrial warfare between owners and workers as social disorder and the betrayal of republicanism.

Violent confrontation between labor and capital in the latter decades of the century accelerated and shaped social and cultural change. A litany of protest and criticism arose from people squeezed in the hierarchy of control, the centralization of power, and the bureaucratization of command that accompanied the growth of technological industrial society. From the strikes of 1877, the agrarian and labor protests of the 1880s and 1890s, the spectacular growth of union membership and the dramatic spread of strike activity between 1899 and 1905, workers and farmers sustained three decades of resistance, focusing class antagonism and polarizing the public debate with penetrating and disturbing questions about the role of smallholders, artisans, and ordinary workers within industrial society.

Faced with these challenges, energized by the coalescing strength of corporate consolidation and by the technological and managerial demands of efficient production, many of the nation's manufacturers united in their perception of the common enemy and began to reformulate their attitudes toward workers. Exploring the suasive and coercive possibilities of public discourse, businessmen and manufacturers seized and expanded their roles as moral instructors as they recognized the growing inadequacy of more traditional social authorities. "We have been too much inclined to hold a few half starved clergymen chiefly responsible for the moral culture of the masses," charged an *Atlantic Monthly* editorialist in 1878, "capital must protect itself by organized activities for a new object—the education of the people.'"[6] By the turn of the century, many industrial leaders recognized that within their lifetime, urbanization and the concentration of industrial processes had magnified the domain of public life and released the forces of mass society, mass culture, and mass politics, thereby offering new opportunities to develop ideas as tools of social instruction. "While the industrial era has brought new problems of social government," the NAM's David Parry explained in 1906, "it has also fortunately supplied the means for their solution. The dissemination of knowledge is one of the wonders of the age. The minds of men are being constantly broadened, and in this fact lies the hope for the correct solution of industrial questions.''[7]

Editorialists for the nation's newspapers and journals anticipated modern propaganda tactics as they joined manufacturers to seek Parry's "correct solution" by advocating the distribution among workers of "small, low priced books [and] newspapers" to teach norms of "political economy" in a manner simple enough as not to "perplex the brains of workingmen." An *Atlantic Monthly* writer recognized the "persuasive power of public speaking, lecturing, and preaching" when presented simply and repetitively, as the minds of men "are swayed and decided by the continuity of attack, by the cumulative force of the constant iteration of the same idea in varying forms.''[8] In the numerous trade and industrial journals that appeared after 1880, articles such as "How to Handle Men" supplied manufacturers with modern strategies for "meeting and managing, directing and controlling, inspiring and enthusing all sorts and dispositions of human nature." Labor made "thus intelligent," predicted Dexter Hawkins of the New York Association for the Protection of American Industry, "will harmonize itself with capital.''[9]

Armed with such tactical skills, manufacturers and businessmen confronted workers in a struggle for the social authority to appropriate the language of labor republicanism and redefine the republican promise. The history of capital's efforts in this confrontation is best understood in the broad, ideological context of national myths or popular beliefs through which Americans made meaning out of their world. In the late nineteenth century, capital focused on the language of republicanism to illuminate and justify its positions and vilify its enemies. Assaulting working class culture in the nation's cities and towns, manufacturers searched for new ways to organize and control the habits, thinking, and communities of factory workers. The very act of discrediting premodern work habits, resisting strike demands, or adopting modern management techniques spurred manufacturers to redefine traditional meanings of rights, obligations, security, work, workers, unions, wages, strikes, and violence. As the specter of the dangerous classes arose, workers garnered the blame in the popular press for a degeneration of republican virtue, for having betrayed traditions of diligence and deference, and for breaking the connection between work and morality. An entire generation of workers who considered themselves the true upholders of the republican tradition found themselves branded unAmerican, subversive, and even unscientific. In business rhetoric, the term *labor* increasingly signified merely a large unwashed class of dependent, selfish wage earners, rather than the broader antebellum definition of a public-spirited citizenry of small freeholders, shopkeepers, laborers, and artisans. Picturing labor as a natural opposite to capital, businessmen acknowledged an open conflict of class interests, what everyone had come to call industrial warfare. By 1915, the rhetoric of the business elite had transformed the republican ideal of labor into praise of the social contributions of business and condemnation of workers' disruption of the social order.[10]

Manufacturers' new definitions of *labor* necessarily derived from, and were sustained by, the increasingly common assumptions of industrial society at the turn of the century: the value of competition and profit seeking, the need for rising productivity, the benefits of efficiency, and the value of organizing and disciplining work. By World War I, manufacturers' labor terminology had become an integral factor in convincing many workers to accept "modern" work patterns and a belief system that secured compliance with faster paced and more systematized work. In describing this process, historians have provided dramatic insight into the culture of common working people, demonstrating how resistance to new work forms shaped their lives and made bourgeois culture anything but directly "received" or imposed.[11] Yet working class culture did not develop in a vacuum. It must be understood as a process of resistance and accommodation that took place under the influence of manufacturers bent on changing their employees' thinking and behavior. "We mould men while we make commodities," proclaimed James Emery, the NAM's general counsel, summarizing capital's strategy in the struggle against labor's habits and values.[12]

Structural changes in the nation's information flow, such as newly centralized communication technologies, magnified the transmission and range of business ideas and correspondingly left workers less opportunity to claim public sympathy for their plight. Having ownership of, and greater access to, the increasingly hierarchical channels of mass communication, such as large urban dailies and the telegraph, employers' version of "truth" proved increasingly difficult to challenge in the media. By contrast, workers' responses to employers' charges most often appeared in trade union publications that lacked a mass audience.

The new forms of factory work organization demoted many skilled artisans and mechanics to a status a bit above that of specialized operatives and settled wage scales to a point that decreased precipitously any hopes for the promised fruits of diligence—property ownership and economic independence. By its sheer scale and imposing patterns of systematization, standardization, and centralization, the modern factory minimized the work roles of skilled mechanics, a process that left little space for artisanship, "brainwork," creativity, individual expression, or the social rewards that these attributes had brought in preindustrial times. Skilled workers seldom owned tools, controlled time, or planned jobs in modern workplaces sanitized of most traditional social functions save production. As workers' concerted efforts to control work were forced underground, they found outward compliance increasingly built into the modern factory's highly organized and routinized work patterns.[13] Little but rhetoric remained as the payoff for virtuous hard work or the promise of economic democracy. America's wage earning men and women had been demoted from the ranks of aspiring republican property owners to the pool of wage labor.

Equally powerful, if more subtle changes accompanied the new social relations of industrial society, directly and inextricably involving workers and bosses in a complex relationship of obligations that compelled ritualized cooperative behavior. The factory whistle, the clock tower, the rewards and penalties of hiring and firing, promotions and raises—all implied a rendering of reciprocal benefits and duties within an unequal power relationship. Such symbolic and ceremonial exercises of power visibly reproduced the factory hierarchy. Long lines at the hiring window, blacklists, yellow-dog contracts, injunctions, and even the wage contract itself affirmed employers' authority in a buyer's labor market and far surpassed the actual physical coercion these instruments effected. Factory workers vividly described these new relationships with metaphors of domination. Conveyer belt workers, for example, recounted "work on the chain," calculated "to evoke in the minds of their hearts the idea of a convict worker with a symbolic ball chained to his foot." By the 1920s workers could complain, "we have to follow the chain, and often when timekeepers see we are keeping up with it, they *shorten the links*, so that we have to work much faster."[14] The new work discipline "rationalized" workers' ideas and values toward more "modern" definitions of work, wages, and organization; it intensified the hierarchy of authority between employees and employers; it moved complete knowledge of the work process from workers to managers; it deskilled work; and, consequently, it helped lower workers' social value in the public eye.

Although Americans continued to use the traditional language of individualism and the dignity of labor to describe these changed work relations and aspirations, after 1877 the accelerating transition to industrial work patterns prompted businessmen to develop a specialized vocabulary, which defined the relationship of workers to specific tools, usages, technologies, payments, units of time, and the larger institutional framework of shop, union, factory, industry, society, and indeed the entire economic system. Developing a new vocabulary alongside the old, employers and their scientifically trained managers transformed and reshaped the language and perceptions that described capital and labor, ownership and wage work, individual effort, as well as the relationship of public and private endeavor. In short, a new "reality" emerged describing the fundamental relationships of the political and moral economy of the times. By the early twentieth century, techniques integral to scientific management (a) made the new labor vocabulary fundamental to understanding and executing more heavily supervised, subdivided, and disciplined industrial work tasks; (b) used the legitimacy of scientific experts to seek workers' "willing" participation; and (c) urged workers to internalize the new vocabulary and work habits through appeals to self-interest. Minimizing the use of force, these methods were at once more subtle, public, superficially noncoercive, cheaper, and far more effective than driving floor bosses or federal troops.

The everyday material requirements of production sustained the increasingly professionalized language of management and control. Indeed, the politics and techniques of labor control and the language of labor definition are closely connected. By substituting terms like *increased efficiency* for what many workers termed *exploitation*, and *increased productivity* for *speed-up*, or *right-thinking individuals* for *scabs*, and giving wage incentives to "rate busters," the new vocabulary sanitized the implicit criticism inherent in workers' own terminology under the protective rubric of efficiency and scientific progress. By emphasizing the distinction between 'brain work'' and ''hand work,'' one reserved for planners and managers and the other relegated to ''labor,'' scientific management and other new forms of work organization demeaned those who were no longer required to think on the job, thereby repudiating republican definitions of work that did not draw these distinctions.

The economies of scale brought by the factory system reinforced some of the old notions about work and workers, omitted others, and added still others. Diligence, of course, remained central to the worker's task, even as the task changed to routinized, semi-skilled machine tending or repetitive, one step functions scarcely identifiable with the finished product. But managers began to call diligence ''discipline'' and urged it on with the new ''inner compulsion'' of factory time and fast paced work exacted by clocks and orchestrated by an anonymous managerial elite in a hierarchical, systematized machine. In the antebellum world, an individual who worked diligently earned the social distinction of virtue through hard but freely chosen work. In the rationalized factory system, especially where assembly line speed or scientific managers determined the pace, one had less choice about having to keep up. Thus, the modern factory rather than the individual made diligence and hard work no longer moral choices but externally imposed economic obligations.

Such immense changes in the forms of production and management and the corresponding birth of a new symbolic language describing these activities transformed the term *labor* in the public eye. Labor, to antebellum Northern society, did not define a class of people or characterize the activity of the wage worker. Instead, as Eric Foner noted, it represented a classless definition encompassing small businessmen, farmers, and craftsmen, as well as ordinary workers. The ideal goal of work was to accumulate enough capital to obtain a business for oneself, not for the purpose of achieving wealth, but for economic independence. A degree of integration of ownership and work occurred in the small shops and manufactories of pre-industrial America where artisans, handcrafters, and cottage producers often had daily, face-to-face social interaction, where discipline was casual, and productivity not entirely geared to profit maximization and cost efficiency. By the advent of a mature industrial society later in the century, the term *labor* had come to denote a distinct class of wage workers, separated by the growth of workers' neighborhoods, widened by the ''alien'' ways of immigrants, and distanced by the growing inequities of economic distribution. In the context of rising national power and progress, borne on the administrative power of a bureaucratized technocracy and spurred by the fruition of bourgeois cultural power that turned material gain to its own advantage, labor became isolated and targeted as one of the main barriers to efficient industrial production and conduct of the good society. The factory system eroded the virtuousness that had automatically accompanied work, reducing ordinary factory work to an activity that a relatively homogeneous Anglo-Saxon middle class increasingly abandoned to immigrants and blacks.

Even the popular rhetoric of work developed new forms in the late nineteenth century. It became clear to writers of success literature, for example, that industrialization had created a society in which diligence and hard work would not necessarily guarantee anything. In Horatio Alger novels, it took pure luck and patronage, not just good habits, to boost an aspiring youth out of the factory into worldly success.[15] Self-help literature continued to give lessons in good character and hard work, but it concentrated increasingly on the bureaucratic and managerial level and ignored the factory wage earners who were no longer candidates for mobility, even in fiction. Despite its "democratic logic," which disguised the narrowness of opportunity, success literature targeted white collar sons of the middle class, reflecting what most of society had come to accept, as did John Mitchell in 1903, that the average wage earner "must remain a wage earner" and give up the "hope of the kingdom to come, when he himself will be a capitalist."[16] If Americans openly continued to believe in mobility, they also secretly knew it was more and more denied to the bulk of the factory wage force.

It is important to understand the national climate of criticism in the late nineteenth century that denounced capital's excesses but that also helped shape businessmen's and manufacturers' thinking about proper social relationships within capitalism. Arguing that the Jacksonian democratic promise of political equality could be sustained only through economic equality, unionists, Populists, socialists, and anarchists posed a broad spectrum of demands, which called upon leaders of industrial society to recognize their own traditional social obligation and moral responsibility and agree to more equitable definitions of the good society. Their collective responses were inspired by the original promise of republicanism as well as various visions of utopian worlds without special privilege wherein everyone produced and nobody lived off the labor of others. Calling for the radical restructuring of society, the redistribution of wealth, the recognition of unions, workers' welfare, and even the complete elimination of capitalism, each of these movements offered specific criticisms of corporate capitalism.

A protest movement based in the staple crop agricultural and mining sectors in the late nineteenth century, populism arose from the social strains of rapid industrial expansion, the commercialization of agriculture, and the consequent decline and marginalization of rural America, developments that seemed to benefit unduly the manufacturers, businessmen, and financiers at the top of the pyramid of economic concentration. An amalgam of Western wheat and Southern cotton farmers hindered by rising costs and falling prices joined with inflationists, debtors, and anti-monopolists in a cooperative crusade against a "conspiracy of monopolists." Populists portrayed bankers and large-scale manufacturers as selfish, corrupt financial manipulators who profited at the people's expense by controlling freight rates and market prices, maintaining a high protective tariff, deflating currency, and stealing from shareholders through stock watering. Populism's dramatic images pitted small producers against nonproducers, the virtuous against social parasites, "the people" against "the great trusts and combinations."[17]

Populist remedies envisioned revolutionary changes in the nation's political and economic life. Rather than reject modern industrial society, they embraced its promise but called for a more equitable distribution of its opportunity and wealth. Confronting corporate "money power" in an "intense democratic effort" to force a restructuring of the nation's financial, monetary, and banking systems, they organized cooperatives and planned for mutual aid and insurance, the subtreasury system, and government ownership of railroads, banks, utilities, and lands. Greenbackers and inflationists challenged the financiers' control of the nation's banking and monetary systems, arguing for a continually expanding money supply to bolster prices and ease credit.

Beginning with the great strikes of 1877, worker militancy produced cooperative organizations that directly threatened industrial concentration, monopoly, and special privilege through wage and hour demands, workers' control, sabotage, calls for workplace democracy, and demands that industrialists share more equitably the fruits of labor. As the number of industrial workers had quadrupled between 1860 and 1890 to over 3 million, craft unions grew in trades where skilled workers could harness their bargaining power. The Knights of Labor represented a remarkable and visionary approach to organization. Founded in 1869, the Knights' utopian vision of a cooperative commonwealth of producers promised to emancipate labor from the grip of monopolists through collective ownership of businesses and factories. Organized as a large nationwide union of skilled and unskilled workers, enrolling blacks, women, and immigrants, the Knights' program rejected the permanency of wage servitude and affirmed a labor theory of value wherein each worker received a just proportion of the wealth he or she created. The Knights defied the dominant culture of individualism, competition, and acquisitiveness, and promoted the traditional values of cooperation and commonwealth. A series of strikes after 1884 boosted membership to 700,000 in 1886. But a weak administrative structure, internal jurisdictional disputes, lack of strike funds, and most important, the backlash against radicalism after the Haymarket bombing and the failure of the Great Southwest Railroad Strike of 1886 cut the Knights' membership to 100,000 by 1892.

American Federation of Labor pragmatism emerged after 1886 as the dominant form of labor organization and working class action in the United States. Groups of tightly organized skilled craftsmen accepted the permanence of wage labor within the corporate state, gave up visions of a society without privilege, abandoned hopes for broad organization of all producers, and formally rejected socialism in favor of a dogged realism focused on narrower, more palpable benefits for a small sector of the workforce. No longer seeking to overturn the system, AFL leadership exhorted member locals to find economic justice within capitalism, avoid sympathy strikes, forego independent political activity, and honor contracts. The goal became equitable treatment within industrial society, not

revolution against it. The AFL nevertheless reminded Americans of the contradiction between the rhetoric of promising just rewards for hard work and the
reality of the lives of ordinary skilled and semi-skilled workers. Within this more
focused organization, AFL member unions created solidarity and social identity
among members of a craft and attempted through closed shops to provide job
security and ensure craft standards. They publicly affirmed the mutualistic values
of cooperation, solidarity, and equality among members and repudiated the
aggressive materialism and individualism of the age. By 1915, the AFL organized
2.5 million tradespeople, or approximately 8 percent of the workforce.[18]

With the formation of the Socialist Labor party in 1877 and the Socialist party
in 1901, socialism in America evolved into a broad-based radical political movement. Although rank and file radicalism continued in the labor movement even
within the AFL, radical unions had been marginalized, nullified, or destroyed
by 1910. Socialists, who represented at times as much as 40 percent of the vote
at AFL meetings, had no trade union base themselves. Having undertaken a
direct political challenge of the established order, the Socialist party's membership in 1912 of 112,000 represented the high point of socialism in the United
States and appears even more significant in the context of an increasingly individualistic and acquisitive culture. The great appeal of socialism, especially
in the person of Eugene Debs, lay in its defense of the still esteemed preindustrial
values of America—democracy, equality of opportunity, the rights and obligations of citizenship—all in opposition to the rise of the corporate industrial state.
Debs and the Socialists fought to relocate America's cultural symbols within the
ideal of the "workers' republic." Couched in the language of democratic egalitarianism, socialist dissent reasserted the historically patriotic quality of a critique of class relations.[19]

The major protest strikes of the industrializing period called into question
whether the basic democratic promise of American life was being fulfilled for
the nation's workers. The eight hour movement had gained wide popularity
among workers by 1886, prompting twice as many strikes that year as in any
other to date. From the Chicago, Burlington, and Quincy strike in 1888 to the
founding of the Industrial Workers of the World (IWW) in 1905 and through
the postwar strikes of 1919–1921, the nation's workers sustained three decades
of protest, which profoundly shaped businessmen's strategies in response to
labor's demands. Seeking union recognition, better pay, and decent working
conditions, the famous strikes of the 1890s, most notably Coeur d'Alene, Homestead, Pullman, and coal miners in 1897, fixed the nation's attention on the
demands and tactics of strikers and employers alike. Boosted by dramatically
increased union memberships, strikes intensified after the turn of the century,
with the decade of 1900 witnessing struggles by steelworkers and machinists in
1901, anthracite miners in 1902, textile workers in 1903 and 1904, meat packers
in 1905, and garment workers in 1909, all sustaining working men and women's
critiques and calling for a reorganization of society. The common factor in
historical accounts of these great strikes and thousands of lesser ones is that they

were often discredited in the public eye. Espousing a remarkably similar body of arguments, businessmen and manufacturers, as well as the much of the nation's press, castigated labor for having disrupted social order and praised business for promoting efficiency, progress, social order, and American patriotism.

How did capital enter the great social debate that raged at the turn of the century, meet the criticisms put forth by socialists, unionists, and populists, overcome its image as the parasitical corrupt money power, and mount a counterattack against its class adversaries? On an ideological level, businessmen had to overcome the negative image inherited from the republican and Jacksonian eras that pictured bankers, speculators, and the idle rich as parasites living off the efforts of honest men. At the same time they wished to restore a republican era politics of deference, which had established national leadership by a natural aristrocracy of wealth, learning, respectability, and honor, dedicated to selfless public service. Jacksonian politicians had modified and in some ways rejected political deference with demands for political and social equality and for equal participation by the common man in governance. Through the 1830s, as republican politics of deference gave way to the Jacksonian call for egalitarianism, political leaders and national elites continued to speak in classical republican terms while at the same time acknowledging the Jacksonian challenge with rhetorical doses of egalitarianism, a recognition of the growing tension between ideals of virtue and the public good versus the social strains of capitalist expansion. Jacksonians created liberal party politics, a system based on competition for office between free individuals who disparaged, at least publicly, traditional political power derived from family wealth. Speaking for ''the people'' as they assaulted the political and class privileges, the monopolies and banks of the aristocratic and wealthy, Jacksonian politicians actually affirmed rather than challenged capitalist values. They merely represented men of more recent wealth, building a political party based more upon wealth and notions of bourgeois virtue than honor, reputation, or family connections. Thus, the antebellum republican politics of deference was transformed after the war into liberal republicanism, that acknowledged the new ''virtues'' of materialism and acquisitiveness and incorporated bourgeois liberal concepts of property, markets, wages, and labor into evolving definitions of the American promise.[20]

After the Civil War, the survival of the ideal of equality was called into question by the growth of the national market and increased participation in market activities, factors which together had greatly altered the distribution of wealth, fostered the growth of innumerable social evils, and brought questions of class politics to the fore. Populists, socialists, and unionists insisted that political and social equality was inextricably linked with economic equity, and based their critique of modern capitalism on its inequities. Thus, while new national elites had to reaffirm traditional democratic ideas of individualism, self-reliance, and free enterprise, they also needed to reconcile these with the growing scientific and technological demands for stability, predictability, and efficiency in production and distribution, and especially for order within the workplace.

To reconcile the apparent contradiction between traditional values and new imperatives, businessmen proposed a new classless corporate social order based on class-neutral progress and scientific technology but controlled by private corporations. Within this, they asserted new moral ground for themselves and altered traditional definitions of the social role of labor and capital to fit the new order.[21] The rapid and profound material changes that industrialization brought to American society made easier the task of posing a new social order based on the pursuit of individual wealth. The rise of corporatism in business, the centralization of cultural authority, and the emergence of a more tightly structured society necessarily altered cultural perceptions, bringing to the fore energetic visions of efficiency and social betterment through scientific progress.[22] As the business elite formulated its definitions of the new corporate liberal order, it drew upon, and finally adopted as its own, the new vision of progress.

Business' reaction to the Populist revolt furnished an example of its attempt after the Civil War to garner political support for the new order or, failing that, to silence its critics. The first significant effort of the business elite to consolidate political power involved the struggle in 1896 with popular forces represented in the Democratic party over which interests were to provide leadership, determine fair economic distribution, define the national good, and fulfill the promise of the nation's democratic and republican forbears. The Republican campaign in 1896 presented a new political form to the nation, what Lawrence Goodwyn termed "aggressive corporate politics in a mass society."[23] With Mark Hanna's financing of William McKinley's victory over the combined Populist and Democratic parties, big business sponsored "American's first concentrated mass advertising campaign aimed at organizing the minds of the American people on the subject of political power, who should have it and why."[24] That campaign argued that William Bryan, the Populists, and the silverites threatened the "very foundations of the capitalist system." Picturing the election's issues in grand symbolic terms, the themes of the Republican campaign posed to the nation's voters Hanna's "progressive society" of peace, progress, patriotism, and prosperity in stark contrast to the Democrats' threat to dismantle the financial system and bring chaos and economic ruin. During the election campaign, Republican political rhetoric so assaulted the "immorality" of inflated money that the term "greenback" became "actually inadmissible," while the gold standard acquired the morality of sound money.[25] In direct response to Bryan's call for the free coinage of silver, Republicans distributed American flags, sponsored Flag Day spectacles, and started Sound Money Clubs to symbolize the connection between the preservation of the gold standard and the very survival of the American nation.

The Republicans had become the unapologetic party of business that, having abandoned blacks, Catholics, and foreigners, campaigned in 1896 against a Democrat speaking for "the people." The Republican party no longer saw a need to actively seek any but white Protestant Yankee support, done easily enough by denouncing revolution and anarchy in the guise of Populist resistance and using patriotic stereotypes from the Civil War to maintain its constituency.

Republican notions of the "progressive society" became more narrowly conceived within the scope of enterprise and progress, closing the arena of permissible debate and ultimately pushing the most challenging Populist issues outside accepted political discourse.

The demise of the Populists silenced a powerful national voice that had asked the market to function fairly in the interests of small producers in the name of economic democracy. With this silence, Goodwyn wrote, "the idea of substantial democratic influence over the nation's financial system passed out of political dialogue," surrendering descriptions and definitions of the new capitalist political economy to the capitalists. Citizens became "culturally intimidated . . . so that some matters of public discussion pass[ed] out of public discussion."[26] They settled into an "acquiescence" and a "settled resignation" that at once reasserted the politics of deference, reaffirmed elites as the cultural heirs of received patterns of political deference, and signalled the triumph of the nation's elites in the political and ideological confrontation of 1896.

Populism represented the nation's last significant political challenge to the new economic order of industrial capitalism. In the Republican victory of 1896, won in part through the support of urban labor, national elites understood that for their system to survive, it had to be flexible enough to make good on at least some of society's promises to debtors and farmers. In defeat, the Populists' economic analysis lost public legitimacy, discredited by Republicans' arguments for sound money, the American flag, and national prosperity. Republican rhetoric in the 1896 fray initiated a political pattern for the future which, joined with the rhetorical denigrations of strikes and socialism, encouraged a politics of denunciation rather than engagement. Rather than listen and effectively respond to their critics, businessmen shifted the ground of the debate from their protagonists' calls for moral economy to couch it in terms of the search for efficiency, the application of scientific technology, and the freedom of the individual, all of which would ensure the coming of the utopian future. Even more, capital wrapped the language of this defense in a cloak of American eulogisms that by default branded detractors as social misfits.

The work of Peter Dobkin Hall suggests yet another strategy that New England capitalist elites used to strengthen their identity in the face of the Jacksonian and Populist revolutions. In a bid to regain social power lost in the eighteenth century, New England elites, through corporate capital management and the administration of private, nonprofit trusts and endowments, especially those for higher education, were successful in developing a disproportionate influence and asserting their own cultural and moral standards in defining the national interest throughout the nineteenth century.[27] Although their own material success within a context of popular suspicion of monopoly had undermined their claims to moral stewardship and national leadership, business elites proved capable of developing these new bases for authority that synthesized the Jacksonian urge for popular democracy with the national impetus toward unrestrained capitalist development. The Civil War transformed the nation's economic and cultural elites' view of the marketplace. Before the war, elites saw getting and spending in an atavistic jungle as a waste of genteel talent. The war's organization, national-scale mobilization, and national service unified and integrated the New England elite along corporate lines, and transformed the marketplace into "a testing ground on which the practibility of men and ideas could be worked out," evidenced by the shift toward business careers among graduates of Harvard and Yale. The new elite based its "claims for leadership on [the] ability and willingness to compete," emphasized the specialized training of technicians and administrators, and insisted that the process of recruitment was democratic and meritocratic.[28]

Unlike the eighteenth- and early nineteenth-century national elites, the new industrial elites and their managers exuded faith in democracy, adopted a national outlook, and embraced the national marketplace. In their new vision of American society, "democracy and the marketplace were compatible with regulated order." They succeeded in reestablishing moral authority through the mastery of professionalized technocratic bureaucracy and management, and they legitimated this mastery in the public mind through appeals to mass participation in progress and prosperity. A new worldview of corporate-led reform, identifying business and its leaders as instrumental in making the nation's economy more productive and efficient, was a key to widening public allegiance to the goal of national prosperity. Thus, businessmen could overcome capital's negative image and deflect its critics by defining the essence of American society as material progress, gained through democratic participation in the marketplace and led by trained scientific experts, the engineers and managers who ran the industrial plant. "Portraying itself as success," Alan Trachtenberg found, "business thus captured the free-labor ideology convincing the middle classes that in competitive enterprise lay the route to fulfillment, to the true America."[29] By making material success more widely available, the new capitalist elites reestablished their claims to national moral leadership under the ideal of democracy and the promise of material goods. In this manner, they joined morality to utility and technocracy and in doing so reintegrated political, economic, and intellectual authority for the twentieth century.[30]

The contrast between elite values extolling progress gained through aggressive acquisitiveness and republican-era values stressing industry, frugality, and honesty did not escape Mark Twain, who presented this dialogue in 1871:

Q. What is the chief end of man?

A. To get rich.

Q. In what way?

A. Dishonestly if we can, honestly if we must.

Q. Who is God, the only one and True?

A. Money is God. Gold and greenbacks and stocks—father, son and the ghost of the same—three persons in one; these are the true and only God, mighty and supreme; and William Tweed is his prophet.

Q. Who were the models the young were taught to emulate in former days?

A. Washington and Franklin.

Q. Whom do they and should they emulate now in this era of enlightenment?

A. Tweed, Hall, Connely, Camochan, Fisk, Gould, Barnard, and Winans.

Q. What works were chiefly prized for the training of the young in former days?

A. Poor Richard's Almanac, the Pilgrim's Progress, and the Declaration of Independence.

Q. What are the best prized Sunday-school books in this more enlightened age?

A. St. Hall's Garbled Reports, St. Fish's Ingenious Robberies, St. Camochan's Guide to Corruption, St. Gould on the Watering of Stock, St. Barnard's Injunctions; St. Tweed's Handbook of Morals, and the Court-House edition of the Holy Crusade of the Forty Thieves.

Q. Do we progress?

A. You bet your life.[31]

After 1890, professionalization became a method of organizing knowledge under the control of certified, degree-holding, university-trained academics and professionals. The university became the symbol of the new culture of professionalism and the source of new ideas that became the raw material by which people understood American society. This corpus of professional knowledge reduced the legitimacy of traditional sources of authority across American institutions from churches to trade unions and established a new intellectual base, that of social science and technocratic experts. In their quest for a progressive social science, doctors, lawyers, engineers, civil servants, social scientists, and psychologists established social opinion and redirected American self-definition toward notions of efficiency, progress, order, discipline, growth, stability, and bureaucratic control.[32]

This professionalized world came to dominate national social thought in the late nineteenth century, helping to solidify middle class behavior toward seeking success and providing a new source of personal prestige and a new perception of the world as a fluid environment subject to manipulation according to bourgeois needs and values. Best of all, this new perception offered an interpretation of society that placed the root of success in personal achievement rather than privilege or inherited wealth. Thus, it represented an individualist, democratic, universal method of achieving success and prestige in the anonymous capitalist market.[33] While workers asserted mutuality, equality, and communal values through union organization, the newly emergent paradigm of America as a corporation based on individual acquisitiveness elevated the authority of the professionalized leaders of that corporation, the technocrats.

Through curriculum reform in Ivy League universities, elites sponsored a new framework for, and definition of, national leadership within the rubric of the democratic, meritocratic society. America would achieve "historical progress," elites promised, led by a "meritocracy of talent" open to all, chosen through academic success, promoting values that continued the republican and Jacksonian heritage: democracy, social development, order and progress, freedom of choice, self-discipline, and nationalism. These were the ''administrative cadres,'' the very foundation of progressivism, who held power in universities, professions, and the federal bureaucracy, managed production and distribution, and furnished elite leadership to the new industrial order and the corporate liberal state. This educated aristrocracy would serve the national goals of progressive and democratic social evolution, Hall wrote, thereby ''reassert[ing] the connection between wealth, learning, respectability and the masses.'' Confusing national success with that of their own class, they saw their moral, cultural, and historical mission as the ''reorganization of their country's economic, political and social institutions.''[34]

Business endorsed the new educational view and the universities' interests through increased endowments to Yale, Harvard, and later Columbia and the Massachusetts Institute of Technology. In the years after the Civil War, as the social thought of Brahmins and businessmen shifted toward a more technocratic, activist worldview, the general public likewise embraced new attitudes toward the institutional role of the nation's wealthy and powerful. ''Public and patrician were moving towards one another in a broad ideological consensus,'' Hall continued, which accepted a national elite based on university-acquired knowledge and business success. If elite educational institutions had ''project[ed] on the nation an enlarged image of themselves,'' they were nevertheless able to create public approval for their definitions of morality, in this case national self-fulfillment defined in their own class terms.[35]

It is important to understand the role of technocratic managers in the science-based industries as they applied modern technology and management techniques to achieve unlimited growth. Science, as a productive force, was separated from traditional craft knowledge, monopolized by professionals, and brought under control of corporations. Modern technology, ''pressed into the service of capital, became a class bound phenomenon,'' David F. Noble observed.[36] Large corporations provided the only social medium for heavily capitalized research and development, the control of patents, and the application of science to production. It was partly the massive institutional presence of the large corporations, especially electricity, oil, and chemicals, which gave credibility to the new science and its practitioners and connected science and the proprietorship of science in the public mind. Corporate organizational power and control of scientific research fostered, in turn, the professionalization of engineering between 1850 and 1900. Engineering graduates went to work for corporations and became the managers of applied science. Between 1884 and 1924, two-thirds of engineering graduates had become managers within fifteen years. These engineer-managers emerged as corporate liberal reformers, seeking not just to rationalize technology and production in industry, but to shape other social institutions and values in a manner compatible with capitalist social organization. They sought to remove irrationality not just from factories but from ordinary social behavior by encouraging employers and educators to instill "correct" attitudes to heighten efficiency. This meant industrial and vocational education that would prepare workers for a life of labor and higher education to ready college graduates for a life of managing labor. Both forms of education stressed teamwork, loyalty, obedience, and diligence, values which, like those of other professionalized social scientists, became acceptable to a broad spectrum of society.[37]

As a newly emergent stratum in the employed workforce, managers adopted new references for self-valuation apart from those of traditional craft origins. Engineers "identified themselves publicly as servants of business," Noble found, and developed their social identity as scientists and their new status as managers and white collar professionals within the corporate bureaucracy.[38] They viewed their mobility into corporate management as evidence of their superiority, equating success in the competitive marketplace with personal success. Thus, engineers became "staunch individualists" who never acquired the collective sentiments of trade unionists. Moreover, since success so depended on their status within industry, they never developed an independent life apart from corporations as did other professionals such as doctors.

After the new generation of engineers developed various forms of modern management at the turn of the century, factory organization focused on engineering men rather than materials. "The wise manager," advised scientific management consultant Robert Valentine in a speech to the New York Taylor Society, appropriates "the great mass of unorganized forces—the rights, the desires, the opinions, etc., of the workmen" and transforms them into "agencies of co-operation in the conduct of his plant." Such a "machinery of contact" adds human beings to the industrial stock of raw material for the "inventive organizer."[39] The emphasis on the importance of organization and leadership by professionally trained management in science-based production reduced the social as well as technical value of skilled workers' craft knowledge obtained through work experience. Workers no longer controlled either the technology or the descriptive terms of their labor. Loss of control lowered the social status of skilled workers in managements' eyes and, almost certainly, in their own self-assessment. Mechanical engineers emphasized their reliance on science and new industry-based standards of measurement to distinguish themselves from the rule-of-thumb, "imprecise" methods of mechanics. As managers, they thought unions fostered mediocrity. Thus, the class control of science allowed the class appropriation of its legitimacy. In time, popular science's appeal and promise became "a banner which confounded the opposition" and produced a "mystifying and numbing effect on the mind of the worker," Noble wrote.[40]

Modern managers encouraged workers to accept the social habits and relations of corporate capitalism, arguing that it would offer them a better life. Similarly, businessmen pictured themselves to the public as the agents who, through their managers, would transform the nation's unmanageable, disruptive working population into a smoothly running, rationalized corporate machine capable of providing social progress, equilibrium, and prosperity. Within this worldview, workers would achieve higher wages, more purchasing power, respect as team players, and their rightful place in industrial society rather than garner social opprobrium as problem causers and misfits. Larger businesses often joined and even steered Progressive reform and regulation of the corporate economy, in part, for more efficiency and often to escape the strains of unrestricted competition. Corporate liberals supported welfare reform and joined with labor leaders to form working partnerships geared to extract the greatest efficiency from the industrial plant and provide the optimum conditions for workers to advance themselves.

As the century moved to a close, many Americans remained fundamentally ambivalent about big business even in the flush of national prosperity. Republicanism had taught them to fear the growth of monopolies, the power of speculators and financiers, and the degradation of workers, conditions that grew more urgent as the nation's industrial plant expanded, consolidated, and matured. But republicanism had also lauded honest, small-scale entrepreneurship, while prosperity and the material promise of the machine had whetted appetites for the social prestige and personal rewards of self-betterment. Such an atmosphere made it easier to assert the authority of business as tenders of the machine and guarantors of progress and to posit a new society based on the pursuit of private wealth. If still unconvinced of business' beneficence, Americans nevertheless found themselves spurred on by its promise and the ideology of equality. Some continued to denounce monopoly even as others admired the excesses of the millionaire barons. Americans wanted to believe these gains were gotten fairly and squarely and that such opportunities were there for the taking and open to everyone on an equal basis. Within a rising climate of progress and prosperity, business rhetoric played to the hopeful, holding out the rewards of the republican dream of property ownership, security, and, most of all, a stake in the future. It was the promise of machine industry that mattered—progress, prosperity, material goods, mobility—and it paid businessmen to argue that those who disrupted or broke the machine denied its promise. Thus Americans held on tightly, Daniel Rodgers observed, to an abstracted ideal of the virtuous and moral basis of work, even as it became separated from the reality of industrial society.[41]

While business elites found it politically unwise to reject the Jacksonian heritage of political equality, they could separate the marketplace and the workplace from politics and meet the challenge of those who questioned this separation by arguing that a hierarchical workplace was necessary for efficiency, growth, and national progress. New market forces reinforced rather than threatened political democracy, businessmen argued, for the workplace itself fostered open, equitable competition among free individuals. While growing less democratic toward the end of the century, the marketplace was increasingly enveloped in a rhetorical aura that emphasized equal opportunity for all. The market emerged as the most important cultural arena where white men could identify themselves as earners, heads of family, producers, and achievers. The values emphasized in the market—aggressiveness, competition, ruthlessness—seemed to ensure material success, an attribute that became the definition of manliness. The hierarchical, undemocratic social organization of industrial factory production demanded compliance with factory work imperatives and obedience to the next authority above in the chain of command. Many workers resisted these demands and repudiated manager's democratic claims, as David Montgomery has aptly demonstrated. The language of modern management portrayed factory authority as "democratic" by picturing it driven not by men or special interests but by the "rational" logic of individual self-seeking and efficiency. Once the market was separated from "politics," made apolitical, "meritocratic," and apparently interested only in social beneficence, business elites found it easy to support political and social equality in the public sphere. In reality, modern corporations established new patterns of authority under an entirely new managerial, scientific factory elite and an ethos of progress and self-advancement.[42]

In the intense struggle to achieve public legitimacy and at the same time discredit its detractors, corporate enterprise "took on the guise of an efficient, well oiled mechanism—the very embodiment of technical reason," David F. Noble wrote, "against which individual opposition could not but appear 'irrational.' "[43] The public saw workers' and unions' economic theories, disruptiveness and inefficiency as inimical to progress and as an alien presence within national culture. As capital made its own claims to truth based on scientific legitimacy, workers became less and less able to get any ideological mileage from either their vision of progress or their skilled use of science and technology. The values that corporate capital directed against its critics, were, in the language of the times, loyalty and cooperation over industrial sabotage, individuality over collectivity, the national interest over selfishness, a natural harmony of interests over divisiveness, social order over instability, industrial peace over industrial warfare, and cooperation over conflict.

HEGEMONY AND HISTORICAL INQUIRY

Before examining the three case studies, we must clarify the concept of hegemony, a theoretical framework for exploring the complex mechanism through which dominant meanings and values govern the social process. For the Italian theorist Antonio Gramsci, hegemonic social domination occurs when the particular ideology of ruling classes "tends to prevail, to gain the upper hand, to propagate itself throughout society—bringing about not only a unison of economic and political aims, but also intellectual and moral unity." Hegemony is not produced simply by the conscious exercise of ruling elites' power, however; it also results from the aggregate, anonymous, and cumulative effect on public consciousness of manipulations and "independent decisions" made not only by economic and political elites, but professionals, bureaucrats, religious and military spokespeople, and other advocates for society's most powerful and influential institutions. Hegemony constitutes the "central, effective and dominant system of meanings and values, which are not merely abstract, but which are organized and lived,'' Raymond Williams observed. Not to be understood as simple manipulation, hegemony is a "whole body of practices and expectations; our assignments of energy, our ordinary understanding of the nature of man and of his world. It is a set of meanings and values which as they are experienced as practices appear as reciprocally confirming. It thus constitutes a sense of reality for most people in the society.''[44]

The hegemony of ruling elites is never a static system imposed upon pliant masses; it is, rather, a social process that must be constantly recreated in the face of oppositional social forces and ideas. The dominant ideology must often acknowledge the claims of, and make concessions to, subordinate, alternate, or residual groups in order to achieve legitimacy. Thus, the dominant ideology, like social behavior, is contested terrain, as George Lipsitz observed, "something to be struggled *for* rather than imposed *on* society from the top down.''[45]

Forms and patterns of social control are as old as society itself, and modern hegemonic methods continue patriarchal and authoritarian forms begun in the ruling hierarchies of early social groupings. However, the hegemonic structure of late nineteenth-century society differed from preindustrial forms in several ways. First, the intensely focused, short-term, profit-oriented demands of production in a competitive market drove employers to rationalize the factory. Next, the application of technology to production weighted the struggle for efficiency heavily on the side of owners and managers; then labor resistance forced employers to search for new, "democratic," and less obviously manipulative forms of workplace control. Finally, a growing sense of class power energized elites to exercise social and cultural leadership. Workplace hegemony began to take shape when manufacturers struggled for greater control of workers in the factory and in society by producing a socially marketable set of ideas surrounding "labor" and using them as a weapon.

To understand how the ideas of ruling elites pervade society and how the resistance of subordinate groups to these ideas often adapts them to the very demands they resist, one must begin with primary socialization and the reproduction of culture. Individual knowledge, which most people take for objective reality, is a social product. Human social interaction occurs within a highly structured body of ideas, the "social stock of knowledge," which constitutes "reality" for most persons and determines how they relate to the institutions, beliefs, and other individuals in society.[46] In short, social being determines much of ordinary consciousness.

During early socialization, individuals experience the various social institutions such as family, school, or religion as being "given," or inevitable, and thus hardly distinguishable from the reality of the natural world. Beyond the level of the individual psyche, society constitutes an agglomeration of institutions, a network of public symbols, shared beliefs, and behavioral norms through which people communicate and make sense of one another and the world around them. Institutions maintain this social stock of knowledge that includes the rules and norms of each institution and provides definition, direction, and stability to social interaction. Socialization makes the individual "want to do what he has to do," as Christopher Lasch observed. The more conduct is institutionalized, "the more predictable and thus the more controlled it becomes," Peter Berger and Peter Luckmann wrote; "if socialization into the institutions has been effective, outright coercive measures can be applied economically and selectively." Thus, what an individual might be certain is spontaneous, freely chosen behavior is actually "spontaneous" only "within the institutionally set channels." As institutionally determined conduct is taken for granted, "the more possible alternatives to the institutional 'programs' will recede, and the more predictable and controlled conduct will be."[47]

In this manner, the "givenness" or reality of institutions reduces the opportunity for individuals to think or act outside institutionally patterned boundaries. Although they may allow some latitude for the exercise of choice, these boundaries ultimately serve as the arbiters of both what is allowed and disallowed and the means by which individuals perceive the boundaries themselves. Historically, as institutions such as religion change or new ones such as the industrial factory system appear, their requirements for proper thought and behavior assume a similar "givenness" because they draw upon traditional, familiar norms and reinterpret and transform them into the new setting. Thus the work ethic and the democratic promise when translated into the modern factory system provided its owners with a broad-based, almost universally approved, symbolic legitimacy rooted in the language of labor republicanism.

Hierarchical systems of authority within institutions assert the unspoken inevitability of concentrated power and knowledge, which, for most people, constrain conscious choice. Here lies the slippery realm between knowing acceptance and unconscious compliance, crucial to understanding different degrees of hegemony. On one level, such "obedience" forms part of the sometimes unthinking deference and spontaneous ritualized behavior toward powerful authority figures within the institutional order: parents, priests, teachers, editors, judges, businessmen, and politicians. In premodern societies, the greatest "spontaneous" institutional socialization and unconscious deference occurred among slaves, serfs, untouchables, sharecroppers, or tenants within a predictable institutional order characterized by a minimal and rigidly hierarchical distribution of knowledge.

Modern industrial capitalist society, however, with its high division of labor, greatly differentiated social structure, and rapid social change added new institutions and social hierarchies that undermined the collective nature of traditional society and placed in its stead a society of relatively atomized individuals, more easily "recombined" into modern hierarchical and rationalized educational, governmental, penal, industrial, political, media, and even labor institutions. New methods of persuasion in such institutions as national politics did not provide elites with the means to monopolize all competing definitions of reality at all times. On the contrary, the ideological grounds for modern worker rebellions indicate that while they may have varying degrees of hope about changing the system, they do not see social domination as inevitable or just. Against these perceptions, an increasingly national-minded business elite skillfully orchestrated and disseminated pro-business ideology and developed a doctrine and method of public discourse among a literate, urban population that, by the turn of the century in Europe and America, rivaled, reinterpreted, and sometimes even replaced traditional forms of social authority.[48]

The primary form of hegemony may be the legitimative value and coercive weight of language itself. In many respects, words are not free for the choosing. Language includes formal social discourses that both proscribe permissible vocabulary for activity in the public sphere and delineate the "proper" relationship of individuals to social authority and to one another. Certain dissenting ethnic, religious, and class subcultures, poets, or political radicals violate the boundaries of these discourses with words most people might label as incomprehensible or unthinkable. Most people, however, remain within the confines of permissible discourse, allowing its "definitions" to serve as real references for thought and action. Moreover, they often vehemently defend the exclusivity of specialized discourses, as Thomas Kuhn suggested in his study of the historical evolution of scientific paradigms.[49] Thus, for example, to name another person cousin, jailer, or apprentice calls up and affirms a whole range of relatively unexamined behavior and thought appropriate to kinship, imprisonment, or work relations, specifying, for instance, that one would not ordinarily consider marrying one's cousin. Governments engage in ritual legitimations of such abstractions as "nation" through public demonstrations and discourses on patriotism and sacrifice that portray the prevailing political system as logical, valid, moral, and God given. On the highest level, legitimators such as teachers, politicians, or priests "make sense" of the various institutional realities by integrating them into universal, symbolic wholes which, in the West, have had successive historical designations—divine will, natural law, and more recently, scientific progress. The idea of apprentice, or cousin, then, represents a small portion of a grand theory of the universe and its people.[50] Hierarchical patterns governing the organization of knowledge prescribed and reinforced authority relations in the late nineteenth century. This leads to the question of how these authority relations are reproduced.

While most individuals share a common "social stock of knowledge," ordinary consciousness reflects social hierarchy and thus is neutral neither to policies, ideology, class, race, nor gender. In industrial society, different economic classes or ethnic and religious groups adhere to beliefs that reflect and promote their own self-definition and self-interest. In the Gilded Age, many ideas of the business elites reflected a desire to enhance their social standing and confront their critics or their quest to profit from the social organization of factory labor. Since labor loomed as the primary threat to these goals, industrialists sought docility, diligence, predictability, and allegiance among their workers by enforcing upon them "modern" time and work discipline and a "scientific" form of plant and human management.[51] The most direct coercion of workers occurred at the point of production, which provided the structural, institutional, and ideological means of subjecting and utilizing workers' labor power. With the application of technology to the factory, the vast increases in on-the-job supervision and constraint brought workers face to face with manipulative and coercive employers and managers. The labor ideas of manufacturers played an important role in convincing workers to follow the more systematized, centralized, supervised, and hierarchical factory administration. While scholars disagree over the ease with which workers accepted the new factory discipline, they eventually accommodated to the new work habits and institutions. This transition and its accompanying values had far-reaching effects legitimizing the institutional forms of corporate capitalism.

The power of business elites found further reinforcement in public and private architecture, especially the modern skyscrapers built of steel and concrete after the 1880s, which furnished massive, costly, and seemingly permanent expressions of corporate power. Factories, government buildings, and the churches and homes of the wealthy all supplied visual sustenance to the "reality" of elite institutions and belief systems. Messages encoded in the material presence of their walls signified the special ability of elites to govern public space and to influence, and even intimidate, persons entering those spaces. By comparison, the scale and significance of the buildings that represented working class institutions—union meeting halls, public parks, local bars, residential neighborhoods, factory towns—provided relatively less dramatic reinforcement. Thus through ritualized public behavior, symbolic legitimacy, and control of public space, elite institutions specified appropriate behavior and provided most of the information and vocabulary governing the social relations of industrial society. This "received" vocabulary began to delineate the conscious limit of admissible ideas and discussions.

Labor ideology of employers furnished an important element in the attempt to create new kinds of thinking and habits among workers. Workers' defiant public pronouncements polarized the debate with capital, posing dramatic questions about wages, unions, and strikes. Businessmen countered by attacking workers' demands for shorter hours and the right to organize and control work and by attempting to censor and discredit working class arguments in the debate. On a wider scale, the bitterness of industrial warfare and the plight of urban workers prompted businessmen to expand their ideological justifications of the distribution of wealth, patterns of property ownership, forms of labor utilization, and state police tactics. Businessmen's increasing influence over the social definitions of "reality" became a political tool as they sought to "assign" workers' "rightful" place and justify the distribution of power and goods within industrial society.[52]

Communication between businessmen and workers took place within unequal social and cultural power relationships and almost always carried a coercive element that ultimately enhanced the ruling elites' authority. As manufacturers organized the structure of debate in the factory and in public, they set the boundaries of acceptable discussion and injected their own forms of knowledge and logic, their own science-based terminology, and their own notions of acceptable behavior. Thus, the very framework of discourse profoundly affected the nature and flow of information. Working people's definitions of terms such as *justice* or *a fair day's work* almost certainly differed from those of elites; yet workers realized that they lived in the real world of elite-defined justice, structurally regulated to exact a fair day's work and often only thinly masking its actual political intentions.

Workers' relatively subordinate position in the institutional structure of public discourse meant that their "arguments" in the debate with owners gained less credibility in the public sphere. As news accounts of strikes and violence filtered to the public through hostile editorial accounts in the nation's newspapers, most worker "input" into the social stock of knowledge possessed a negative value. Terms like *strike* or *union* became increasingly tainted as they entered public discourse through the prism of the corporate ideas that dominated most of the nation's newspapers, universities, courts, civic organizations, and public forums. Writers in popular journals acknowledged the effects on the public mind of business rhetoric. Although Louis F. Post welcomed strikes in 1886 because they "make the people talk and think about the labor question," he lamented that "so long as the 'boss' class controls news channels, strikes will appear to be tornadoes of wickedness."[53] As strike activity increased between 1880 and 1900 and the nation's media increasingly exposed "lawless and socialistic unionism," approval of workers declined among the middle class.

Such contextual differences in the political impact of words points up the historical paradox that found workers, particularly recent immigrants, simultaneously resisting their employer's labor ideas while they accommodated to the new factory work discipline. Between 1880 and 1910, the variety of working class ethnic values, religious beliefs, and class consciousness socially distanced workers from employers. Workers maintained separate cultural institutions, which offered ethnic and religious solidarity that often empowered their resistance to the demands of industrial acculturation. As E. P. Thompson and Herbert Gutman have demonstrated, however, after a period of shock and friction, workers gradually accommodated to the lessons of industrial "rationality."[54] While the first generation of workers chafed most harshly against modern factory discipline, later ones reacted less strongly as the insulating qualities of their subcultures weakened under the influence of the dominant Victorian culture with its emphasis on the rewards of hard work, science, individualism, and progress. In this transition period, Milton Cantor adds, "industrialization severely tested and frequently overwhelmed [workers'] traditions and institutions."[55]

Work traditions brought from the old country, however, were not necessarily archaic or premodern and actually may have aided the transition to modern factory life and eased accommodation to dominant values. Rowland Berthoff, for example, traces "republican" notions of an ideal community of self-sufficient, hardworking, prudent, frugal yeomen to its origins in the English,

Irish, German, and Scandinavian peasantry. Successive waves of immigrant smallholders and artisans throughout the nineteenth century brought with them an affinity to "republican" moral economy, its work ethic, and its quest for self-sufficiency through property ownership.[56]

It is important to emphasize that hegemonic relationships, whatever their origins, never determined a one-way process wherein the dominant culture "defined" institutional forms and behaviors and subordinates accepted "correct" ideas and followed their appointed roles. Hegemony assumes a conflict between often irreconcilable historic groups, the outcome of which is never certain. Bourgeois hegemony in modern society, Lipsitz wrote, is unstable and in need of constant re-creation because the dominant ideology involves "concessions to aggrieved populations as well as control over them." Business elites and working people communicated in an interactive, continual, if unequal struggle for advantage which constantly reshaped definitions and meanings. This relationship featured a continual dialectic between working class and elite cultures and ideologies, which provided space for the development of oppositional cultures *and at the same time* for the downward flow of elite cultural authority. In the context of social conflict, the fluid dynamics of this ideological struggle offered room for resistance and reinterpretation by all parties. Popular criticism of the growth of corporate-managed, profit-driven society provided an alternative notion of private property used to maintain individual autonomy and civic virtue. Labor republicanism, Leon Fink found, "affirmed the significance of the nation's political commitment to independent citizenship" based on an alternative vision of cooperation, equality, and social responsibility.[57] Workers demanded certain guarantees and tried to preserve traditional rights, obligations, and privileges within new industrial relationships as they fought manufacturers over whose labor ideas would prevail.

Individual workers internalized the "objective" reality of business ideology in varying degrees, if at all, depending on the relative influence of radical elements in working class culture, union experiences, on-the-job formal training and informal socialization, family conditions, and ethnic and religious background. Even within the consciousness of a single individual, there remained public and private spheres, the former more easily governed by public discourse and the latter a realm where workers were, for a time, more successful in retaining traditional values.

If workers eventually accommodated to the material aspects of the new work discipline, many, perhaps most, did not wholeheartedly accept employers' definitions of reality. Depending on their degree of radicalization, or their desire for upward mobility, or their resignation, or even a combination of these sentiments, workers made different adjustments to, and established varied personal attitudes toward, employers' workplace demands and definitions. These included a range of responses from blind acquiescence, to grudging compliance, to knowing and even energetic complicity. Some clearly recognized their own exploitation but felt paralyzed and unable to make a defense. "The laborer is conscious of the wrong,'' Louis Post observed in 1886, ''though he may not know its cause or how to remedy it.''[58] Many of these continued to work despite a clear feeling of having been wronged. Other workers expressed an eager compliance derived from the hope of the new industrial order, notions about work that the middle class popularized in late nineteenth-century America. The pervasiveness of these ideas, whether from a middle class or yeoman source, was borne out in the observations of Sir James Kitson, a steel manufacturer and one of a 300 member British Iron and Steel Institute expedition to the United States in 1890 to inspect methods of production in heavy industries. Judging the comparative capabilities of English, German, and American workmen, the visitors were struck by the greater effort put forth by Americans. Kitson's impression was strengthened upon encountering one of his former employees from England at Carnegie's works in Pittsburgh. The workman spoke of his experience in America: ''I am a quite different man here from what I was in the old country; I don't know why it is so; whether it is that I live in a stimulating atmosphere, or whether it is the example set me; but I know I have got the go in me here. I can do more work; I feel I have it in me, but I also feel and I know it won't last. I shall be done in ten years.''[59] Thus caught in the promise, this worker continued to work, perfectly aware of his own plight.

It was not only workers who were caught up in the eager, competitive, energizing spirit of capitalist expansion and reward for the self-seeking individual. Businessmen, too, Kitson discovered, worked at ''high pressure'' in a ''terrific struggle for possession of the markets,'' although the fierce competition ''reacts on the men.'' Moreover, the energetic spirit of the employers made workers more obedient and less willing to organize. ''We were surprised to find,'' Kitson continued, ''that the workmen had so little power, and were to such a large extent the docile instruments of energetic employers.'' This he attributed to the factory bosses' faculty for ''driving the men and getting the maximum amount of work out of them, and the men do not seem to have the inclination or power to resist the pressure.''[60] Both Louis Post and Kitson's employee registered degrees of consciousness somewhere between accommodation and consent, however eager, grudging, or resigned. This is the ''inner compulsion'' that encouraged many workers to strive for an immediate, tangible success in a reputedly democratic, meritocratic workplace, however palpably undemocratic. Thus, it is clearly possible, as Jackson Lears suggested, that some workers internalized the work rules of factory culture even as they recognized its forms of domination, thus manifesting what Gramsci called ''contradictory consciousness.''[61]

Resignation to the inevitable demands of feeding oneself and one's family may have guaranteed subordination to the factory regime without ascribing to it legitimacy. One should not assume that ideological support lay behind faithful compliance. One can ascribe a measure of inner resistance and ideological nonconformity to the seemingly most compliant worker. The very act of appearing at the factory gate, working, and drawing a wage, whether resentfully or wholeheartedly, possibly inured many to patterns of social control and work ideology, and certainly affected each worker's perception of his or her role in the system and sense of possible strategies of resistance. Yet the visible and invisible lines of authority in such an accommodation were a form of coercion sufficient to reproduce authority relations in the factory and society. For employer hegemony to succeed, then, the dominant ideology does not have to be internalized; rather, subordinate classes merely have to comply with the outward, material requirements of authority.

It was possible, too, that workers and farmers in America could remain ideologically radical while basing their critique on stated values within the commonly held framework of classical republicanism. In other words, rather than anesthetize subordinate classes, a dominant ideology can furnish the raw material for its own critique, creating a dialogue over the proper direction of the social order within agreed upon norms. It was not necessary, then, for workers and farmers to think outside the republican dream of liberty and equality of late nineteenth-century America in order to send out radical criticisms of elite power. Historically, class conflict, as James C. Scott found in studies of peasant resistance, arises in response to the "failure of a dominant ideology to live up to the implicit promises it necessarily makes." Peasant grievance was based on the perceived gap between the promises and the professed values of the elite and the failure to deliver the promises. "Properly understood," Scott continued, "any hegemonic ideology provides, within itself, the raw material for contradictions and conflict," although conflict necessarily occurs within an existing hegemony.[62] When Populists and unionists pressed their claims against the business culture, their arguments were based on the ideals and professed values of personal liberty and economic justice grounded in a preindustrial social order, itself hegemonic and valid. They demanded a meritocracy of virtue and denounced favoritism, monopolized markets, the concentration of power and capital, unequal access, and the unrestrained pursuit of material self-interest. They denounced unemployment, low pay, and poor conditions that denied the fruits of hard work and served as barriers to upward mobility. They advanced a labor theory of value that rested on the respect for labor's rewards imbedded in the republican promise. In short, they offered a radical critique of existing relationships based on alternate interpretations of values that were deeply embedded in the dominant ideology.

The Populist critique advanced a set of arguments that likewise demanded fulfillment of the republican promise of just rewards for the labor of virtuous smallholders. Seeking to restore political power to "plain people," they railed against the forces in America that violated the original intent of its founders: monopolists, trusts, usurers, railroads, industry, banks. They argued free trade against high tariffs and the credit needs of small producers against financial monopoly. If some of their program calling for an end to private banking, transportation, and communication was revolutionary, it is also true that they would allow other production to remain in private hands. Indeed, they sought to preserve small producers' capitalism, attacking not its substance but its scale.[63]

Populists made a radical critique of existing relationships based on the arguments of classical laissez-faire economics and the language of republicanism, both elements of the dominant ideology.

Since the end product of hegemony is mass allegiance to the established order, it is risky for elites to tolerate too great a degree of experience or consciousness completely outside the dominant ideology. In its nascent period, Raymond Williams observed, bourgeois, capitalist society tolerated residual or emergent religious, artistic, or private spheres without significant concern.[64] By the twentieth century, however, changes in the social character of labor, communication, and decision making prompted elites to define deviance more narrowly and incorporate more spheres of life into the affairs of state. The expansion of a universalized public consciousness in modern society extended the "necessary area of effective dominance" and reduced the level of elite tolerance of ideological diversity. What businessmen perceived as labor's violation of this line after 1877 prompted them to repress deviant ideas and legitimate the machinery of repression: censorship, court injunctions, imprisonment, private armies, and federal troops. "Nihilation," to use Williams' term, is a specific form of repressive machinery that discredits or dismisses deviant notions and antagonistic behavior. Gilded Age industrialists "nihilated" labor's defiance by branding their words and deeds moral depravity, lawlessness, mental disease, ignorance, folly, madness, and downright evil. They achieved the ultimate nihilation of dangerous ideas by imprisoning or destroying some workers who held them.[65]

Businessmen made skillful use of their ideas to reinforce power relationships beneficial to themselves, and often obscured their own class biases by presenting their ideas and efforts as a progressive force that developed national energies. Political questions inherent in the labor-capital struggle were masked by universalizing capital's particular interests into the public interest. Modern political society makes this process easier by fragmenting members of a social class, representing them as individual citizens, voters, or workers, and then reuniting them into what Stuart Hall terms class neutral "ideological totalities"—the community, the nation, public opinion, consensus, the popular will, the general interest, or society.[66] This fragmentation and recombination enabled progressive business elites to generate unity and consent within liberal bourgeois notions of tradition, liberty, freedom, equality, or morality.

Economic elites disguised class interests as general interests through a process Williams calls the selective tradition, which emphasizes certain facts and actively excludes others in order to present "history" as *the* actual, most meaningful past.[67] The power of ruling elites rested on and was reinforced by their claims to embody history, tradition, and the "universal" moral values of antebellum America. Scientific management "simply emphasized" moral and ethical principles "stated in the New Testament nearly two thousand years ago," explained Morris Cooke, Philadelphia's director of public works.[68] Similarly, leaders of the National Association of Manufacturers claimed their chief aim was the "purely patriotic one of defending human liberty. Business and patriotism go hand in hand. Industrialism is beneficent, civilizing and uplifting. It is the enemy of war, of despotism, of ignorance and poverty. In truth, its foes are the foes of mankind.'' Ignoring contemporary social experience, selective history nevertheless passed down from generation to generation as "truth" or "reality." Always, Raymond Williams said, "selectivity is the point." In this manner, selective tradition incorporated and institutionalized historical dissent in the public mind and, in that process, made social defiance abstract, one dimensional, and disconnected.[69]

National advertising and the professionalization of the advertising industry represented another form of hegemonic symbol-making to emerge in the nineteenth century. Mass produced luxury goods had begun to come off assembly lines toward the end of the century just as the democratic franchise broadened, discretionary income became available to more potential buyers, and mass public education and mass literacy all helped create a climate of consumerism. Advertisers like Walter Dill Scott learned to play mass concern effectively, to "appeal to ruling interests and motives, the desire to be healthy, to hoard, to possess, to wear smart clothes, to get something for nothing, to be like the more privileged and successful classes." These motivations played upon envy, shame, greed, and jealousy and sought to persuade the worker-consumer to accept the mores of a consumption-oriented society.[70]

Twentieth-century consumer culture assigned a different role to labor than the work and thrift of the republican vision. In the culture of consumption, workers evolved into installment purchasers, encouraged by advertisements to buy beyond their means. Savings and economic independence gave way to using credit at the cost of fiscal responsibility. This had the effect of adding interest to rents as the two most important means of shifting working class earnings into the pockets of landlords and financiers. Workers began to substitute the consumption of mass produced goods for any actual power in decision making in production or public policy, Richard Fox and Jackson Lears observed. While workers could no longer anticipate being their own bosses or owning property, they could, nevertheless, exercise "personal power" through "choice" in the consumer marketplace. By the 1920s, consumption had become a "cultural ideal, a 'hegemonic way of seeing,' " Fox and Lears wrote.[71]

The process of subordinating oppositional working class ideas within the dominant employer ideology was not entirely due to the hegemonic power of employers. Their ideology, tempered and challenged by subordinate groups and classes, did not unilaterally determine what was thought about labor, either by the public or by workers themselves. But it did bring to bear a network of ideas and interests that profoundly influenced any discussion about workers, unions, or strikes. In short, their ideological power may not have been absolute or monolithic, but it was systemic and legitimating. It rested, ultimately, on the coercive power of the state. It did not instantly drive out workers' ideas, but by the second half of the twentieth century, it prevailed in popular political economy. Anti-capitalist ideas exist today among members of the U.S. workforce, but they are often so sporadic, discredited, and penalized that they cannot be considered part of any significant challenge. Today, most U.S. citizens and unionized workers alike support the political and economic institutions of American society for reasons that echo many of the ideas expressed by owners in this period, ideas about work, workers, unions, rights, and the social function of capital.[72]

This national consciousness concerning labor seems to have taken shape in the short span of years between 1880 and 1915. It is important to remember that this dominant norm was less created or established by businessmen, although they played a crucial role, than it was derived from a broad social collage of ideas already circulating in the air of national consciousness. These ideas included religious arguments for the colonization of America, Puritan notions of social labor, nineteenth-century success and self-help literature, experience with more benign antebellum marketplaces and workplaces, and European peasant and smallholder traditions, all reinforced by remarkable postwar economic growth and whetted by imperial expansion and the creation of an advertised consumer culture. Businessmen took up these norms of virtuous independence, individual progress, and social fulfillment and made them their own to advance arguments for the democratic legitimacy of competitive work and marketplaces.

The three case studies that follow demonstrate the formation of employer ideas concerning labor and outline dialogues that contributed to the formation of this national consciousness. The first provides an example of the labor rhetoric generated during the acute national crisis brought on by the Pullman strike in the summer of 1894. This confrontation, together with the major protest strikes of the previous decade, crystallized the sense of class warfare in the nation and intensified the resolve of large corporations to meet militant labor's challenge with increasingly organized and publicly sanctioned force. The Pullman study also examines George Pullman's attempt to create an ideal industrial setting at the town of Pullman in the decades before the turn of the century. It asks whether it was possible to remold workers in capital's image even within a tightly controlled, seemingly hegemonic system, which to all observers did encourage middle class habits. A second case study explores modern management techniques that sought to apply technological and psychological expertise to production. Modern management's techniques and beliefs played a major role in the formulation of professional attitudes toward work and workers and became particularly associated in the public eye with progress, efficiency, and the notion that the common good lay in the hands of scientifically trained professional experts. The third case study examines the National Association of Manufacturers' purely propagandistic attempts to sway public opinion as it embarked on an assault against unions and workers in the decade after 1903. These three studies illuminate a number of factors critical to understanding the late nineteenth-century evolution and codification of the labor ideas in modern business ideology, particularly as a tool of working-class discipline. They seek to explicate relationships between workers and owners in the realm of knowledge-as-power, in the control of the production and distribution of goods, in the appropriation of "science" and technology, in the use of architecture and public space, in the use of influence on law and public policy, and above all, in the purchase of labor power. And they argue that the capital-labor confrontation involved an ideological struggle in which public opinion counted, not just in the outcome of strikes or shop floor struggles, but in the definition of labor's place in the new corporate order.

NOTES

1. Alan Trachtenberg, *The Incorporation of America: Culture and Society in the Gilded Age* (New York, 1982); Parry quote, National Association of Manufacturers, *Proceedings of the Annual Convention*, 1904, 72.

2. For discussions of the relation between technology, industrialism, social change, and the centralization of knowledge between 1877 and 1914, see Peter D. Hall, *The Organization of American Culture 1700–1900: Private Institutions, Elites, and the Origins of American Nationality* (New York, 1982), quote 1, 2; James Gilbert, *Designing the Industrial State: The Intellectual Pursuit of Collectivism 1800–1914* (Chicago, 1972); Alexandra Oleson and John Voss, *The Organization of Knowledge in Modern America, 1860–1920* (Baltimore, 1979); Nathan Rosenberg, *Technology and American Growth* (New York, 1972); David F. Noble, *America by Design: Science, Technology and the Rise of Corporate Capitalism* (New York, 1977); William Akin, *Technocracy and the American Dream* (Berkeley, 1977); on the maturation of industrial society, see Karl Polanyi, *The Great Transformation: The Political and Economic Origins of Our Time* (Boston, 1944); T. J. Jackson Lears, *No Place of Grace: Antimodernism and the Transformation of American Culture, 1880–1920* (New York, 1981); for analyses of capitalism in contemporary culture, see Herbert Schiller, *Culture, Inc.: The Corporate Takeover of Public Expression* (New York, 1989); and Stuart Ewen, *All Consuming Images: The Politics of Style in Contemporary Culture* (New York, 1988).

3. For discussions of cultural hegemony, see T. J. Jackson Lears "The Concept of Cultural Hegemony: Problems and Possibilities," *American Historical Review* 90 (June 1985): 567–93; David B. Davis "Reflections on Abolitionism and Ideological Hegemony," *American Historical Review* 92 (Oct. 1987): 797–812; and discussions by Leon Fink, T. J. Jackson Lears, George Lipsitz, John Diggins, Mari Jo Buhle, and Paul Buhle in "A Round Table: Labor, Historical Pessimism, and Hegemony," *Journal of American History* 75 (June 1988): 115–61; Alan Dawley, *Class and Community: The Industrial Revolution in Lynn* (Cambridge, Mass., 1976), shows the emerging hegemony of capitalism in the industrializing process; James C. Scott, *Weapons of the Weak: Everyday Forms of Peasant Resistance* (New Haven, Conn., 1985), especially chapter 8, "Hegemony and Consciousness," 304–50; Raymond Williams, "Base and Superstructure in Marxist Cultural Theory," *New Left Review* 82 (1973): 3–16.

4. Lawrence Goodwyn, *The Populist Moment* (New York, 1978), 271; Trachtenberg, *The Incorporation of America*, 73.

5. See Daniel Rodgers, *The Work Ethic in Industrial America, 1850–1920* (Chicago, 1974), and Eric Foner, *Free Soil, Free Labor, Free Men: The Ideology of the Republican Party Before the Civil War* (New York, 1970), 2–15; Hall, *Organization of American Culture*, chapters 4, 9, and 12. It was "enlarging capital," after the 1850s, Hall says, that "required the creation of the mutual trust and common values essential to effective

collective economic action,'' 179–180; for discussions of early economic thought, see Joseph Dorfman, *The Economic Mind in American Civilization* vols. 2 and 3, (New York, 1946 and 1949), and Paul K. Conkin, *Prophets of Prosperity: America's First Political Economists* (Bloomington, 1980); Harold U. Faulkner, *American Economic History* (New York, 1924); Arthur Perry, *Principles of Political Economy* (New York, 1885).

6. Jonathan B. Harrison, ''Certain Dangerous Tendencies in American Life,'' *Atlantic Monthly* 42 (Oct. 1878): 402.

7. National Association of Manufacturers, *Proceedings of the Annual Convention* 1906, 13; Martin Schiesl, *The Politics of Efficiency: Municipal Administration and Reform in America, 1880–1920* (Berkeley, 1977); on earlier social control, see David Rothman, *The Discovery of the Asylum: Social Order and Disorder in the New Republic* (Boston, 1971) and Samuel Bowles and Herbert Gintis, *Schooling in Capitalist America: Educational Reform and the Contradictions of Economic Life* (New York, 1976); for a discussion of business elites, see Lee Soltow, *Men and Wealth in the United States 1850–1870* (New Haven, Conn., 1976), and Louis Galambos, *The Public Image of Big Business in America: A Quantitative Study of Social Change* (Baltimore, 1975); for business ideology see Thomas Cochran, *Railroad Leaders 1845–1890: The Business Mind in Action* (Cambridge, Mass., 1953); Edward Kirkland, *Industry Comes of Age: Business, Labor and Public Policy 1860–1897* (New York, 1961) and also his *Dream and Thought in the Business Community 1860–1900* (Ithaca, 1956); Sidney Fine, *Laissez-Faire and the General Welfare State: A Study of Conflict in American Thought* (Ann Arbor, 1965); Robert Sobel, *The Entrepreneurs: Explorations within the American Business Tradition* (New York, 1974); James Weinstein, *The Corporate Ideal in the Liberal State, 1900–1918* (Boston, 1968); Martin Sklar, *The Corporate Reconstruction of American Capitalism 1890–1916: The Market, the Law, and Politics* (New York, 1988).

8. Harrison, ''Certain Dangerous Tendencies in American Life,'' 398.

9. ''How to Handle Men,'' advertisement for the journal *System* in *Factory* 1 (Dec. 1907): 60; United States Senate, *Report of the Relations Between Labor and Capital*, 5 vols., (Washington, D.C., 1885), first quote vol. 1, 1090, second quote, vol. 2, 155.

10. Trachtenberg, *The Incorporation of America*, 77; Sean Wilentz, *Chants Democratic: New York City and the Rise of the American Working Class, 1788–1850* (New York, 1984), 13–15.

11. Dawley, *Class and Community;* Herbert Gutman, *Work, Culture and Society in Industrial America* (New York, 1967), 80; and E. P. Thompson ''Time, Work Discipline, and Industrial Capitalism,'' *Past and Present* 38 (Dec. 1967): 56–97. For a critique of the notion of progressive acculturation of workers, see Daniel Rodgers, ''Tradition, Modernity, and the American Industrial Worker: Reflections and Critique,'' *Journal of Interdisciplinary History* 7 (Spring 1977): 655–81, and Rowland Berthoff, ''Writing a History of Things Left Out,'' *Reviews in American History* 14 (March 1986): 1–16.

12. James Emery, *Party Platforms and Industry* (New York, 1920), 9; Roy Rosenzweig suggests that it was the very ''insularity and separatism'' of Worcester, Massachusetts' ethnic workers' cultures that limited workers' influence in the nation's civic culture. Furthermore, he claims the issue is not just resistance versus accommodation, but he demonstrates that alternative working class culture was not necessarily directed by workers against the perceived power of employers. Worcester's workers responded to employers' demands on the job, never unionized, and rarely struck, but they still preserved ethnic neighborhoods and culture away from the job. Eight hours for the employer, eight of rest, and eight for what we will describe a deliberately compartmentalized consciousness

rather than what Gramsci identified as contradictory consciousness. In any case, "consciousness" for Worcester's workers produced a weak labor movement. Rosenzweig located reasons for this in a combination of factors: manufacturer' mobilization through trade associations, blacklists, suppression of strikes and unions, influence in public schools, propaganda, paternalism, and welfare policies. Rosenzweig, *Eight Hours for What We Will* (Cambridge, Mass., 1983), 15, 31. See also E. J. Hobsbawm, "Labor History and Ideology," *Journal of Social History* 7 (Summer 1974): 371–81.

13. David Montgomery, *Workers' Control in America* (Cambridge, England, 1979), 10, 44, 102; and also his *The Fall of the House of Labor: The Workplace, the State, and American Labor Activism, 1865–1925* (Cambridge, England, 1987), 215–16.

14. Haycinth Dubreuil, *Robots or Men: A French Workman's Experience in American Industry* (New York, 1930), 102; italics in original; the sound of the factory whistle "instantly curtailed" workers' lunchtime play in parks; Rosenzweig, *Eight Hours for What We Will*, 222.

15. Rodgers, *The Work Ethic in Industrial America, 1850–1920*, 39.

16. John Mitchell, *Organized Labor* (Philadelphia, 1903), ix, cited in Rodgers *The Work Ethic in Industrial America*, 39; for a general discussion of republicanism and technology see John Kasson, *Civilizing the Machine: Technology and Republican Values in America, 1776–1900* (New York, 1976).

17. Goodwyn, *The Populist Moment*, 103.

18. Douglas Dowd, *The Twisted Dream: Capitalist Development in the United States Since 1776* (Cambridge, Mass., 1974), 147; See Ronald Radosh, "The Corporate Ideology of American Labor Leaders from Gompers to Hillman," in James Weinstein and David Eakins, eds., *For a New America: Essays in History and Politics from Studies on the Left* (New York, 1971).

19. Nick Salvatore, *Eugene V. Debs: Citizen and Socialist* (Urbana, 1982); William Dick, *Labor and Socialism in America* (Port Washington, N.Y., 1972); James Weinstein, *The Decline of Socialism in America* (New York, 1967).

20. Sean Wilentz, "On Class and Politics in Jacksonian America," *Reviews in American History* 10 (Dec. 1982): 56.

21. Noble, *America by Design*, xxiv.

22. Trachtenberg, *The Incorporation of America*, 3, 4; see also Daniel Howe, "American Victorianism as a Culture," *American Quarterly* 27 (1975): 507–32; H. Wayne Morgan, *Victorian Culture in America* (Ithaca, Ill., 1973); R. H. Tawney, *The Acquisitive Society* (New York, 1921).

23. Goodwyn, *The Populist Moment*, 271.

24. Ibid., 280.

25. Ibid., 10, 281.

26. Ibid., 269.

27. Hall, *The Organization of American Culture*; Gabriel Kolko argues that Boston's traditional elite was also its new industrial elite in "Brahmins and Business, 1870–1914: A Hypothesis on the Social Basis of Success in American History," in Kurt Wolff and Barrington Moore, eds., *The Critical Spirit: Essays in Honor of Herbert Marcuse* (Boston, 1967), 343–63. Similarly, Christopher Lasch maintains "the old elite preserved much of its influence and imposed its values on the emergent national ruling class," in *The World of Nations: Reflections on American History, Politics and Culture* (New York, 1973), 82, 89.

28. Hall, *The Organization of American Culture*, 238.

29. Trachtenberg, *The Incorporation of America*, 87.

30. Hall, *The Organization of American Culture*, 236–37, 268.

31. Quoted in Philip Foner, *Mark Twain: Social Critic* (New York, 1958), 90–91; see also Tawney, *The Acquisitive Society*, 35; F. W. Taussig, *Inventors and Money Makers*, (New York, 1915).

32. Thomas Haskell, *The Emergence of a Professional Social Science: The American Social Science Association and the Nineteenth Century Crisis of Authority* (Urbana, 1977); Schiesl, *The Politics of Efficiency*; Robert Gordon, "Legal Thought and Legal Practice in the Age of American Enterprise, 1870–1920" in Gerald L. Geison, *Professions and Professional ideologies in America* (Chapel Hill, 1983); Edwin Layton, Jr., *The Revolt of the Engineers: Social Responsibility and the American Engineering Profession* (Baltimore, 1986), especially chapter 2.

33. Burton Bledstein, *The Culture of Professionalism: The Middle Class and the Development of Higher Education in America* (New York, 1976).

34. Hall, *The Organization of American Culture*, 250–51, 258–59, 275, 279; Layton, *The Revolt of the Engineers*, 53–74.

35. Hall, *The Organization of American Culture*, 262, 270, 279.

36. Noble, *America by Design*, 43; see also Samuel Haber, *Efficiency and Uplift: Scientific Management in the Progressive Era, 1890–1920* (Chicago, 1964).

37. Noble, *America by Design*, 41–43, 168, 263–64; Hall, *The Organization of American Culture*, 251.

38. Noble, *America by Design*, 42.

39. Robert G. Valentine, "The Progressive Relation Between Efficiency and Consent," *Bulletin of the Taylor Society* 2 (Jan. 1916): 8, 12.

40. Noble, *America by Design*, xxv, xxi, 41–42, 179.

41. Rodgers, *The Work Ethic in Industrial America*, 37.

42. Julie Matthaei, *An Economic History of Women in America: Women's Work, the Sexual Division of Labor, and the Development of Capitalism* (New York, 1982), 101–19; Irvin G. Wylie, *The Self-Made Man in America* (New York, 1954); John Cawelti, *Apostles of the Self-Made Man* (Chicago, 1965); Montgomery, *Worker's Control*.

43. Noble, *America by Design*, xxvi.

44. Antonio Gramsci, *Selections from the Prison Notebooks* ed. and trans. Quinten Hoare and Geoffrey Smith, (New York, 1971), 121–25; see also Karl Marx, *The German Ideology* (New York, 1947); Joseph Femia, "Hegemony and Consciousness in the Thought of Antonio Gramsci," *Political Studies* 23 (Mar. 75): 29–48; examples of the use of hegemonic theory in historical writing include Edward Said, *Orientalism* (New York, 1978); Eugene Genovese, *Roll, Jordan, Roll: The World the Slaves Made* (New York, 1974); Christopher Hill, *The World Turned Upside Down* (New York, 1972); Eugene Genovese and Elizabeth Fox Genovese, *The Fruits of Merchant Capital* (New York, 1983), especially part 3, "Ideology"; a discussion study of ideology occurs in John Higham and Paul Conkin, eds., *New Directions in American Intellectual History* (Baltimore, 1979), especially section 3, "History of Cutlure"; Williams, "Base and Superstructure in Marxist Cultural Theory," 8, 9.

45. Lipsitz, "The Struggle for Hegemony," 147; Williams, "Base and Superstructure in Marxist Cultural Theory," 8, 10–12.

46. Peter Berger and Thomas Luckmann, *The Social Construction of Reality: A Treatise in the Sociology of Knowledge* (New York, 1966).

47. Christopher Lasch, *Haven in a Heartless World: The Family Besieged* (New York, 1977), 4; Berger and Luckmann, *The Social Construction*, 62.

48. Alvin Gouldner, *The Dialectic of Ideology and Technology: The Origins, Grammar and Future of Ideology* (New York, 1976), 33; Scott, *Weapons of the Weak*, 322–34; Raymond Williams, *The Country and the City* (New York, 1973).

49. Thomas Kuhn, *The Structure of Scientific Revolutions* (Chicago, 1970).

50. Berger and Luckmann, *The Social Construction*, 66, 103; see also Nicholas Abercrombie, *Class, Structure, and Knowledge: Problems in the Sociology of Knowledge* (New York, 1980), 56–58, 68.

51. Montgomery, *Workers' Control*, 18.

52. Gouldner, *The Dialectic of Ideology and Technology*, 34; for a contemporary assessment of how wealth furnished the foundation for public esteem in the Gilded Age, see Tawney, *The Acquisitive Society*, 35; similarly, a Harvard economics professor argued genetic bases for business behavior, including the urge for power, domination, money making, and an inborn love of rule; Taussig, *Inventors and Money Makers*, chapter 3, "The Psychology of Money Making."

53. Louis Post, "What Rights Have Laborers?" *The Forum*, 1 (May 1886): 298; it is unclear whether this Louis F. Post was the same Post as the author of *Ethics of Democracy* and later assistant secretary of labor in Woodrow Wilson's administration.

54. Gutman, *Work, Culture, and Society*, 80; and Thompson, "Time, Work Discipline," 56–97; for a critique of this position, see Rodgers, "Tradition, Modernity and the American Industrial Worker: Reflections and Critique," 655–81.

55. Milton Cantor, *American Working Class Culture* (New York, 1979), 13.

56. Rowland Berthoff, "Peasants and Artisans, Puritans and Republicans: Personal Liberty and Communal Equality in American History," *Journal of American History* 69 (Dec. 1982): 589–91.

57. Lipsitz, "The Struggle for Hegemony," 146; Fink, "The New Labor History and the Powers of Historical Pessimism: Consensus, Hegemony, and the Case of the Knights of Labor," 116.

58. Anthony Giddens writes of workers, "To mistake pragmatic, ironic (for example, working to rule), humorous, distanced participation in the routines of alienated labor for normative consensus was one of the great errors of the orthodox academic sociology of the 1950s and 60s." *Central Problems in Social Theory: Action Structure and Contradiction in Social Analysis* (Berkeley, 1977), 148, cited in Scott, *Weapons of the Weak*, 321; Post, "What Rights Have Laborers?" 303.

59. James Kitson, "The Iron and Steel Industries of America," *The Engineering Magazine* 1 (July 1891): 484–87; testimony of John Jarrett, president of the Amalgamated Association of Iron and Steel Workers, U.S. Senate *Report of the Committee of the Senate upon the Relations Between Labor and Capital*, 5 vols. (Washington, D.C., 1885), 1:1138–39.

60. Kitson, "The Iron and Steel Industries of America," 486.

61. Lears, "The Concept of Cultural Hegemony: Problems and Possibilities," 567–93.

62. Scott, *Weapons of the Weak*, 336, 338.

63. Trachtenberg, *The Incorporation of America*, 174–79.

64. Stuart Hall, "Culture, Media and the Ideological Effect," in James Curran, et al., eds., *Mass Communication and Society* (Beverly Hills, 1979), 315–48, quote 333; Williams, "Base and Superstructure in Marxist Cultural Theory," 9.

65. Raymond Williams, *Marxism and Literature* (Oxford, 1977), 109; Williams, "Base and Superstructure in Marxist Cultural Theory," 11.

66. Gramsci, *Prison Notebooks*, 181; Hall, "Culture, Media," 332.

67. Williams, "Base and Superstructure," 9.

68. Morris Cooke, "Scientific Management, Collective and Individual," address to the Philadelphia School of Commerce and Accounts, October 27, 1913, Carl Barth Papers, cabinet 1, drawer 1, Baker Library Manuscript Collection, Harvard University.

69. National Association of Manufacturers, *Proceedings of the Annual Convention*, 1906, 13; Williams, "Base and Superstructure in Marxist Cultural Theory," 9.

70. Richard W. Fox and T. J. Jackson Lears, eds., *The Culture of Consumption: Critical Essays in American History, 1880–1980* (New York, 1983); Judith Williamson, *Decoding Advertisements: Ideology and Meaning in Advertising* (New York, 1978); Roland Marchand, *Advertising the American Dream: Making Way for Modernity, 1920–1940* (Berkeley, 1985); Smithsonian Institution, *Images of an Era: The American Poster, 1945–75* (Cambridge, Mass., 1976), 19.

71. Fox and Lears, *The Culture of Consumption*, x.

72. Roger Blough, *The Free Man and the Corporation* (New York, 1959); the author, chairman of the United States Steel Corporation, restates much of the late nineteenth-century ideology, for example, that unionization constitutes a loss of freedom for workers.

Chapter 2

The Pullman Strike: "The Solidarity of Society" versus "The Solidarity of Labor"

The Great Chicago Strike in the summer of 1894 paralyzed the nation's rail transportation for weeks and riveted attention on a grand symbolic struggle between capital and labor. The strike by Pullman's workers, the American Railway Union's boycott of Pullman cars that spread civil violence throughout the country, and the use of troops and court injunctions to quell the strike generated a body of employer rhetoric through which capital defined and defended its and the nation's interests and prescribed labor's proper role in society. In the course of events, George Pullman and the General Managers' Association, and finally the federal government handed the American Railway Union a major defeat that denied its members the right to strike and boycott, defused their organized resistance, discredited them publicly, jailed their leaders, prevented their communications, and refuted their arguments in the nation's press.

Although events of the strike are well known, it is important to examine them in light of capital's promotion of its ''rights'' and its quest for public appearance of its position, both important aspects of its expanding cultural domination. The strike created ''an intense excitement throughout the country,'' an editorialist in the *Nation* wrote in November 1894, ''and the general feeling that the existence of the Government and of society itself was at stake.'' The crisis decade of the 1890s had witnessed the emergence and consolidation of new corporate-led leadership and organization, as well as the rise of a coalesced political challenge to capital in the form of Populism and the 1896 Democratic party. Together with series of major strikes that seemed to herald class warfare, these events prompted capital to assert its own social role aggressively and propose a new view of what constituted public welfare.[1]

The Pullman Company and the General Managers' Association (GMA) took advantage of the public interest surrounding the momentous events of 1894 to argue, against the strikers, their philosophy of markets, property rights, employer-employee relations, arbitration, regulation, strikes, unions, violence, and government action. The public debate over these issues in the months following the strike prompted a national self-examination of civil and economic law, public interest, interpretations of human nature, the proper direction of the social order, and, finally, the durability of the American republic itself. The popular journals that dissected the strike indicated that many of America's opinion leaders had come to equate union tactics with mob violence. As with the heated national discourse generated during other important labor conflicts near the turn of the century, such as the Knights of Labor strike against the Texas and Pacific Railroad in 1884, the strike against Carnegie's Homestead plant in 1886, and the coal strike of 1902–1904, the anti-labor rhetoric of 1894 represented a concerted attempt on the part of businessmen to use publicity and public opinion as a union-busting tactic and to sway the minds of Americans against labor violence, public inconvenience, and even against workers as a class.

This attempt was an exercise in the tactics of cultural warfare as the nation's business elite sought to construct and maintain its cultural power against working class Americans whose lives and actions represented the threat of chaos. Pullman and the GMA, as representatives of an expanding capitalist elite, came to define their own economic and social principles and their own tactics of control as universal reason and mortality, inextricably bound up with the cult of national progress. And they attempted to portray their particular economic interest as that of the state.

The strike assumed especial importance in the public debate because it began in the model factory town George Pullman had created fourteen years before. The town of Pullman had gained national attention as an example of a prominent employer's social theories in practice, a demonstration of a sophisticated welfare scheme that attempted to change employees' cultural patterns, and a realization of an ideal social environment he and, by implication, many manufacturers would have were they to control the work and leisure habits of their employees.[2]

Cultural forms are anchored in the material world where their messages supply socialization as surely as does language or the use of force. Thus, at Pullman, the spatial and hierarchical arrangement of streets, homes, and living space, the temporal arrangement of work and leisure, the nuances of bourgeois display in public space, and the technology of production on the job established social relations and conditioned ways of thinking. They also furnished the sites of struggles between owners and workers over work control, time discipline, and living habits. The story of Pullman town indicates how material organization and ritual rooted the ideas of capitalism in everyday domestic, civic, and working life. It shows how the ideologies of class domination in the form of middle class definitions of the good and proper society are developed on the level of every day life.

PULLMAN TOWN

George Pullman established the Pullman Palace Car Company in 1867 with a capital investment of $1 million. By 1880, prosperity and patent protection had guaranteed him a monopoly on railroad sleeping car manufacture and service on three-fourths of the nation's rail mileage. The fiscal year ending in July, 1893, found the company capitalized at $36 million, having a $25 million surplus of undivided profits, paying yearly dividends to stockholders of 8 to 12 percent, including $2,520,000 in 1893, and distributing wages of $7,233,000. The panic of 1893 forced the company to lower wage payments in fiscal 1894 to $4,471,000, although in the same year it raised stockholder dividends to $2,880,000.[3]

By 1880, financial success spurred Pullman to construct a new car plant and, alongside it, the planned community of Pullman town. Situated fourteen miles south of Chicago between Lake Calumet and the Illinois Central tracks, Pullman's town served as a public demonstration of his principles of order, harmony, economy, efficiency, and social control. His desire to create such an environment equalled, however, his goal of realizing a profitable return on his original investment. Conceived as "strictly a business proposition," he said, the town remained an investment designed to take advantage of the "commercial value of beauty" while yielding a minimum annual return of 6 percent.[4]

Pullman's ideas about working men and women had taken shape within the context of the harsh reality of boomtown Chicago. Between 1870 and 1880, Chicago's population almost doubled to 500,000, and it became the nation's busiest rail center. In the decade after 1880, the city's population tripled. To the city's business leaders, the rapidly built, overcrowded, and dirty working-class housing districts bred the social unrest that had continually dogged the city. The labor disturbances of the 1870s culminated in the great nationwide railroad uprisings of 1877, during which Chicago witnessed four days of rioting that left more than forty dead and scores injured. Chicago newspapers predicted "Civil War," "Horrid Social Convulsion," and "Red War."[5] In 1886, the Haymarket Square bomb established Chicago's reputation for harboring the nation's most radical workforce and generated a national outcry among businessmen and the public against the dangers of anarchism.

Determined to avert what seemed to be an impending social revolution, George Pullman and other Chicago business leaders searched for new institutions to alleviate the workers' plight and bring order to urban life. Pullman involved himself in Chicago's civic sphere, promoting education through the Young Men's Christian Association (YMCA) and the Chicago Manual Training School, supporting youth temperance through the Citizen's Law and Order League, and seeking civil improvement through commercial clubs. As early as 1873, he began welfare work in his own plants with the Pullman Mutual Benefit Association, promising to provide workers with eating, bathing, reading, and social facilities. No amount of welfare work, Pullman came to believe, could correct the unruly habits of Chicago's working people. The social and moral evils of working class neighborhoods—drinking, filth, idleness, unhealthful living, transience—all of which fostered poor work performance, could be eradicated, he thought, only by forcing workers to live in a clean, orderly, stable, moral environment.[6]

Pullman's desires to acculturate workers in middle class behavior reflected a larger middle class attempt to create order in a world of social upheaval by defining the world in bourgeois terms. As the middle class grew stronger in the late nineteenth century, it sensed the need to discriminate itself from the working class and to present itself as representing progressive universal culture. It attempted to define taboos in working class life that had to be rectified. The negative qualities of the working class targeted by Pullman's managers—drinking, dirtiness, bad manners, immorality—furnished a symbolic inversion of the positive values through which the middle class defined itself and upon which it built its hegemonic social differentiations. Pullman's elite both depended upon and opposed the workers who provided it with the opportunity to construct order from chaos and define itself as the progressive agent of that process. The social distance from workers that the middle class could construct through cultural symbols and meanings created images and meanings of its own superiority and worthiness. The middle class security and confidence instilled by orderly homes, parks, playgrounds, and workspaces exposed both the anxiety and the agenda of Pullman's constant cultural warfare against the people who represented the threat of chaos.

Cultural warfare is carried out through the use of symbols that identify the acceptable and the taboo, that define "self" and the "other," and that maintain boundaries between them. The nation's bourgeoisie made claims to social leadership based upon its superior morality, its habits of order and cleanliness, its self-control, responsibility, and thrift, and its belief in rational, scientific progress. Order was the primary virtue in the bourgeois life and worldview. Public and private life at Pullman was organized in symmetries of space and time. The bourgeoisie used working class disorder and underdevelopment as a mirror for its own cultural sophisticated and social progress.

The physical surroundings and moral regimen at Pullman town were an attempt to transform workers' social habits through the benefits of a pleasant, healthful, uplifting atmosphere, free from disorder, drink, and corruption. Attracting the "best class of mechanic" and excluding "baneful influences," Pullman maintained, would achieve "elevation of the employees." In this manner, commercial motives and social goals blended into a utopian project in which material beneficence provided the basis for moral uplift and guided workers' thought and behavior toward Pullman's goal of more efficient and profitable plant management. If Pullman anticipated the welfare work and paternalistic reform of the early twentieth century, he sought at the same time to re-create between employer and employee the stable, paternal, hierarchical, deferential social relations of an earlier age. Modelled on the Krupp company's planned community at Essen, Germany, Pullman town inherited the regimented pattern of factory towns like Lowell, Massachusetts, which, together with asylums, schools, orphanages, prisons, reformatories, and barracks, represented bourgeois efforts to contain the disruptive forces of urbanizing and industrializing society in the nineteenth century.[7]

Pullman town's physical arrangement furnished a visual representation of its patriarchal authority system with Pullman himself at the head. Pullman's name, or that of his family members, appeared on buildings, streets, the town's bank, church, school, and its leisure organizations. Pullman's authority, ultimately grounded in his actual ownership of plant and town, was, in turn, reinforced by the visual legitimacy embodied in its imposing, formal, elegant architecture. Intended to shape residents' attitudes as well as meet their needs, the town provided workers with tangible models of hierarchical class differences in housing and income. The entire social space of Pullman furnished a backdrop for the owners' and managers' ceremonial and ritualized enforcement of caste through the public display of clothing, carriages, fine homes, expenditures, and leisure activity. Theoretically, residents of all classes were to use services and interact with one another on an equitable basis; actually, the town's work, living, and social spaces remained segregated along class lines. Pullman admitted that the town's very design reinforced social relations on the "business level of employer to employee and landlord to tenant." This appeared obvious to Richard Ely who visited Pullman town in 1885. "It is avowedly part of the design of Pullman to surround laborers as far as possible with all the privileges of large wealth," he observed.[8]

Thus, worker socialization was designed to instill middle class habits but, more importantly, to ensure that workers remained workers. Pullman town was not just an attempt to teach workers middle class habits, but to define workers as the "other," through segregation and the provision of relatively poorer social services, and housing and wage differences. Through its supervised work and leisure activities, and in everyday use of public space, the town juxtaposed the prosperity and propriety of Pullman's elite with the deplorable habits of its working people.

The town was constructed entirely of red brick in a uniform design, a palpable, substantial, permanent, institutional embodiment of ideas of utility, order, and harmony in social space. Streets were patterned in a 1/2 × 2 mile grid, offering a repetitious, orderly, predictable public space designed to reinforce deliberate, respectable, rational habits. Located at one end of town near workers' living quarters, the manufacturing plant signified production and the ultimate reason for all other contingent activity. Covering 30 acres and dominated by a 190 foot tall water tower, the shops and offices of the Pullman Palace Car Company included a foundry, wheel manufactory, brickyard, lumberyard, gas works, wood and machine shops, tool shops, and auxiliary buildings. The car manufacturing shops were dominated by a main construction shop 700 feet long, whose center administrative section featured a bell tower that rose 140 feet and displayed to a world still largely without watches and clocks four great, lighted clocks facing the points of the compass with the front-facing one reflected in a pool below.

Pullman's clock tower, like those of other factory towns, routinized workers' goings and comings, as Daniel Rodgers wrote, signalling a visual and audible "mechanization of work and time, the narrowing and tightening of the injunction to diligence" at the center of the industrialized world. When operating at full capacity in the years before the depression of 1893, the plant used 6,000 to 8,000 employees to turn 50 million feet of lumber and 85,000 tons of iron into 12,500 freight cars, 313 sleeping cars, 626 passenger cars, and 939 street cars in one twelve-month period. The entire plant and town implied order, symmetry, punctuality, austerity, utility, and a self-proclaimed "no-nonsense" business atmosphere.[9]

The town proper consisted of park, residential, and commercial areas. Bordering Lake Calumet, the park offered spacious greens, seating areas, sports fields, and tennis courts. At lakeside, beds of flowers spelled Pullman's name. From the park, a bridge led to an island in the lake that sported a lavishly constructed boathouse and race track that doubled as a skating rink in winter. The regularity of street patterns and residential architecture was broken by dignified public buildings, the Arcade, the Market, and the sumptuous Florence Hotel. The Arcade, a large building 256 feet long, 146 feet wide and 90 feet high, was designed to force residents to combine commercial and community activities in one central, company-supervised location. It contained large passageways running north-south and east-west, lined on either side with booths and shops. The second floor housed a theater, kindergarten, library, and meeting rooms all opening out onto an interior balcony. On the main floor was the Pullman Loan and Savings Bank. Pullman required that all the town's shops other than grocery markets be located in the Arcade. Since the "bosses" of the Pullman works rented the store spaces and owned the shops, "woe betide the poor man or his family who fails to patronize the Arcade," reported Thomas Grant, one of the journalists who visited Pullman in 1885 at the owner's invitation. "It is possible for the company to dictate these matters," observed a former employee, "as it controls every inch of ground."[10] Such requirements reflected bourgeois notions of workers as consumers who could be encouraged to use leisure time for shopping or browsing and partaking of community services in the Arcade.

Pullman's library of 6,000 volumes was richly upholstered and decorated with "Wilton carpets and plush-covered chairs," clearly intended for the clean and well dressed, not to mention the literate and leisured. The small, austerely furnished Men's Reading Room had a separate entrance that led directly to the street, allowing workers to enter from the outside without passing through the sumptuously furnished library. These arrangements replicated class differences in the town proper. Sensing this, the average worker avoided the library, according to Pullman town's Methodist minister, the Reverend W. H. Carwardine, for it appeared too luxurious and created "a spirit of caste in the little town." Pullman expected the library to promote the community's moral and intellectual development. Only 31 percent of its books were fiction, the remainder devoted to what the librarian termed "more serious education." In an age of free libraries,

Pullman's library patrons paid an annual fee of $3, equal to a day and a half's work for an ordinary laborer, which, coupled with the intimidation of its luxuriousness, kept annual membership near 200 patrons, out of a pool of 5,500 workers in 1893. The library also charged for its classes in stenography, history, languages, literature, and civics. Like the library, the richly appointed, 800 seat theater separated those who paid 35, 50, and 75 cents a seat for the more wealthy occupants of the Moorish-design boxes in the balcony. In an attempt to refine theatergoers' tastes upward, the company excluded ''immoral'' theater presentations in favor of ''innocent amusement.'' The town's other public buildings included a free school for employees' children, a church, a casino, a firehouse, and a stable, which housed both the town's work horses and wealthy residents' pleasure horses. A carriage and horse could be rented for $3.00 a day for excursions.[11]

The most imposing building in the town proper was the Florence Hotel, a huge, two-story, elaborately constructed and decorated ''gingerbread'' building surrounded on three sides by public squares covered with flowers and shrubbery. It was here, the *Chicago Evening Post* reported, that the ''aristocracy of Pullman hold forth.'' The hotel rented rooms from $3.00 to $4.00 a day, offered 75 cent meals in its restaurant, and contained banquet rooms to let for weddings and parties. It also housed the only bar allowed in town, which, by its location and luxurious appointments, was clearly intended for managers only. One of Pullman's employees reported that he had ''looked but dared not enter Pullman's hotel with its private bar.''[12] Such deference clearly suited George Pullman, who revealed his class perceptions of the effects of drink in an interview in the *Ottowa Daily Free Press* in 1882: ''We allow no liquor in the city; now take strong drink away from men who have been accustomed to it, and not furnish something to fill the gap is all wrong—there is a want felt, a vacuum created and it must be filled; to do this we have provided a theatre, a reading room, a billiard room, and all sorts of outdoor sports, and by this means our people soon forget all about drink, they find they are better off without it, and we have an assurance of our work being done with greater accuracy and skill.'' Thus, ''the temptation to drink does not constantly stare one in the face,'' one of the town's visitors observed, ''and this restriction has not entirely failed to accomplish its end, the promotion of temperance.''[13]

City planners located grocery shops in Market Hall, which, like the Arcade, provided areas for supervised social activity and relaxation, most of which were centered on encouraging workers to engage in middle class sports and recreations such as theater, reading, shopping, touring, ice skating, and picnicking in parks. Pullman anticipated that the town's middle class would, during these activities, set good examples for workers and discourage that favorite working class pastime, drinking. Nowhere, the Reverend Carwardine and other visitors noted, did the planned society provide for working men's clubs or designate official space for separate working class pastimes, where ''men may congregate and chat with each other and where, for the benefit of young men there should be games such as checkers, chess.'' Despite the opportunities for supervised play amid Pullman town's greenery and luxury or the presumed benefits of temperance, many workers did not avail themselves of the leisure activities provided. True to the working-class traditions of group public leisure and lacking homes with ''living'' space, workmen preferred instead to congregate in the thirty saloons in nearby Kensington and Roseland. They understood, perhaps, as Roy Rosenzweig later pointed out, that the ''essential ingredient in supervised play activity is supervision.''[14]

If it did not provide for separate working class leisure activity, Pullman town did offer living accommodations in the form of 1,799 dwelling units which, by their different amenities, denoted separate income and job classifications. Thus, while the town's physical symmetry stood for order, it also publicly designated relative gradations of class rank and, presumably, social value. Although Pullman denied any connection between renting his apartments and working in his plant, workers testified to the United States Strike Commission that they were compelled to reside in town when space was available. Pullman's average rent of $13.50 per month was 20 to 25 percent higher than in neighboring working class communities. Many families sublet to individual boarders in order to survive, although Pullman's managers deplored the practice since exposing wives and daughters to unmarried males in an unsupervised domestic setting appeared to the managers' middle class sensibilities to encourage immorality.[15]

Pullman fought immorality from external sources too. His refusal to sell or rent space to outside commercial interests, for example, protected the town from ''baneful elements which it was the chief purpose to exclude.'' Claiming ''very satisfactory success'' with such exclusions, Pullman boasted, ''there are no saloons in Pullman; there are no brothels or other objectionable houses; no such places of resort.'' Pullman saw the results of his benevolent social organization and paternalistic control in visits to employee homes, ''as I had occasion to do often,'' and from their appearance in the streets. He estimated that employees and their families lived ''about 40 percent better than people in ordinary manufacturing towns . . . that did not have the advantages of cleanliness and order and the elimination of bad influences.'' He concluded that ''the general expression of people was in the direction of a higher class.''[16]

Workers' residences were situated on paved, landscaped streets arranged in a crosshatch pattern. These homes consisted of unbroken rows of brick tenements where, in each block, up to 500 persons lived under one roof in nearly identical two-to-five family dwellings. Each building had a narrow strip of front lawn and a small back lot that, one worker complained, barely accommodated a clothesline and allowed no space for a garden. Carwardine found that ''the monotony and regularity of the buildings gives one the impression that he is living in a soldiers' barracks.''[17] If this were true, it fulfilled the intent of Pullman's designers. The daily ritual of living in such imposed visual and spatial order helped impart values of stability, regularity, and predictability, and it implied the static ''assignment'' of each person to his or her rightful place in a rational, orderly universe.

Tenement apartments renting for $8 to $9 per month housed both ordinary laborers, who represented 20 to 25 percent of Pullman's population and earned $1.30 a day, and carbuilders, who earned $2.50 to $3.00 daily. Each apartment included a cook stove, gas lighting, sink, and water tap. A water closet was shared with other apartments on that floor. Skilled craftsmen, who represented about 60 percent of the workforce, usually resided in more comfortable, five room duplexes that occupied separate plots of ground and rented for $15 to $25 a month. Pullman's company officers, merchants, and professionals lived in individually constructed homes with lawns bordering the wide Florence Boulevard. Considerably larger, these had up to twelve rooms and rented for up to $75 a month. Relatively high rents and coercive collection procedures guaranteed prompt monthly income from the residential section of the town. Each worker received two paychecks, one for the rent due that was immediately signed over to the company, and one for the remainder in actual wages. The checks were issued payable by the Pullman Loan and Savings Bank "to accustom [employees] to its use and encourage them to make deposits."[18]

Pullman advertised his model town as a public demonstration of his notions of economic efficiency and social organization and encouraged Chicago's citizens, the press, and other businessmen to visit the plant and town to see how a company simultaneously promoted its own and its employees' interests. "It was an age of advertising," observed Thomas Grant, "and Mr. Pullman was shrewd." The town's paid professional propagandist, Colonel Duane Doty, a historian and statistician, professed a "profound admiration for the system upon which the town is based." Disseminating literature, conducting tours, editing the *Pullman Journal*, and writing newspaper and magazine articles, Doty delivered "delightful impressions of the town" to the many visitors who arrived daily from Chicago. He distributed copies of Mrs. Doty's *Pullman Illustrated* to the thousands of guests who visited the Chicago World's Columbian Exposition in 1893 and took the train out to Pullman town.[19] "Imagine a perfectly equipped town of 12,000 inhabitants," the official *Story of Pullman* read, "built out from one central thought to a beautiful and harmonious whole" and "bordered with bright flowers and green stretches of lawn, [and] shaded with trees and dotted with parks and pretty water vistas, where the homes are bright and wholesome, filled with pure air and light, where all that is ugly, and discordant, and demoralizing is eliminated, and all that inspires to self-respect, to thrift, and to cleanliness of person and of thought is generously provided." Pullman's official preacher, the Reverend Doctor Oggel of the town's nondenominational church likewise lauded the "great experiment." In a sermon from the Biblical text "Thou hast made him a little lower than the angels, and hast crowned him with glory and honor," Oggel sanctified Pullman's "service to his age." On the first Sunday after the strike began, he admonished workers who had complained of drastic wage cuts that "a half loaf was better than no loaf."[20]

Pullman planned the town's physical and social arrangements to produce an obedient, moral community by providing a closely monitored, centralized setting free from liquor and "bad influences." By the visual examples of regularity, cleanliness, and spaciousness, he intended the city environment to foster "habits of respectability," making workers punctual, mannerly, respectful of superiors, moral, saving, educated, and uplifted. Company literature portrayed the town's ideal worker who went directly from home to work in the morning and spent his time and money on his family rather than at the saloon in the evening. The company attempted to enforce images of the bourgeois family in its provision of single family space, its policy on boarders, privacy, cleanliness, and its prohibition of saloons and brothels. "The building of Pullman," a company official reported to the press, "is very likely to be the beginning of a new era for labor." Interestingly, workers did not destroy property or initiate violence at Pullman town during the strike. Pullman's interpretation attributed this to the company's having provided its townspeople with "various sources of elevation of character."

Despite its attempts at social control, however, the company claimed that it fostered independence among the workers, helping them to "help themselves without either undermining their self-respect or touching their . . . absolute personal liberty." In eleven years of residency, reported W. T. Stead, visiting the town in 1893, the Pullman worker "has developed into a distinct type" with all the "external indications of self respect," including thrift, refinement, tidy dress, clearer complexions, brighter eyes, and a "bearing and demeanor" reflecting "the general atmosphere of order and artistic taste which permeates the town."[21]

This was the goal, then, of the industrializing bourgeoisie in the late nineteenth century, to reorganize the lives and habits of workers so that they no longer represented dirt, disorder, violence, or immorality. Pullman town's managers remained content with the "external indications" of self-respect, morality, cleanliness, and thrift, but they were mindful that no matter how acculturated workers became, it remained necessary to maintain class distinctions of income and status for purposes of bourgeois self-definition.

Pullman often repeated his ideas about the social and psychological characteristics of his employees in implicit and explicit messages to town residents. The company's interests were identical to those of its workers, he maintained; the company was competent to ascertain such interests; order and hierarchy were to be maintained at every point of contact between labor and management; and the company rightfully supervised and controlled workers' lives outside their regular hours. Mindful of employee discontent, company spies, or what the residents called "spotters," practiced a system of surveillance and tendered to managers weekly reports concerning residents' attitudes and conversations. Housing leases included written permission for company officials to enter residences "at all times."

Employees expressed their resentment of the weight of company intrusion into their lives on and off the job. Women in car shops, for example, protested the abuses of shop forewomen, "whose delight it has been to make the girls' life one of discontent, humbling and crushing them in spirit, forcing many of them to become pliant tools and debased informers," a grievance committee reported to the American Railway Union (ARU) convention in 1894. Another resident found Pullman "all very well as an employer" but complained that "to live and breathe and have one's being in Pullman was a little bit too much." Town residents, he continued, felt their "lives were bounded on all sides by the Pullman Company," having "paid rent to the Pullman Company, bought gas from the Pullman Company, walked on streets owned by the Pullman Company, paid water-tax to the Pullman Company, sent children to Pullman's school and attended Pullman's church." Indeed, even when residents "bought gingham for their wives or sugar for their tables at the arcade or market-house, it seemed dealing with the Pullman Company." "It seems to me," said Carwardine of Pullman's authority, "that imperialism on the part of a gentleman so powerful in influence as Mr. Pullman is unpleasant to say the least, and capable of producing harm whether intentional or not toward those in authority under him."[22]

Many town residents found their only escape from company presence in that "Pullman did not sell them their grog." The long row of saloons in adjacent Kensington, which the press called "bumtown" and which was often found "give over to disorder," also served as meeting places where workers aired their grievances and, once the strike commenced, plotted their resistance. Pullman did not allow labor unions in town and forbade labor organizers to hold meetings or give speeches. To Federal Strike Commissioners who later assessed the significance of the tightly controlled social system, "the conditions created at Pullman enable the management at all times to assert with great vigor its assumed right to fix wages and rents absolutely, and to repress that sort of independence which leads to labor organizations and their attempts at mediation, arbitration, strikes, etc."[23]

Despite the company's vigorous attempts at repressing independence, employee criticism of the Pullman system surfaced often enough to indicate the impossibility of maintaining control over workers' lives even within such a grand experiment in social engineering. Subjecting themselves outwardly to the work discipline in car shops and social discipline in the town, workers nevertheless routinely complained to the company about its favoritism, arbitrary blacklisting, and interference with their political activities. As resentment built in the town over the gradual reduction of piecework rates in the five years preceding the strike, workers charged that no redress or grievance system existed to deal with inequities in the shops. "They had come to feel they could get no justice," charged Carwardine, citing instances in which workers had left the company's employ rather than endure Pullman's "absolutism."[24]

Pullman's attempt to extend his power over his employees' electoral choices brought him face to face with their resistance. An active Republican, he was well known in Washington as a generous contributor, "much esteemed by party treasurers." It was widely known among his workers that Pullman could not endure "stiff-necked rebellion politically," as evidenced by his response to one of his employees, John P. Hopkins, who organized the town's workers and returned a Democratic majority in the presidential election of 1888. Hopkins, later mayor of Chicago during the strike, had been rapidly promoted through the ranks at Pullman from laborer to paymaster, earning the respect of his fellow workers along the way. His reputation as a staunch individualist came from having openly sympathized with the workers in an earlier unsuccessful strike. Pullman had demanded his resignation as punishment but later reinstated Hopkins at a higher salary "because of [the workers] admiration for the brave fellow who had stood unabashed and victorious before the company," according to a former co-worker of Hopkins at Pullman. In 1888, despite rumors of "official vengeance," the popular paymaster organized a successful Democratic turnout. "It was not an easy thing to do," Hopkins' co-worker remembered, for "the people were accustomed to subserviency, and yet more so since the unsuccessful strike." By his "magnetic presence" and his example, Hopkins "brought manhood and courage to the surface in men who had never given any signs of either before, and have since lapsed into the old lack-lustre, subservient mode of life."[25]

By 1892, Pullman had geared up to ensure this docility, taking upon himself the political organization of his workers. In an *American Industries* article of August 1894, editors of the National Association of Manufacturers' magazine reported Pullman's attempts to influence his employees' voting in the campaign of 1892. The article reprinted Pullman's July 10, 1893, interview in the *New York Herald* in which he expressed anger and disgust over the election of Grover Cleveland in 1884 and 1892, whose policies Pullman considered directly responsible for the panic of 1893. Pullman town traditionally returned a Republican majority of 2,000 to 2,500 votes in presidential elections. Confidently expecting the same for Benjamin Harrison in 1892, Pullman had fought Cleveland's election "with all my power." Pullman told his employees during the 1892 summer campaign that he wished to avoid "unduly" influencing their votes and that he sincerely hoped that no worker regarded his speech as an "attempt to coerce you into voting any way against your convictions." Nevertheless, he threatened workers with economic disaster should Cleveland be elected. "This is a business campaign," he warned, "if Cleveland is elected, it means an end to the protective tariff . . . and the biggest financial disaster which this country has ever seen. If Cleveland is elected, business in this country will come to a standstill. Pullman will have to shut down or to run along on half pay. In other words, the cold fact is just this: That any man in Pullman who votes the Democratic ticket is simply voting bread and butter out of his mouth and out of the mouths of his wife and children. If you want to do that, go ahead and do it. But I appeal to you not to commit such a folly."[26]

Reprinted in Chicago newspapers, this speech angered many of Chicago's workers and, in the opinion of the *Herald* editor, contributed to the unexpected vote Cleveland received in that city. *American Industries* reported that a "more impolitic speech could hardly have been delivered" and that Chicago Republicans had tried unsuccessfully to counteract its "boomerang effect." Pullman admitted surprise when his town returned a majority of more than 2,000 votes for Cleveland. "The workingmen were simply crazy," he fumed. Claiming that he had done as much for labor as any man alive, he felt betrayed and lashed out in a vindictive fury. "I made up my mind," he told the editor, "that that was the last of my sympathy for the workingman." He decided that since his employees had voted "against their own interests and against my interests," he would cut wages "to the bottom notch" and "see how they like it." The *Herald* correspondent and other writers attributed Pullman's "vengeful, retaliatory policy" during the strike to his having been provoked by the 1892 vote.[27]

In addition to outright political pressure, however effective, other company policies drew workers' complaints: the company's refusal to assume liability for plant accidents, its coercive bill collection policies, its full occupancy requirements for company housing, and arbitrary dismissals and blacklisting. Since no channels existed for employee complaints, however, criticism remained problematic and was most often driven underground by the presence of spies and the pervasive, intimidating atmosphere. "Owing to the peculiarity of the paternalistic government of Pullman," Carwardine concluded, "no one feels like openly criticizing the Company."[28] When wage cuts came in late 1893 and early 1894 and Pullman's workers resorted to union organization, they argued that there was no other way to get the company to talk to them.

In the 1880s and 1890s, the Pullman experiment received substantial coverage in the nation's press, much of it centering on what W. T. Stead, British social critic and author of the influential expose *If Christ Came to Chicago*, called its "too paternal despotism." An interest in oppressive social systems reflected the nation's preoccupation with large-scale production that stifled the free individual. An examination of this lively debate indicates that contemporaries analyzed social coercion at Pullman in terms that anticipate those of hegemonic analysis. Some writers like Charles Eaton, who visited Pullman in 1894, found that "no pressure of any kind is brought to bear upon the men," and described them "talking with entire freedom, praising and blaming overseers and officers with an easy manner borne only of long habit."[29]

An investigation of the Pullman experiment undertaken by the National Convention of the Commissioners of State Bureaus of Labor Statistics attested to a palpable degree of behavior modification in the closely monitored town. The convention, led by H. A. Newman, Missouri commissioner of labor statistics and including Carroll D. Wright, Massachusetts commissioner of labor statistics, met at Pullman for three days in September of 1885 and studied the city's "economic, sanitary, industrial, moral, and social conditions." The commissioners produced a glowing report, published by the Massachusetts Bureau of Statistics of Labor in 1885, that lauded "one of the most attractive experiments of the age seeking to harmonize the interests of capital and labor." The report cited workers' high morale and "generously confirmed" earlier good impressions reported in the Chicago press. It attributed Pullman town's low death and accident rates to good drainage and sewage treatment, clean air, temperance, and general health. And the commissioners confirmed the coercive but nevertheless beneficial operation of social pressure that ensured the good behavior claimed in Pullman company pamphlets. The "silent but powerful influence of public opinion" inside the town, for example, quickly induced new residents to abandon unsanitary habits "such as making yard cesspools." Families soon replaced "dirty broken furniture" with that "more in accord with their surroundings." Likewise "men who are accustomed to lounge on their front stoops, smoking pipes, and in dirty shirt sleeves, soon dress and act more in accordance with the requirements of society. All this accomplished," the commissioners maintained, "by the silent educational influence of their surroundings." Members of "untidy families," as they walked the streets, "learned the ever-present lesson" taught by "orderly ways, well-kept lawns, tidy dwellings, [and] clean workshops." It was true that the constant social pressure of "perfect order and cleanliness" was "often felt as a restraint" by those brought up "under disorder and uncleanliness" and "causes a sigh for the looser ways and consequent looser morals of other communities." These types of people found Pullman uncongenial and soon left. In answer to charges that Pullman's civic atmosphere oppressed workers, the commissioners concluded that its benefits outweighed any drawbacks and, indeed, that workers should appreciate what they had. "If the workman at Pullman lives in a 'gilded cage,' we must congratulate him on its being so handsomely gilded; the average workman does not have his cage gilded," the commissioners admonished.[30]

Anticipating an important issue in the coming strike, the commissioners recognized that Pullman had "merely proposed to manufacture railway cars for profit" and assumed no obligation to jeopardize his investment in a "costly experiment." Taking a cue from promotional company literature, they granted that Pullman's good will prompted his "nobler uses of great wealth." For his part Pullman had made no claim to being a philanthropist, disdaining "promiscuous charity" in favor of "business principles [which] should net a fair return for efforts made." This, the commissioners agreed, constituted "true philanthropy."[31]

Other observers, however, found that while Pullman had made generous provisions for the residents' social life, the town's features, in their beauty and regularity, were "so artificially perfected as to give one the impression of a machine-made town." The town might appear benevolent, observed Thomas Grant, who visited in 1885, but a "very unreal and false notion of the place is apt to be carried away by the visitor." He indicted Pullman's "modern satrapy" as a "crude attempt . . . to resurrect . . . the ideas . . . of medieval barons who took pride in fostering villages beneath their castle towers . . . from which they looked down in lordly condescension on their humble retainers." Lamenting the loss of individuality, Grant described the "blight" that "suspended like a black cloud over Pullman City, and crushes out the spirit of fun, of humor, and of independence, from the hearts and thoughts of the people." In the entire city of 12,000, he feared, there was not "a single independent man—outside of Mr. Pullman."[32]

With Richard Ely's *Harper's Monthly* article that appeared the same year as the labor commissioner's report, the issue of paternalism and social control at Pullman received national attention. An assistant professor of economics at Johns Hopkins University, Ely rejected the "dogmatic assumptions of classical political economy" and criticized the town from the Christian and "scientific" standpoint of a liberal reformer. He praised Pullman's use of scientific principles to undertake "social experimentation of a vast scale," one that gave the individual worker a chance to participate "as fully as his nature will allow in the advantages of the existing civilization." Like earlier observers, Ely confirmed that social beauty indeed fostered habits of utility and order. In the car shops, the "wholesome, cheerful surroundings enable the men to work more constantly and more efficiently." Keeping the town's streets sprinkled with water, the lawns trimmed, and the exteriors of workers' homes tidy was certain to "exert its proper effect on housewives, stimulating them to exertion on behalf of cleanliness and order."[33]

Yet Ely condemned the evident paternalism for creating a dependence that subverted the workmen's personal liberty and individualism and emphasized class gradations. He cited conditions that produced this effect, in particular the company's exercise of an all-pervading, absolute power and a "needless air of secrecy," which frustrated even his efforts to obtain reliable statistics. The monotony and "mechanical regularity" of the town's design and physical setting dismayed Ely for it reinforced "machine made" habits among the residents. As an extension of Pullman Company, the city's "every municipal act" was that of a private corporation. Pullman's authority reminded Ely of royal absolutism in which "the citizen is surrounded by constant restraint and restriction, and everything is done for him, nothing by him." Pullman's experiment "desires the happiness of people, but in such a way as shall please the authorities." In order to avoid strikes, the "chief of social sins," Pullman's social atmosphere repressed individual initiative even in the residents' private affairs, producing what Ely deemed a "dependent, servile population." Ely furthermore lamented the reinforcement of class in Pullman's treatment of its unskilled laborers, both through subsistence pay and poor housing. "They are crowded together in the cheap flats, which are put . . . out of sight . . . and present a rather dreary appearance," he noted. Even the scope of Pullman's social experiment hardly touched them. "The social problem in their case remains unsolved."[34]

Ely also discerned the attempts to transform workers into consumers of middle class culture. The company, for instance, purchased "great quantities" of wallpaper at discount and sent a representative around to "the poorer houses" with samples from which each housewife was to select and purchase cheaply for her own home. Friends and neighbors expressed "great interest" in helping one another choose styles and colors, and the laborers' wives developed "a very general desire to adorn and beautify their dwellings." A local architect involved in the project remarked to Ely that this was "doubtless the first time many women had been called upon to exercise taste." One must guard against assuming, however, that internalized pressure against dirt and in favor of neatness and "beauty" meant that workers and their families surrendered to middle class cultural colonization. The working class wife may have adopted the quiet, well-kept, wall-papered parlor as a refuge against the overcrowding and drudgery of ordinary life, appropriating the middle class parlor but giving it a symbolic meaning different from that of the middle class.[35]

For all its beauty and instructiveness, Pullman town symbolized to Ely industrial society's assault upon the free individual. He correctly identified the core elements of Pullman's social experiment as the physical reproduction of ideal notions of order within a hierarchical, corporate structure. And he understood this experiment as an attempt to transform older communal forms of social organization based on mutuality and morality into an efficient, profit-oriented, corporate-led culture.

One must ask if the town's physical surrounding, surveillance, moral example, planned leisure time, prohibition of alcohol, encouragement of thrift and industry, and penalization of improvidence kept workers sober or made them thrifty, respectable churchgoers or elevated their choices in spending and leisure activity. Did they willingly or grudgingly accept the communal experiment? And, regardless, were they enriched or oppressed? Even more, was it long-sustained resistance to company oppression that finally exploded in an act of defiance, or a momentary breakdown in an otherwise intact system of control? The answer is not clear, since observers like Charles Eaton reported visible moral uplift and cheerful participation by freedom-loving citizens at the same time as others like Ely and Stead reported numb compliance under stifling paternalism. Workers, too, spoke in varying tones. In public testimony, Thomas Heathcoate exposed the company's blacklist and union prohibitions, criticized its rent policy, and challenged its claim to be operating at a loss and its offer to prove this by allowing workers to examine the books. Yet he allowed that "employees were very favorably disposed toward Mr. Pullman," at least until an inexperienced foreman appeared in the car shop two years before the strike.[36]

However, it may not simply be either one or the other, and one must guard against "pigeonholing every expressive gesture as either 'accommodation' or 'resistance'," as Jackson Lears has cautioned. Furthermore, to call it accommodation may be to assume that employer dominance was something completed or achieved, when it was more a dialectical process that took place on contested terrain and never culminated in any definitive outcome. The question may be less, "Did workers capitulate to absolute social dominance, or did they resist by preserving their dignity and social norms against company power?" than "On what terms was the original accommodation forged in the town? How was it broken? How was it re-established?" It is clear that Pullman's workers aired grievances when and where they could and that when the crisis arose took matters into their hands and acted with great determination against the company. It is also clear that intimidation and coercion took place, that a job at the Pullman works required a measure of outward compliance no matter what the degree of inner resistance, and that the more workers submitted to these demands, the more they were in the grip of society.[37]

It is revealing to examine workers' assessment of their situation in the Pullman Strike Committee's official statement to the American Railway Union convention on June 15, 1894. Strikers defined their grievances within the context of a community of workers and owners wherein each side was mutually obligated to uphold its responsibilities. Pullman had provided the raw material for the conflict by drawing on shared republican norms, by creating a community of *imposed* responsibility, decency, self-respect, independence, and healthy life. Hence, conflict between the Pullman Company and its workers took place within the context of these established norms and through the dynamic of paternalism *and* mutuality.

Workers eloquently described their aggrieved situation, which had produced a "dance of skeletons bathed in human tears." Yet they spoke fondly of their home. "Our town is beautiful . . . , we are peaceable, we are orderly"; the town's moral uplift guaranteed that "no word of scandal has arisen against one of our women. What city of 20,000 can say the like?" In this spirit, Pullman's workers served night and day as guards during the strike to "save the Pullman property." Pullman officials "started out on the basis that their system is paternalistic," Carwardine testified; "they founded their system upon a desire to improve the workingman and to solve the industrial situation on a basis of mutual recognition." That this moral community existed within a corporate entity underscored the workers' understanding of, and response to, both the coercion and beneficence at Pullman. Workers saw themselves as a moral community whose patron had reneged on his responsibility by "not feeding us" and then run away from adverse public opinion. When Pullman cut wages and refused to talk to his employees, workers rebuked their employer for his failure to abide by community norms. "We could get no redress," said Thomas Heathcoate, explaining recourse to union organization. Theodore Rhodie, a painter and Pullman resident for twelve years, felt that Pullman had asked him to "give up my principles, my right as an American citizen."[38]

Thus, workers made claims against their patron not in terms of a radical alteration of property or power relations but simply for failing to provide what he had promised, a wholesome family existence in a benevolent, if business-oriented, atmosphere. They demanded that he return, face the situation, and rectify the wrongs in order to restore what the workers termed the town's "harmony and peaceableness." To make his triumph appear legitimate, Pullman would have only to re-establish the bonds of this moral community by making concessions to its population, to "share up a little bit," as Carwardine said, based on his own stated norms of gentility and fair play, however subsumed under, and tied to, the "ethos of corporatism" these bonds actually were.

Commissioner: If rents had been reduced to any reasonable extent, along with the reduction of wages, would the employees at Pullman have been satisfied?

Heathcoate: Yes, sir; if they had reduced the rents in proportion to the reduction of
    wages.[39]

In short, Pullman workers had both submitted to and resisted his heavy handed
methods but consented to the republican notions of communal responsibility that
held the Pullman community together. Samuel Gompers, too, observed the deference to Pullman's notions of community on the part of his employees. Pullman
had made workers dependent entirely on his "generosity and foresight in all
things" and warned them not to unionize against their mutually profitable "joint
enterprise." Hindsight prompted Gompers to remark that the workers had been
"wholly misled by false promises and covert threats."[40] Hegemony, then, involves the ability of elites to organize meaning, in this case around republican
norms reinforced by paternalism and mutuality and backed by coercion. Pullman
town offers an example of a hegemonic relationship based on shared economic
interest and good will whether or not workers were "misled." Workers resisted
based on different interpretations of stated norms, but the worker-owner relationship remained hegemonic in the sense that the resistance took place and order
was restored within the wider context of an employer-led and employer-defined,
profit maximizing, corporate community.

   Pullman city's "model" and tactics of social control did not long survive
Pullman, who died in 1897. Technological changes in industry after 1900 that
reduced the need for skilled labor coupled with demographic changes in boomtown Chicago caused the town to lose its community identity. Housing deteri-
orated and many homes and buildings stood vacant or were occupied by Pullman's
new unskilled workforce from southern and eastern Europe. By 1915 the town
contained fifteen saloons. Three years later, one-third of the Arcade lay unoc-
cupied. The Pullman Company experienced increasing unionization in its plant
and a succession of strikes after 1902, culminating in a victorious union-busting
lockout in 1904. Thereafter, the company rehired only those it could deal with
as individuals. Although Pullman town remained famous as an experiment in
corporate social engineering, few U.S. industries followed Pullman's example
of creating company planned and owned residential areas.

THE STRIKE AND BOYCOTT

   The greatly increased organization of both owners and workers in the railroad
industry during the last quarter of the nineteenth century made the 1894 strike
a test case between capital and labor. Between the great strikes of 1877 and the
summer of 1894, the railroads experienced seventeen years of struggle against
their workforces. The formation of the General Managers' Association (GMA)
on a national basis in 1886 furnished railroad leaders with the most powerful
employers' organization in the United States in the decade of the 1880s. Composed of the twenty-four railroads centering or terminating in Chicago, it represented $2,108,552,617 in capital, 52,088 stockholders, annual earnings of

$102,710,917 and control of 221,097 employees. The GMA received dues from members for the purpose of recruiting strikebreakers during labor disturbances, maintaining blacklists, deflecting employee grievances, and fixing among its members standardized rates for service and wages. During the strike, it served as an administrative body which determined overall strategy, coordinated daily tactics, hired strikebreakers, organized state, local, and federal civic authorities, and endeavored to manage public opinion.[41]

Once the railroads organized the General Managers' Association, their employees formed the American Railway Union at Chicago in 1893. Led by Eugene Debs, the ARU represented the first attempt to unite the nation's railroad workers in an industrial union that would transcend the Brotherhoods' conservatism and protect labor against the rapid concentration of railroad capital and management. As an official of the Brotherhood of Locomotive Firemen, Debs had observed the railroads' successful exploitation of the Brotherhoods' rivalries, their reluctance to act, and their willingness to work as strikebreakers against one another. Early success in the Great Northern Railroad strike of 1893 boosted ARU membership to 150,000 by the spring of 1894, out of a national pool estimated at 1 million railroad workers. This compares to a combined Brotherhood membership of 140,000, AFL membership of 230,000, and Knights of Labor membership of 150,000 at the same time.[42]

The depression of 1893 forced layoffs and wage reductions in most U.S. industries and railroads. Pullman began lowering wages in August and reduced the workforce from 4,500 to 1,100 between July and November. By April of 1894, the employment level climbed to 1,300, but average monthly salaries had fallen 30 to 50 percent, and the company had, despite workers' resistance, converted many jobs from day rates to piecework, as it "readjusted to suit the necessities of the times." Despite wage reductions and layoffs, the company offered no corresponding reduction in workers' rents nor did it cut salaries of officials. As rents in nearby towns had fallen, resentment grew among workers suffering throughout the winter of 1893. By March 1894, Pullman's employed and unemployed swelled the membership of the town's nineteen new ARU locals to over 4,000. On May 7, a workers' committee formally asked Pullman's Vice-President Thomas Wickes for either a return to the June 1893 wage scale or a reduction in rent and for an investigation into shop abuses. On May 10, the company fired three members of the workers' committee despite George Pullman's prior assurances that their jobs were secure. As this news spread through the shops the next day, most workers struck and Pullman closed the plant. The strike continued in a peaceful stalemate for over a month with strikers aided by Chicago's Civic Federation, private individuals, and the city's trade unions while Pullman refused to give in to public pressure for negotiation.

In the tense atmosphere of nationwide strikes and violence associated with the depression, the American Railway Union's national convention met in Chicago in the early summer and immediately took up the Pullman workers' cause. On June 21, 1894, the ARU voted to boycott Pullman cars after June 26 if

Pullman refused to arbitrate. Ignoring this threat, Pullman again rejected arbitration on June 22 and turned the matter over to the General Managers' Association. The ARU began a nationwide boycott of Pullman cars on June 26, and
Debs threatened a general rail strike if the railroads attempted to use strikebreakers. The GMA met on June 29 and resolved to uphold the Pullman Company's
stand against its employees, to find workers willing to handle Pullman cars, and
to "act unitedly" to break the boycott and crush the ARU. The GMA declared
that member railroads would run Pullman cars on every train and that no striking
worker would ever secure work on the road whose employ he had "forfeited."
By the end of June, almost 25,000 railroad men had crippled the nation's rail
movement, especially along Western routes, blocking two-thirds of the lines
leading to Chicago and all but isolating the city. Random violence and sabotage
alarmed city officials and prompted the railroads to ask for police protection.
As rumors abounded amid fears of general insurrection, the Pullman strikers
began to lose the press sympathy they had enjoyed in Chicago and throughout
the nation. Ignoring evidence that street mobs rather than strikers were implicated
in the violence and destruction, newspapers printed dramatic headlines: "From
a Strike to a Revolution"; "Mob Bent on Ruin—Debs' Strikers Begin Work of
Destruction"; "Wild Riot in Chicago—Hundreds of Freight Cars Burned by
Strikers—The Torch in General Use"; "Anarchists and Socialists said to be
Planning the Destruction and Looting of the Treasury."[43]

On June 28, U.S. Attorney General Richard Olney appointed Edwin Walker
as special U.S. attorney in Chicago and instructed him to break the strike. Two
days later, the GMA secured from Olney the right to import private detectives
and to deputize a private army of U.S. marshals. The railowners immediately
recruited, armed, paid, and directed this army throughout the course of the strike.
To isolate and paralyze ARU leadership, Walker obtained from the Circuit Court
of Chicago blanket injunctions effective July 2 that cited forcible obstruction of
mail carriage and claimed that, in Cleveland's words, "a combination and conspiracy exists to subject the control of such transportation to the will of the
conspirators." The injunctions sought to ensure mail delivery and prevent "carrying into effect such conspiracy." Although the ARU offered special crews to
guarantee the movement of mail trains, the railroads attached mail cars to regular
trains carrying Pullman cars. Since the injunction forbade the union to obstruct
the movement of mail, this tactic furnished the federal government with a reason
to intervene. The federal injunction also prohibited ARU officials from sending
telegrams or communicating with one another or with strikers. Federal courts
issued similar injunctions in eighteen other states where ARU locals had enforced
the strike.[44]

On July 2, Walker informed Olney that neither the passage of mail trains nor
the court injunctions could be enforced without aid from the U.S. Army. Olney
agreed and on July 3, despite protests of Illinois Governor Altgeld, an entire
federal garrison entered Chicago and began clearing tracks, guarding trains, and
fighting mobs. Federal military intervention increased popular violence, which

in turn resulted in the enlargement of the federal garrison and the calling out of the Illinois State Militia. For two days, July 5 and 6, 50,000 strikers and sympathizers "held undisputed control over the suburbs of Chicago," according to W. T. Stead, burning cars, looting railway sheds, tearing up rails, and "spreading devastation through the city, including the burning of most of the famous buildings of the White City of the Chicago World's Fair."[45] Not since 1877 had Chicagoans felt the massed physical force of armed federal troops.

Once the federal government intervened in the strike, John Egan, acting manager of the General Managers' Association and former general manager of the Chicago Great Western railroad, announced that the railroads were no longer party to the dispute. Now, events pitted the government against the strikers, further reinforcing the symbolic if real struggle of social order against social chaos. On July 5, Debs promised an end to the strike in return for Pullman's agreeing to arbitrate his employees' original demands. On July 10, the Chicago Circuit Court issued an arrest warrant for Debs and three other ARU leaders for "open, continued and defiant disobedience of the July 3 injunction," forcing Debs to appeal to Samuel Gompers and the AFL to declare a general nationwide strike in support of the rapidly failing boycott. Gompers declared that his union would neither join a sympathetic strike nor support the ARU boycott, and he advised strikers to return to work. On July 17, Debs and other ARU leaders were jailed for a week. Together with the decline of popular support and the refusal of the railroads to re-employ active union members, these events effectively killed the strike and crippled the ARU. Mob violence in Chicago abated by the middle of July and most troops were withdrawn by July 19. On July 18, the Pullman Company announced the resumption of work in its shops. By August 24, it had employed 1,778 former workers and 559 new ones. In September the company shut down for two weeks and re-opened as a non-union plant. Debs was convicted of violating a federal court injunction and served six months in jail in 1895, transformed by the events into a political activist.[46]

THE ISSUES

In the course of the strike, Pullman and the General Managers' Association mounted an ideological assault in the popular media against the strikers, their union, and their sympathizers and in favor of capital and its conduct. With the nation's attention on Chicago, the Pullman Company and the GMA made a series of official public pronouncements concerning property ownership, wage and rent theory, public safety, labor and street violence, unions, sympathetic strikes, the rights of strikers, the rights of capital, arbitration, and the nature of working class people. Their most vehement public assertions maintained that owners of property had the exclusive right to control it, that their interests were guided by the legitimate principle of safeguarding capital, that their hands were tied by economic law, and that they wished to protect the public from being victimized and inconvenienced by the strike. Their other arguments and practices flowed from these assertions and presented capital's "side" in the public debate over the events and outcome of the strike.

In the company's statement in the *Chicago Herald* at the height of the strike in June, Vice-President Wickes insisted that the main issue in the conflict was Pullman's and the railroads' right to govern themselves. To Pullman spokesmen, the inalienable right to conduct business as they saw fit superseded workers' claims for "fairness" and negated the call for a negotiated settlement. The ARU, Pullman charged, "seeks to dictate to the railway systems of this country what cars they shall use." Likewise, the GMA held that the strike arose from the railroads' unwillingness to allow the ARU to dictate to them. "There was a principle involved," Wickes argued, defending the refusal to arbitrate, "that the company felt in justice to itself it was bound to maintain; that was the control of its own business. If the company had allowed its employees to dictate upon what terms it should do its business . . . , the control of its business would have been a very serious matter for years to come."[47] To the company, control meant that employees should not "dictate" company policy or enter into negotiations concerning wages, rents, or work conditions.

The strike commissioners, led by Carroll D. Wright, questioned Pullman's sense of duty toward his employees, suggesting that a profitable company should have borne some losses, shared some profits, and carried workers through the depression. In vehement rebuttal, Pullman insisted that his loyalty belonged exclusively to company stockholders who had wisely invested years ago in a company that prudently created profits and accumulated a surplus. Even if the company "happened to be prosperous," Pullman saw no reason why he should turn over profits rightfully belonging to the 4,200 shareholders to workers who obviously had not made equally smart investments of their own. "The Pullman company divides its profits with the people who own the property," Pullman attested. Paying profits to workers would be giving them a "contribution," which would reduce their self-respect. By this reasoning, railowners attempted to remove the debate from the "soft" social and moral realm that took into consideration workers' lives and livelihoods to a nakedly economic realm of hard-driving, pragmatic, rational decision making where the ownership of property carried no obligation beyond that of efficient management. Thus, in their rhetoric morality gave way to the allegedly scientific and rational arguments of economic law.[48]

At the forefront of the public dialogue between workers and bosses was the controversy over wages. Pullman, supported by the GMA, blamed the strike on unreasonable wage demands and looked upon wage reductions as easily the most justifiable method of cost cutting in hard times. Neither Pullman nor the general managers acknowledged workers' claims to the right to a living wage. The Chicago press raised the issue of unfair wage cuts, prompting Pullman to explain the factors determining wage rates in his public statement of July 14. During the depression, he argued, the company operated at a loss in order to share the cost of hard times with workers by providing work, although at reduced wages.

Since the depression reduced plant activity to small repair contracts from hard-pressed railroads, Pullman based repair bids on the lowest possible estimates and postponed the question of profit until better times. For his part in meeting the economic crisis, Pullman contributed a "business loss." In return, he expected workers to "work a little harder . . . at a less price." Employees should "show proper appreciation by helping themselves over hard times," he announced. Lacking or ignoring information to the contrary, company officers assumed that wage reductions were "acceptable to the employees under the circumstances." While calling on workers to sacrifice, Pullman did not reduce management salaries.[49]

The wage question, Wickes testified to the Strike Commission, "is settled by the law of supply and demand. We were obliged to reduce wages . . . in order to compete with other people in the same business, that were doing the same thing. I suppose the wages we were paying were practically the same wages they were paying." Wickes further emphasized: "we go into the market for men, just as we go into the market for anything else." To pay more than the law of the market allowed was to give a "gift of money." If high wages kept costs too high to remain competitive, the plant must close. "The economic law is inexorable," he insisted.[50] Hence, with appeals to laissez-faire and the inevitable working of natural law, Pullman officials attempted to counter the public sympathy the strikers enjoyed before the summer's violence began.

Despite Pullman's insistence that fixed economic law governed company practice, the Strike Commission found that it had kept the plant running "mainly for its own benefit as a manufacturer, that its plant might not rust, that its competitors might not invade its territory, that it might keep its cars in repair, that it might be ready for resumption when business revived with a live plant and competent help, and that its revenue from its tenements might continue."[51] Pressed by the commissioners on this point, Pullman admitted that operating at a loss was cheaper than shutting down entirely. Company testimony to the Strike Commission also revealed that shop foremen arbitrarily determined daily piece rate payments. Plant managers avowed the "principle" that a day's wage should be a "reasonable wage for ten hours at that particular work for a competent workman, not an expert," and they claimed to be able to tell "by experience" the amount of work a "faithful, competent" worker could perform in one day. However, the company also admitted using piece rates to penalize "less industrious" workers by paying them "less than the reasonable day's wage," while rewarding the "expert and more industrious" with the "just benefit of his superior energy and skill." Managers automatically adjusted piece rates downward when "experience" discovered that "undeserving" workers regularly received an "unreasonable day's wage." Company managers claimed they never lowered piece rates for competent workmen, but in the same breath accused them of automatically limiting their output on a piece "excessively priced" so as not to attract company attention. When the depression hit in 1893, the company officially abandoned its "principle" of paying a reasonable day's wage and reduced piece rates to the going rate in comparable industries. Just as the company argued the separation of morality and economics in the case of property rights, it as easily reinjected moral arguments, in this case the need to punish laziness and reward diligence, into "fixed" economic law as its needs required.[52]

Until the entrance of federal troops, complaints that strikers were squeezed between reduced wages and fixed rents garnered them public sympathy. Company officers, however, never considered reducing rents and maintained that wages and rents were separate issues. Ownership of employee housing provided the company a captive market for its rental business and a means to recoup almost half the money paid to workers in salaries in prosperous times. Since the two paycheck system guaranteed that the company first deducted rent, many workers received a second check of only a few cents for wages during the depression. Employees realized that Pullman considered rents more important than any other obligation, even feeding their families. From the company's perspective, however, legitimate "business practice" required that employers hire labor as cheaply as the market allowed and that landlords keep rents profitable, regardless of what wages tenants received. Ignoring its own propaganda touting the mutual obligations of community, the company defended its wage and rent policy by claiming both the legal right and the power to operate according to such procedures.[53]

Although fixed at a rate to return 6 percent on the original investment after taxes and repairs, actual rental profits were never more than 4.5 percent and fell to 3.8 percent in 1893. With curious logic, Pullman felt that rents could hardly be as high as workers charged since his own rental income was so low "that there was no room for reducing the rent and bringing any income from it." In his mind, and in his public defense of his position, he judged their livelihood entirely by the balance sheet of his own income. If he did not profit as a landlord, then rents were not too high. Although workers owed $70,000 in back rent by the time of the strike, Pullman did not attempt to collect, intending to recoup through the two paycheck method when good times returned.[54]

Pullman's insistence on the absolute prerogatives of property ownership also dictated his refusal to meet with ARU representatives or arbitrate workers' grievances either before or during the strike. When the ARU committee requested arbitration on June 15, Pullman refused since he could not believe that the union represented his own plants' strikers. The next day, Wickes informed a workers' committee that the company felt there was "no proper subject for arbitration." It would be "business folly," Pullman insisted, to operate the shops at a loss on the recommendation of a third party. The business loss did not figure in Pullman's view of arbitration, rather the "principle involved," that the company, not a "third party," should decide such concerns. Matters of opinions, he conceded, were proper subjects for arbitration, but not "whether a fact that I know to be true is true or not." Such truths "could not be made otherwise by the opinion of any third party."[55] In a press statement, he warned Chicago's reading public concerning the dangers of arbitration: "The public should not permit the real question which has been before it to be obscured. That question was as to the possibility of the creation and duration of a dictatorship which would make all the industries . . . and the daily comfort of millions dependent upon them, hostages for the granting of any fantastic whim of such a dictator. Any submission to him would have been a long step in that direction.''[56] When the ARU committee threatened to boycott Pullman cars unless Pullman agreed to arbitration, he refused to acknowledge any communication from the ARU on the subject. As the ARU announced the boycott, Pullman vehemently denounced its action in the *Chicago Herald*.

Not surprisingly, George Pullman's thinking on the question of arbitration was echoed by the railowners. Asked by a strike commissioner if he had attended any of the meetings of the railroad officers or the GMA, he admitted that he had not, but that he had held a ''casual conversation in the [Chicago] Club with some railroad men'' whose opinion on arbitration ''agreed with my own.'' Like Pullman, the presidents of the Lake Shore and the Eastern Illinois railroads considered the question of arbitration ''an absurd proposition.'' After the boycott began, Pullman insisted that questions of arbitration ''are now entirely under the control of the railway companies, and could not be influenced . . . by the Pullman company in any way.''[57]

On July 3, Chicago Mayor John P. Hopkins advised the company of the need for ''settling the trouble.'' Despite similar urging from fifty other mayors, Wickes adamantly refused to negotiate with ''lawbreakers.'' On July 6, a committee composed of ARU officials and Chicago city aldermen requested that John Egan of the GMA meet with them. He refused. Two days later, the same committee called at the Pullman Company office to arrange for the appointment of a board to ''arbitrate the question as to whether there was anything to arbitrate or not.'' The workers' and aldermen's committee sought ''not to arbitrate the difference between the Pullman Company and its employees, but to see whether there were any differences.'' The company again rebuffed the committee and threatened to move the entire Pullman plant and town to New Jersey.[58]

On July 13, Mayor Hopkins personally delivered a communication from Eugene Debs and other ARU officials to Everett St. John, chairman of the GMA and president of the Chicago, Rock Island and Pacific. St. John informed Hopkins that the general managers would not communicate directly with the union, but that out of respect for the mayor, he would deliver the message personally to GMA members. The next morning, Hopkins received a note from John Egan stating that the managers had ''expressed themselves in the most positive terms that they will receive no communication whatever from the parties whose names are attached.'' The note requested that Hopkins return the ARU's message unanswered.[59] Egan publicly rebuked Mayor Hopkins for acting as the ARU's ''messenger boy.'' Asked if he found the ARU communication offensive, Egan answered that any party that attacked railway companies and found itself ''whipped'' as did the ARU, displayed ''considerable cheek to dictate the terms of their surrender.'' Egan explained that the GMA's employment of strikebreakers had beaten the union and settled the strike. Egan admitted to federal commissioners two months after the strike ended that breaking the strike required a refusal to arbitrate:

Commissioner Wright: Was there no time you cared to negotiate?

A: No, I don't think so.

Commissioner Wright: Was it or not the policy of the managers' association at all times during the pendency of this difficulty to crush the strike as a matter of policy?

A: They considered it necessary to crush the strike; yes sir.[60]

During the strike, Pullman and the railways denied and even ridiculed the claimed right of strikers to remain employees while on strike. Wickes automatically relegated the men on the workers' committee who visited him after May 11 to the status of "former employees." When the shops re-opened, the company acted as sole arbiter in rehiring and forced former workmen publicly to tear up and hand over their ARU cards before being rehired. The railroads pursued an equally firm policy. The General Managers' Association, mindful of a reserve of 60,000 unemployed railworkers on the Chicago lines alone, announced on June 30 that it considered strikers "as employees who have resigned their positions and who are not anxious for work." Illinois Central Superintendent Albert Sullivan endeavored by "every effort" to induce workers to "see the errors of their ways" and return to work "before the opportunity of obtaining reemployment was lost to them." He served an ultimatum to the 3,599 Illinois Central strikers to return to work or lose their jobs. Although railroads maintained that strikers could be re-employed without giving up ARU membership, most striking workers quit the union before being rehired.[61]

To Debs and other ARU officials, crushing the ARU was the object of the federal government as well as that of the railroads. Debs charged that Attorney General Olney planned to use Sherman antitrust legislation to break up every labor union in the country. Furthermore, the strike raised the question of the creation of a private army of deputized U.S. marshals under employer control to police rail yards, move trains, and exercise federal authority for private strikebreaking. Although Attorney General Olney ordered troops to Chicago to protect the mail and keep order, both the U.S. Army and the deputy marshals cleared tracks and ran trains. On the day of his arrival in Chicago, Federal Troop Commander General Nelson Miles reported directly to the general managers' headquarters and began working closely with the railowners. The following day, Miles boasted to local newspapers that he had broken the back of the strike.[62]

The General Managers' Association resolved from the start to break the ARU and completely destroy it as an institution of collective workers' power. While it served their interests, the owners tolerated the docile railroad brotherhoods but did not acknowledge labor's right to use militant organization to protect its interests. Although Debs maintained that the ARU did not seek official recognition from the railowners and insisted that union recognition had no part in the controversy, the GMA made the ARU's very existence an issue. By refusing to recognize or communicate with the ARU, Pullman and the GMA denied its existence and, by inference, its grievances. The Pullman Company, explained Wickes, "would not treat with our men as members of the American Railway Union, and we would not treat with them as members of any union. We treat with them as individuals and as men."[63]

Before, during, and after the strike, Pullman made it clear to his employees that unions had no place in town. Thomas Heathcoate testified before the Strike Commission that company policy forbade union representatives to trespass on company property, forcing workers outside the grounds to organize. Evening gatherings in their very homes were subject to company surveillance. Even though there was no open order against unions, a workman explained, "when a man goes to the company for a job they ask him, 'Are you a member of the American Railway Union.' 'Yes sir.' 'Have you got a card?' 'Yes, sir.' 'Give us that card.' The card is handed to them and then the applicant signs a paper that he will have nothing to do with the [ARU] . . . for five years if he wants a place in the Pullman shops."[64] After the boycott ended, Pullman rehired workers as they publicly surrendered their ARU membership cards to company officials. "We never discriminated against any labor union," he said, "except the American Railway Union."[65] Vice-President Wickes was more succinct concerning the rights of organized labor:

Commissioner: Don't you think that the fact that you represent a vast concentration of capital entitled [the worker] if he pleases to unite with all the men of his craft and select the ablest one . . . to represent the cause?

A: As a union?

Commissioner: As a union.

A: They have the right, yes sir. We have the right to say whether we will receive them or not.

Commissioner: Do you think you have any right to refuse to recognize that right in treating with the men?

A: Yes, sir; if we chose to.

Commissioner: If you chose to. Is it your policy to do that?

A: Yes, sir.

When asked if he thought that the preponderance of capital's power over labor was subject to abuse, Wickes answered "it is a man's privilege to go to work somewhere else."[66]

Explaining to the Strike Commission the general managers' refusal to accept the ARU's communications, Everett St. John stated that "in our judgment, there was no room for an organization of that kind." The commissioner questioned St. John further on the refusal:

Q: Was it based on a determination not to recognize any union of all railway employees?

A: It might have been upon a determination not to recognize this one of all others.

Q: Did [the GMA believe] that an association of all railway employees would not be recognized?

A: I think the general feeling was that the parties who had been instrumental . . . in destroying our property, decreasing our earnings, not permitting us to operate our trains, setting fire to our buildings, were not worthy of very much consideration at that time, when their power was limited.[67]

When asked by the commissioner, "Do you believe in the principle of organized labor in general?" John Egan gave a curiously vague answer. "There is no doubt," he testified, "but what organized labor at times has done good to some classes of labor, but in many cases they have paid dearly for it." A labor union, however, does not help workers "to any great extent," except providing well-paid jobs for its grievance committee members. St. John denied union legitimacy in similar language while insisting, as did his business colleagues, that it was "perfectly natural" and "perfectly right" for railroads to organize, "where an assault is upon all, for all to protect themselves."[68]

To Pullman and the railroad managers, the "unjustifiable and unwarranted" boycott amounted to a labor conspiracy against the railroads. In the owners' view, the ARU itself constituted a combination not only against the railroads but the nation. "It is my belief," charged Pullman in a statement released to the press on July 14, "that the controversy excited at Pullman was merely a move in the greater scheme . . . to a simultaneous and causeless attack upon the railways of the country." Albert Sullivan, Illinois Central manager, pointed out the "utterly helpless condition . . . of the railroad to protect itself" against the irresponsibility of the conspiracy to stop traffic. Such a labor conspiracy would quickly produce social chaos, Egan reported from railroad strike headquarters.[69]

During the strike, Pullman and the general managers told the news media that railroad workers were easily influenced, emotional, irresponsible, and immoral, especially when they repudiated what Albert Sullivan termed the "moral obligation of the contract." For his own purposes, Pullman himself distinguished the "best men [who] don't give us any trouble with unions or anything else" from the "inferior men . . . , the least competent, that give us the trouble as a general thing." If the best men "allow themselves to be led by incompetent men," he added, "that is their misfortune." Pullman believed that workers had rights as individuals, mainly the right to quit if dissatisfied. When they conspired in groups, surrendering their individuality to the control of leaders, however, they forfeited their rights and became lawbreakers. S. C. Wade, a Rock Island Railroad attorney who was appointed a captain of the U.S. Marshals during the strike, blamed working-class disorder on the influence of liquor. During the strike, he observed that "persons who were pointed out to me as dangerous strikers" also frequented "low-class" saloons. Keeping lists of these persons,

Wade came to believe that saloons served as strikers' headquarters. Had city officials taken the precaution to close them, Wade argued, the city would have escaped property destruction during the strike.[70]

Pullman's official doctor for the ten years preceding the strike, John McLean, echoed Wade's notions of economic propriety, blaming the high wages Pullman had paid in 1893 for spawning workers' "profligate habits" and "extensive" intemperance. Workers earning as much as $150 per month engaged in "constant drinking," which the doctor held to be the indirect cause of "all labor troubles." High wages discouraged personal discipline and made economizing difficult in hard times, an important issue, to McLean especially, since workers often paid saloon keepers before they paid doctors. Alcohol, coupled with the abrupt change from prosperity to depression, "prepared the minds" of highly paid workers "for the destructive influences of the labor agitators," the doctor observed, while those earning small wages displayed more temperate and frugal habits.[71]

Both Pullman and the general managers blamed the strike on "labor agitators" and "leaders of disorder" who transformed a minor dispute into a major confrontation. Pullman claimed that his model town had produced workers of high caliber who were immune to union organizers. He felt certain that meeting with the original workers' committee and agreeing to consider grievances had defused the wage-rent dispute among his employees. It was the intrusion of outside union officials, he charged, that changed his employees' perceptions and understandings. Had the union not interfered, Pullman thought, he could have convinced his workers that "their interests lay in the direction of working with me," despite wage cuts. Yet, in the excitement of the ARU meeting the night the committee had been fired, workers "lost their heads" and allowed themselves to be duped by "persons almost unknown to them." Hence, the ARU took unfair advantage of workers laid off by the depression. "If our men had been left free from outside influences," Pullman argued, "there would have been no trouble." John Egan of the GMA likewise blamed the strike on "labor agitators," who, by the very nature of their jobs, "constantly agitate for increased wages and cause employers trouble." To the railowners, "vermin-ridden" labor leaders constituted the conspiratorial source of all labor problems. Pullman and the general managers agreed with Railroad Commissioner Hampton that "no condemnation can be too emphatic, no punishment too severe, for the unscrupulous labor leaders who manipulated the rank and file."[72]

In searching for a long-term solution to the problem of arbitrary strikes, Albert Sullivan of the Illinois Central called for federal restrictions to prevent the formation of other unions capable of causing similar damage. He had no objection to unions, finding it easy to deal with representatives of the railroad Brotherhoods, but he thought there must be "checks on the wrongful use of [union] power." Devastating strikes such as the present one could happen all over again, he charged, if the easily aroused labor force continued to be led by "organization men who can bring about such an emotional wave that will carry with it the same degree of ardor and eliminate entirely all the elements of conservatism, all the obligations of agreement of contract, all the moral obligations that exist between an employee and employer, simply because the organizations themselves have no responsibility.''[73] Sullivan's solution required unions to assume legal responsibility for their acts to ensure that they were led by men of "intelligence and conservatism." The GMA emphasized the need to force labor unions into a more easily controllable, corporate existence. In making their case for union incorporation, railroad managers cited court interpretations of unions as illegal combinations in restraint of trade. Incorporation would compel unions to forego strikes and honor their contracts. Most importantly, they could be sued in court. Hence, corporations answered social violence by attempting to force corporate and therefore economically rational behavior from labor. Pullman's solution to union disruptions was more simple: those who wish to be employed must realize the "rule of business," namely that the "cost of a piece of work must not exceed its selling price."[74]

Throughout the struggle, Pullman and the GMA used the press to convince the public of the rightness of their actions and viewpoints. Insisting that their companies could "do no more than explain [their] situation to the public," Pullman and the general managers encouraged public indignation over transportation inconveniences and further provoked the fear of insurrection. In his press statement of June 26, for example, Pullman deplored "annoyance to the public by the threats of irresponsible organizations" bent on causing discomfort to rail travelers. Similarly, the GMA charged the ARU with deliberately calling the boycott to "discommode the traveling public and embarrass the railroads in the public eye" and placed public interest squarely with that of the railroads, since "whatever violence threatened the railroads' control or destroyed property, in turn endangered the public interest." Railowners pictured themselves helplessly caught in the vise of union power that had entirely removed the strike situation from their control. And they indignantly denied charges that they had fomented violence themselves to justify their use of private force. When the ARU boycott escalated the confrontation against the railroads, W. T. Stead observed, the battle became a fight for public opinion between the strongest organized representatives of both capital and labor. "I am glad the matter has become a sharply defined issue," Pullman declared as he retreated to New York in July, leaving the railroads to face the ARU. The railroads, for their part, courted public approval by declining to prosecute Debs, since such open confrontation would, in John Egan's words, "enable [him] to pose as a martyred man." Instead, their strategy from the beginning was to portray the ARU "conspiracy" as a threat to society and enlist public support on the side of federal intervention. Government prosecution of Debs, railowners reasoned, would in and of itself present the strike to the public as a contest between the "people" and the strikers.[75]

Labor leaders also recognized the importance of public opinion and the ideological nature of the struggle. During the deliberations of the ARU convention,

Vice-President George W. Howard cautioned that a general strike would cause a "revulsion of sentiment" and a loss of "universal opinion" favorable to a peaceable settlement at Pullman. Although a strike observer reported "Americans hate railways" and "regard them as tyrannical, unjust . . . and generally enemies of the human race," still railroads served as America's first corporate symbol of national progress. Most Americans were at least ambivalent toward the railroads and many favored government supervision and regulation of their "evil monopolies." The ARU and the Pullman strikers had appealed to and intensified this public distrust of railroads at every turn. The public initially blamed the strike on Pullman's refusal to negotiate while editors and public officials repeatedly called for arbitration. Moreover, police, city mobs, and relief organizations in Chicago, San Francisco, and other cities had openly sided with the strikers.[76]

From the end of June and into July, however, the combination of the boycott, rail stoppages, violence, public discomfort, armed federal intervention, and an anti-labor press barrage gradually swung press and public opinion to the side of "law and order." Publicists denounced the inconvenience to travellers and consumers as "a reproach to the community at large" and deemed obstruction of the "free passage of the United States mails an offence which came little short of treason." *Harper's Weekly* thundered conspiracy, criminality, demagoguery, blackmail, anarchy, socialism, and in a July 14 editorial called for the government to "Suppress the Rebellion." In a like vein, *The Nation* blasted Debs for putting the country "before the world as the sport of lunatics and madmen" and branded "militant trades' unionism as the slavery of our day."[77]

By July W. F. Burns, a contemporary historian, observed that the anti-labor press campaign had been so successful that "every newspaper in Chicago except the *Times* stood by the railroads." He further charged that "whole columns of . . . falsehoods were published and circulated broadcast through the land" against the strikers. In July, for example, newspapers falsely reported that the strike had been called off, which greatly interfered with its conduct. Employers and editors made personal attacks against Debs to make an example of him. In an expression of personal outrage, Burns charged that the "slanders" directed against Debs "simply baffled recountal." Burns summarized descriptions of Debs that appeared in Chicago's newspapers: "He has been called crazy, drunken, revolutionary, criminal, incompetent. Newspapers have at once declared his conduct of the strike as impotent and denounced him for having made it so effective. Labor has been entreated to throw him over as a puerile leader and capital has been warned that he is a dangerous man because of his surpassing ability." The "subsidized press," Burns concluded, was the "most dangerous enemy of labor and, next to the courts, the most effective weapon in the hand of the railroad corporations in destroying the rights of labor and defeating the strikers."[78]

By August, after two months of vehemently anti-union press, many Americans had come to feel that the ARU had meddled in the Pullman company's internal affairs and unfairly attacked the railroads. "Bad faith on the part of the employers," observed W. T. Stead, an observer whose previous writings had demonstrated his concern for Chicago's downtrodden working people, "is balanced by murder and outrage on the part of the employed." He recounted emotional incidents that had swayed public opinion, where strikers, for instance, "blocked trains full of women and children for days," leaving in one case, "a whole hundred of suffering passengers . . . to lie blistering in the midsummer sun with scant food and no water." "Were these crimes condoned," Stead declared, "society would suffer."[79]

Debs, too, acknowledged the role of the press in the ARU's quick loss of public approval during the strike. In a statement on July 6, he cited the "many misleading reports that have been given currency" in the press and charged that the ARU had been "deliberately and maliciously misrepresented," especially by the erroneous but widely accepted charge that labor leaders and union agitators had induced Pullman's workers to strike in the first place. "The charge is wholly untrue," Debs countered. He further claimed that General Miles circulated the false story that 90 percent of Chicago's citizens sympathized with the Pullman company and the railroads. "The railway managers took advantage of this report," Debs continued, "and spread and distorted it in order to discourage the strikers."[80]

As the strike ended, opinion makers in the nation's journals likewise realized the power of the pro-corporate press to sway the minds of its readers. "Capital effectually . . . controls national feeling through the channels that mold public opinion," wrote Thomas Grant in the August *American Journal of Politics*. Many of the nation's writers seemed energized rather than humbled by this realization. "The most momentous stage in every revolution," observed a *Harper's Weekly* writer in November, "is that which takes place silently in the popular mind," and if the popular mind was uncertain what to think, the press told its readers what "public opinion," in fact, thought. Thus, speaking for, or rather as, the public, the press at once created and reflected public opinion. Thomas Cooley, for example, alerted his readers in *The Forum* to "the sentiment of the country as expressed in its public journals," a sentiment that approved of the federal intervention. "The press is practically unanimous in the position," wrote Henry Fletcher in the *Atlantic Monthly*, "that [the boycott] was both atrocious and insane." Editors of *The Nation* likewise presumed to summarize "American public opinion," discover it arrayed "in a solid mass behind [the President]," and declare that its "overwhelming majority" was convinced that Debs' strike was a rebellion. "Public opinion in America," wrote Harvard Professor of Economic History W. J. Ashley in the April 1895 *Church Social Union*, "determines to brand every great strike as necessarily wrong." Other professionals seconded the importance of official opinion. The strike, for instance, had "discredited in the eyes of disinterested observers all labor organization," observed Edgar Bancroft in a speech to the Illinois Bar Association in January 1895, which was circulated in pamphlet form. While most writers looked favorably on the power of the press to influence the public against the strikers, a few, perhaps those loyal to the cause, remained skeptical. "When we look for light and leading in the press," lamented the Reverend George McDermott in *Catholic World*, "we discover only confusion, contradiction, malice, folly."[81]

How did the press and public opinion become so important in assessing the outcome of the strike? Near the turn of the century, journalists' influence had grown considerably in the United States with the rise of a mass communication culture that included the marketing and distribution by subscription of national journals. These created a nationwide network of opinion making, received and digested by a vast, publicly educated middle class audience. Journalism, like medicine, law, education, and other professions was professionalized through the precise definition of its field and the establishment of technical schools and departments in the nation's universities. Experts armed with new techniques of social analysis and scientific reporting wrote for the nation's monthly magazines and served as legitimators in the popular culture of values and behaviors consistent with a corporate-led, progressive civilization. The expansion of "publicity," Harvard President Charles W. Eliot wrote, represents "a new means of social, industrial, and governmental reform and progress." The mass-marketed ideas of the new journalists, together with the social legitimacy of their professional expertise, bestowed upon them the power to define and interpret issues and crises, provoke reform, and even prepare the nation psychologically for war.[82]

Given the crucial part press opinion played in shaping public thought, it is important to assess how journalists debated the issues raised in the strike and evaluated business' versus labor's interpretations. A sample of forty-one articles by twenty-nine writers that appeared in eighteen opinion-making publications between July 1894 and April 1895 revealed such titles as "Pullman and Its Lessons," "The Real Issues in the Strike," "Are We Awakened?," and "The Relation of the Railway to Its Employees." Together these indicated the national self-examination taking place over the role of labor, corporations, and government in American society.[83]

Pullman and the general managers structured their public arguments on the inviolability of private property rights. They assumed a nakedly economic realm where the bottom line was profits and where employers had an unfettered right to control their property. Sixteen of the twenty-nine publicists, too, eagerly asserted the importance of property. "The great question now at issue before the American people," wrote Nelson Miles in the *North American Review*, is "shall life, personal independence, and the rights of property be respected in this country?" Yes, responded thirteen of the sixteen writers who took up the subject and defended Pullman's and the railowners' actions. "The insurrection was a violent assault on the rights of property," wrote Joseph Nimmo, who supported Pullman's refusal to pay higher wages. Edgar·Bancroft asserted the "fundamental right of the railroads to conduct their business in a lawful manner, without interference on the part of labor organizations." A few distinguished between lawful license to do business and ethical positions that considered labor's position. "The right under existing law," wrote Dr. A.H.P. Leuf in *To-Day*, "of the large capitalist to use his capital as he desires is unrestricted . . . however inequitable in principle, however reprehensible in the abstract." The law protecting property was "inadequate to do justice," he continued, and although it "must be upheld," it should be changed to reflect the nation's "rapid economic advancement" and to provide for the protection of propertyless workers. For most observers, however, the rule of law came before any other social consideration. Few of the writers would have agreed with Albert Shaw, who argued in the *Review of Reviews* that Pullman's workers could demand "as a right" a reduction of rents, or with George McDermot who claimed workers' right to the fruits of their labor.[84]

In perhaps the most far-reaching and aggressive assessment of the role of private property, Harvard's Charles W. Eliot placed corporations and corporate security at the core of national self-identification as he offered "Some Reasons Why the American Republic May Endure" to his readers in *The Forum*. He named the corporation as a stabilizing factor of "incalculable value to modern society," as important as religious freedom, general education, and public health. Corporations contributed to a "new discipline for masses of people," inducing social "stability and durability" by training employees "to the high virtues of fidelity and loyalty—virtues which cannot but secure the state." In this context, corporate rights, while based on private ownership and limited liability, were not simply those of an economic entity, but constituted a significant element of social control. Labor had no claims against property beyond wages received and was easily portrayed as either loyal or disruptive. The strikers, suffering from the "seduction of unions," merely demonstrated that railroad workers, like miners, were, to Eliot, "distinctly of the inferior sort" for they had "little fidelity in the service of corporations" and thus challenged the nation's ability to survive.[85]

The republic would endure, then, only if corporations and private property survived labor's attacks in order to serve society and advance civilization. "The progress of civilization," explained Joseph Nimmo, "has been coincident with the observance of the rights of property." Workers and their activities constituted a threat to civic stability since they had mounted the "war against law and order." Hence, to violate property was not just to challenge Pullman or the railroads, but to threaten social order, a widely held view that made it difficult for the strikers to argue that they, and not the corporations, had been wronged. Even sympathetic writers qualified their acknowledgement of labor's grievances and right to unionize in the context of a higher loyalty to society.[86] Belief in these sentiments virtually guaranteed the railroad's claims that the strike amounted to a workers' conspiracy against the nation rather than Debs' "contest between the producing classes and the money power." Only the "poorer classes," remarked Henry Fletcher, thought the conflict was between wage earners and corporate wealth. That the corporations and not labor successfully assumed the role of guardians of America's future underscores the pervasiveness of pro-corporate thinking among the nation's opinion makers, and, by inference, among their readers. The crisis of 1894 had presented an opportunity to publicly affirm how essential large, privately held businesses were to the very life of the nation.[87]

Carroll D. Wright expressed an important if minority position on property rights, one that would triumph in national policy as the ideas of proprietary, competitive capital gave way to corporate liberal principles in the decades before World War I. "May a Man Conduct His Business as He Please?" he asked *The Forum* readers in December. No, he countered, if he cannot do so in a manner that does not harm society. While he agreed that "the laws of business and the true principles of political economy insist that profits once made shall remain intact," the railroads' quasi-public nature and their ethical obligations to employees required that they be subject to public control. Although unjust treatment of workers had surely caused the strike, the government was nevertheless "duty bound" to intervene against labor when the public suffered loss, inconvenience, violence, or the interruption of trade.[88]

While most writers emphasized labor's social threat and property's beneficence, Wright and a few others focused on the ominous implications of unrestrained corporate power. In the Strike Commission's *Report*, he warned that the railroads' concentrated power threatened rather than guaranteed liberty. Illegal rate fixing illustrated "the persistent and shrewdly devised plans of corporations to overreach their limitations and to usurp indirectly powers and rights not contemplated in their charters and not obtainable from the people or their legislators. An extension of this association . . . and the proposed legalization of 'pooling' would result in an aggregation of power and capital dangerous to the people and their liberties as well as to employees and their rights."[89]

Despite these dangers, corporations remained an integral and necessary part of society to Wright since the country's "business stability" depended largely upon "the prosperity of the railroads." Public danger and public accountability demanded public control of large corporations, a notion that American citizens discovered slowly. In a December address to the American Economic Association, Wright recognized a "revolution . . . quietly taking place" to subject the economic power of "quasi-public servants" to the public will. The Interstate Commerce Act of 1877 and the Sherman Antitrust Act of 1890 represented stages in this revolution to protect property rights against unbridled competition even as it guarded the public against unfair rates. If the Pullman strike had not exactly "crystallized public opinion" in favor of intervention, as Wright claimed, the debate nonetheless advanced in that direction.[90]

Twelve percent of the writers in the sample favored direct government intervention between labor and capital, mostly in the form of compulsory arbitration. To these observers, the purpose of intervention was to protect private property, guarantee social stability, and, in a few cases, uphold workers' rights. For most writers, however, assumptions about the sanctity of employers' property rights conflicted with their growing awareness of the need for governmental control of the economy. A majority agreed on the necessity for government to be more aggressive in protecting private property against socialism, mob rule, demagogues, or even against itself. But few expressed a willingness to protect labor against capital, seeming more interested in corporate rights or public inconvenience than a living wage. Many were uncertain if arbitration would work given the reluctance of the corporations to participate, but almost all remained eager to compel unrestrained labor to bend to social order.[91]

This debate between laissez-faire proprietary competitive capitalism and corporate liberal principles articulated the country's understanding of the importance of subjecting the power of capital, labor, and the market to the law. Eliot and Wright reflected the nation's ambiguity over definitions of capital's social role. Both saw the errors of corporations. Eliot cited their "oppressive monopoly, destructive competition, and political corruption," while Wright named their injustice toward workers. To guarantee their survival, Eliot would leave corporations unrestrained but would have them restrain their employees. Wright would protect corporations through compulsory arbitration and government supervision but demanded equally responsible behavior from labor. For Eliot, from a proprietary–laissez-faire stance, and for Wright, from a corporate-liberal position, the protection of private corporations served as a means to preserve the existing social order. Without being partisans of corporations, both were pro-corporate in order to buttress society through stabilizing institutions and the rule of law.[92] Making corporations more responsible while guaranteeing private property and its privileges would ensure the survival of the corporation as an institutional bulwark of progressive society.

If opinion in favor of regulation sought to protect railroads from unfair rate fixing or unrestrained monopoly, it did not seek the same protection for labor in wage markets as Martin Sklar has pointed out. When Gompers described workers driven to "sheer desperation," Carroll Wright almost alone called for "just and reasonable wages." But Henry J. Fletcher expressed a more typical sentiment among the advocates of "justice for labor" when he proposed laws to protect shippers from unjust rates while admitting that nothing except strikes could force just treatment of employees. The great majority of observers did not understand, much less uphold, workers' complaints. Most understood the wage issue in the context of classical economics, although Henry Holt insisted that the "iron law of wages" was a "stupid untruth" since workers seemed to be making money. Nelson Miles found Pullman's wage arguments "conclusive and logical" and cited both the "immutable law" of unequal distribution and the divine dictum, "the poor ye have always with you." If there was any doubt, an editor at *The Nation* attacked what he derisively termed the "ethical school of political economy" that considered workers' welfare. Most writers would have agreed with Pullman's arguments that his workers' prosperity was tied to his own. As David Means put it, "the interest of workmen is promoted by the accumulation of the greatest possible amount of capital."[93]

While few upheld labor's interests, important journals like *Harper's Weekly*, *The Forum*, *The Outlook*, *The Atlantic Monthly*, and *The Nation* boiled with the language of fear, ridicule, condemnation, and retribution directed against the strikers, their leaders, and their unions. Two-thirds of the writers castigated the strikers as demogogic, unintelligent, miscreant, semi-civilized, sinister, unscrupulous men who "meet in secret and conspire to extort." To these "wild beasts," a "taste of violence was like a taste of blood." The strike itself was "criminal recklessness," the "sport of lunatics and madmen," a "reign of terror." Those who condemned labor offered extreme solutions to the crisis. Henry Holt advocated using the "mailed hand" not "kid gloves" on labor, and, in the case of the anarchist, "there is nothing left but to kill him." Nimmo called for a larger army to restore "law and order." A less vindictive minority of writers distinguished between "good" workers and "bad," blaming irresponsible leaders or immigrant radicals for "all the crazy, destructive talk." A few argued that native-born American workers, while easily misled by "stupid truths" were basically "law abiding," "rational and temperate," and felt, with Cooley and Shaw, that in such emergencies "the worst elements of society come forward."[94]

Half of the writers agreed that the country had experienced social crisis of major proportions. Two-thirds favored the use of government force to put down civil unrest in order to protect the Constitution. Theodore Roosevelt and many editors and writers seconded the GMA's charge that the strike represented conspiracy-driven rebellion against civilization, which, to David Means, had led people to question the stability of the government. "The social fabric seemed to be measurably near dissolution," wrote Harry Robinson in *The Forum*, and "the country was not far from the verge of anarchy." An editor of *The Nation* deemed the strike an "avowed contest for national supremacy."[95] In the *North American Review*, Robinson accused the ARU of conspiring to foment "a general industrial rebellion," an armed insurrection of the "wage earning class against constituted society." Previous labor disturbances were but "sporadic outbreaks"; the strike of 1894 represented the "final onslaught of a deep-seated malady, a cancerous growth, which has been deliberately planted in the social system of the country, and has been fostered there till it struck roots, which will not be torn out without the rending of tissue and the spilling of blood. Its existence is a menace to the nation."[96]

Charges that the American Railway Union threatened the very foundation of civilized society were echoed in the same *North American Review* issue by General Nelson Miles and Wade Hampton, United States commissioner of railroads. Both men defended Pullman's actions, characterized labor as anarchistic and revolutionary, condemned it for usurping power, and described the strike as a national crisis. Miles and Hampton together with Theodore Roosevelt and thirteen others repeated Albert Sullivan's warning of future warfare between capital and labor. "The Republic would go to pieces in a year," wrote Roosevelt, if labor elected its "own chiefs" to power. Organized labor was "only too likely to be replaced by a more revolutionary political socialism," warned Harvard's

Ashley. Such warnings prompted many to agree with a *Harper's Weekly* editor that labor violence "will grow more dangerous unless stopped."[97]

The language of fear and retribution added little to the debate but set a tone that kept emotions high and sustained a desire to retaliate against the strikers and "do something" to forestall class warfare. In a national emergency, "law and order" opinion placed the need to subdue radical labor and preserve social order above labor reform or even above deliberate, unimpassioned analysis. While some writers recognized that corporations should treat employees better to ensure their loyalty, most emphasized labor's obligations to society rather than its claims against it. Labor, then, emerged from these debates as the object of social fears of anarchy, revolution, mob rule, and the strike provided an excuse for a national outpouring of relief over the preservation of the republic and patriotic rededication to the social whole. In articles such as "National Ideals" and "The Solidarity of Society," Roosevelt, Eliot, Wright, and other leaders emphasized common national aims and social unity and aggressively defended the Constitution against those who disregarded the obligations of citizenship.[98]

In the context of this rededication to national ideals, events were judged in light of how much they served the general welfare. "The public is the master," Wright wrote; both the railroads and their employees should bow "under the dictates of lofty patriotism." Many criticized both capital and labor in the name of the higher values of national stability and endurance and called for their respective energies to be channeled into productive forces for the good of the whole. Both were to be responsible and cooperative players rather than antagonists. Capital should no longer practice unrestrained competition or brutalize its workforce. Society, Roosevelt wrote, should restrain the "dangerous criminals of the wealthy class" and "base civic and national betterment on nobler grounds than those of mere business expediency." Labor, for its part, should no longer foment rebellion since violence had no place in liberal society. It was workers who had kept the "spirit of caste alive," an editor of *The Outlook* observed, but "the solidarity of labor must give place to the solidarity of society." Workers must be transformed from a source of chaos into a functioning part of industrial society through restraint, incorporation, legal control, and education, even if it became necessary to pay them more and treat them better. Society should excise the demagogues but keep the loyal. Wright favored making labor "accountable" by treating workers like "businessmen" so that they recognized their "allegiance to the public." Equal participation in the nation's progress guaranteed that all sectors of society could identify with the liberal state as it was described.[99]

Through this debate, national leaders put forth a new definition of what constituted public welfare and legitimated the use of force against strikers to preserve it. By setting the parameters of the public debate within the welfare of the social whole, corporate society collectively drew the boundaries of acceptable behavior and admissible discussion. Militant radicalism lay outside the boundary. Labor existed, as Eliot indicated, either to serve or to disrupt society. As Nelson Miles explained, "Men must take sides either for anarchy, secret conclaves, unwritten law, mob violence, and universal chaos under the red and white flag of socialism on the one hand; or on the side of established government, the supremacy of law, the maintenance of good order, universal peace, absolute security of life and property, the rights of personal liberty, all under the shadow and folds of Old Glory on the other."[100]

In the terminology of good workers versus bad generated by the debates of 1894 and 1895, corporate liberalism upheld the AFL's vision of responsible labor in corporate society and rejected the ARU's tactic of social disruption for the redress of grievances. Few opinion makers saw the issues as did militant labor. The ARU's claims for the necessity of the boycott, the importance of the sympathetic strike, and the labor theory of value seldom found expression in official opinion. A few writers agreed with the right to strike, but none would allow this to be carried so far as to inconvenience the public. A few more favored the right to have unions but, again, found strikes incompatible with social unity. For the most part, however ambiguous they were about large corporations, however sympathetic their feelings toward the strikers, most writers portrayed the events of 1894 as a contest between the forces supporting legal social order and the harbingers of chaos. They preferred the AFL's definitions of labor, which renounced boycotts and sympathy strikes and, above all, foreswore independent political action, all of which affirmed labor's place as a functional part of liberal corporate society. The possibility of bringing workers into liberal society was held out by opinion leaders as real, but only if labor met certain requirements set by corporate and civic necessity.

As a demonstration of employer power, an exercise in employer strikebreaking tactics, a precedent-setting use of injunctions, a clash of opinions, and a message to transportation workers who might again organize and pit a national industrial union against the combined power of railroad capital, the strike and boycott constituted a victory for capital. In a national atmosphere increasingly supportive of state and federal intervention in strikes, the GMA outlasted the strikers and crushed the ARU, discrediting both the leadership and methods of strikers, and sending the message that the railroads would not tolerate militant unionism within the industry. ARU membership declined drastically, and the union disappeared after 1900. No national, industry-wide rail workers' union took its place. Nor did labor organize nationwide by industry until the formation of the Congress of Industrial Organizations in 1935. The demise of the ARU forced railroad workers into the AFL's craft union structure under more conservative leadership who favored honoring contracts and arbitration. Samuel Gompers had objected all along to the militancy of the ARU and at the height of the confrontation had refused Debs' request for a sympathetic strike.

In 1894, the bituminous coal strike and the Pullman boycott involved broadly based, national sympathetic strikes in which striking unions gained support from other unions with no direct stake in the outcome of the strike. Sympathetic strikes represented a consolidation of working class opinion and contributed to class solidarity. The loss of the Pullman boycott demonstrated that the strongest union could not prevail against a determined combination of organized capital backed by the naked force of the federal courts and military. The defeat intensified labor's questioning of the effectiveness of sympathetic strikes and led to a change in tactics. From a high of 11.5 percent in 1891 and 8.8 percent in 1894, the percentage of sympathy strikes declined to 1.5 percent in 1900 and 2.7 percent in 1905. The AFL could not control member locals, and sympathy strikes reappeared between 1901 and 1904, rising to 2.7 percent in 1905 but rarely enjoyed union sanction after 1900. Under the leadership of the AFL, member locals increasingly preferred to honor contracts and negotiate differences with employers rather than express solidarity with other striking unions. Although the absolute number of strikes increased between 1891 and 1905, the pattern shifted away from spontaneous strikes toward union sanctioned ones, called less over wages than to enforce union rules.[101]

The violence and disruption of the strike fueled growing national support for arbitration of industrial disputes. Newspapers reported that many readers believed the railroads' and Pullman's refusal to arbitrate exacerbated the crisis. The move toward state and national legislation requiring arbitration and mediation gained endorsement in platforms of both political parties in 1896. Federal legislation requiring railroad mediation passed in 1898, but even this did not guarantee organized labor the right to union recognition. In the midst of a national union-busting atmosphere, much of the business community expressed outrage when in 1904 President Theodore Roosevelt forced coal company owners to arbitrate with the miners' union.

An exercise in tactics, the Pullman strike pitted workers' weapons of the strike, picket, and boycott against employers' power in their own plants, in the press, the courts, and government. The efficiency of employers' strikebreaking tactics called into question labor's assumed right to organize and strike, its demands for arbitration, its need to have free communication during strikes, its right to recognition of a union as a bargaining agent, and the right to be considered employees while on strike. The adamant refusal of Pullman or the GMA to recognize any of these rights served as an extreme negation of any legal, moral, or economic position but their own. The refusal to arbitrate, wrote Thomas Grant, was "another way of telling the men that they had no status in the case; that they had no rights large corporations need respect; that there was only one side to the controversy; and that the Pullman company alone was the arbiter."[102] The strike established such precedents as the president's use of military intervention against labor and the use of court injunctions as strikebreaking tools, especially in industries engaged in public service, what Illinois Governor John P. Altgeld was to term "government by injunction." Taken together, the GMA's refusal to communicate with the ARU and the federal injunction prohibiting telegraph communication between ARU leaders effected an information blackout and communication crisis inside strike headquarters in other states. The most telling tactic of all on the part of Pullman and the general managers was perhaps encouraging public hostility toward the striking workers by charging them with a range of unpatriotic, immoral, and heinous acts, and helping, finally, to create an atmosphere in which the public condoned the overt use of power.

It is difficult to assess the impact of these events on rank and file union members, let alone among the nation's unorganized railroad workers. Various railroad employees testified to the Strike Commission. Some, like Charles Naylor, fireman on the Pittsburgh, Fort Wayne, and Chicago, reported that workers who witnessed the government supporting the corporations in any emergency "begin to lose confidence." To others like George Lovejoy, a Chicago, Rock Island, and Pacific yardmaster, the strike taught that "no single organization can win," that workers must "get together in one body" when confronted with the combined power of press, clergy, judiciary, and public officials. To ARU Vice-President George W. Howard, the strike and its aftermath also symbolized the power relationship between labor and capital. "The trouble is," he told the Strike Commission, "everything is behind the law . . . and the law never takes the stand against the oppressors." Given such oppression, Howard nevertheless blamed labor's failure to organize for redress of its problems. Were labor to eliminate its jealousies and differences and organize "in one solid phalanx," government and society would recognize its force. But labor failed to organize and necessarily suffered defeats. "Capital has never defeated labor, labor defeats itself through its tragic deeds," Howard lamented.[103] Debs, too, recognized the question as one of power, but power against which no amount of organization could prevail. "The result of [the federal injunction] was to reduce our influence to nothing," he explained. "When all the organized orders of society are against a strike," labor remains powerless. "We have nothing to look forward to defend us in times of troubles," he told the Strike Commission. "We have no recognized influence in society on our side. We have absolutely nothing but the men who begin to starve when they quit work." Against labor's powerlessness, Debs continued, "the corporations are in perfect alliance; they have all the things money can command, and that means a subsidized press, that they are able to control the newspapers, and means a false or vitiated public opinion. The clergy almost steadily united in thundering their denunciations, then the courts, then the State militia, then the Federal troops; everything and all things on the side of the corporations."[104]

The courts defeated the strike, Debs charged, by destroying the ARU leadership and its national network of telegraph communication. "As soon as the employees found that we were arrested and taken from the scene of action," he lamented, "they became demoralized and that ended the strike." The "moneyed power is potential enough to control all this machinery." Yet Debs did not capitulate or resign himself to this power, however immense in his estimation. He continued to serve as one of the most effective radical leaders of his time, although he abandoned labor organization in favor of direct political action as a strategy for opposing the capitalist system. "The change from the economic ARU to the political Social Democracy," Debs later observed, had been "a

matter of grim necessity, forced by the railroad corporations which waged re-
lentless war upon the union and made its existence impossible.''[105]

For many, however, the cumulative effect of ''loss of confidence,'' confrontation with overwhelming power, impatience with their own organizations and
leadership, helplessness or resignation when they realized that the gross machinery of control was out of their hands became an institutionalized social
constraint. To some, the strike reasserted the force, if not the legitimacy of the
law. Perhaps some emerged from the strike accepting the now more visible,
hierarchical political culture as inevitable. In any case, workers did not come
together again to organize in nationwide industries until the 1930s.[106]

To re-establish worker compliance in Pullman town and on the nation's railroads, it was unnecessary for Pullman and the general managers to gain the
workers consensus or agreement to the exercise of their power. It was necessary
only to establish in public discourse the primacy of their argument, to discredit
labor's arguments, and to secure labor's however reluctant or still defiant ca-
pitulation. In the aftermath of the Pullman strike, most strikers gave up their
union cards in return for work at Pullman and on the railroads. Their consent
was not agreement but, more likely, the need to work, which was sufficient for
the needs of their employers. Control only required grudging compliance, not
blind co-optation. It was re-established, as Debs pointed out, through an anonymous, structural rule against which workers came to feel that they had no choice
but to submit. Asked by a strike commissioner, ''Do you believe there is no
solution of any of these troubles under the present industrial system,'' Debs
answered, ''No sir; that is my candid conviction.''[107]

It is important to understand the significance of political action in national
culture, and, especially, the political dimensions of this strike. The state's use
of troops and injunctions to assist employers politicized the strike. When the
state portrayed its actions in response to violent events as part of its overall
responsibility and even its very nature, its role in the strike became a ''strategy
for its transformation,'' as Gareth Stedman Jones has demonstrated. The capital-
labor dispute was taken up by the state which, in turn, acted not as a broker but
as a facilitator for one party against another. This demonstrated a new social
definition of national politics, the identification of the interests of large capital
with the legitimate interests of the whole population. The subordination of labor
that began near the turn of the century did not take place entirely through changes
in the labor process and corporate reorganization nor through middle class reform
efforts but was compounded by the politicization of the labor-capital discourse
in national cultural life and a new ''reality'' represented by the relative power
relationships of the disputants.[108]

Despite Debs' recognition of the political reality of overwhelming state power,
his defiance, as that of many fellow strikers, was undiminished by the experience.
Indeed, he later ran for president ''to teach social consciousness'' within the
context of national party politics, believing that ultimately the public could
understand the relations of power and authority in industrial society. But con-

sciousness alone did not supply the wherewithal for workers to change fundamentally the patterns of authority in industrial relations to their advantage.[109]

NOTES

1. R. Ogden, "The Report on the Chicago Strike," *The Nation* 59 (Nov. 22, 1894):376.

2. William Tolman, *Social Engineering* (New York, 1908).

3. United States Strike Commission, *Report on the Chicago Strike of June-July 1894* U.S. Congress Senate Executive Document no. 7, 53rd Congress, 3rd Session, (Washington, D.C., 1895), hereafter cited as *Strike Report*, xxi; *The Story of Pullman*, official Pullman Company history quoted in W. T. Stead, *Chicago To-day: The Labor War in America* (London, 1894), 117.

4. Testimony of George Pullman, *Strike Report*, 546; Stanley Buder, *Pullman, An Experiment in Industrial Order and Community Planning, 1880–1930* (New York, 1967), 43–44.

5. Samuel Yellen, *American Labor Struggles* (New York, 1936), 30–31; Buder, *Pullman*, 35. In Chicago proper, a gridiron of 1,375 rail miles with 3,000 road crossings resulted in 431 fatal crossing accidents in 1873; Stead, *Chicago To-day*, 198.

6. Stead, *Chicago To-day*, 32–33.

7. Testimony of George Pullman, *Strike Report*, 520–30; John Casson, *Civilizing the Machine: Technology and Republican Values in America, 1776–1900* (New York, 1976); Stead, *Chicago To-day*, 116. On middle class self-definition, see Richard Sennet and Jonathan Cobb, *The Hidden Injuries of Class* (New York, 1972), and Jonas Frykman and Ovar Lofgren, *Culture Builders: A Historical Anthropology of Middle Class Life* (New Brunswick, N.J., 1987).

8. Buder, *Pullman*, 43–44; Richard Ely, "Pullman: A Social Study," *Harper's New Monthly Magazine* 70 (Feb. 1885):459.

9. Almont Lindsey, *The Pullman Strike* (Chicago, 1942), 61–86; Stead, *Chicago To-day*, 116; quote from Daniel Rodgers, *The Work Ethic in Industrial America, 1850–1920* (Chicago, 1974), 154.

10. Stead, *Chicago To-day*, 222; Thomas Burke Grant, "Pullman and Its Lessons," *The American Journal of Politics* 5 (Aug. 1894):202–3.

11. William H. Carwardine, *The Pullman Strike* (Chicago, 1894), 18; Richard T. Ely, "Pullman: A Social Study," 458; Lindsey, *The Pullman Strike*, 24; for a contemporary critique of Carwardine, see Charles H. Eaton, "Pullman and Paternalism," *The American Journal of Politics* 5 (Dec. 1894):573. Carwardine was a Christian Socialist who remarked on the intense pressure against socialist literature among publishers, which resulted in difficulty publishing his account of the strike, which was sympathetic to the workers. He also cited pressure from fellow clergymen against his opinions. See testimony of William Carwardine, *Strike Report*, 449; see also Thomas Wickes' attack on Carwardine's book, testimony of Thomas Wickes, *Strike Report*, 594–97.

12. *Chicago Evening Post*, quoted in Carwardine, *The Pullman Strike*, 20; Pullman employee quoted in Buder, *Pullman*, 66.

13. Buder, *Pullman*, 69; Ely, "Pullman, A Social Study," 457.

14. Carwardine, *The Pullman Strike*, 19; Thomas Grant observed "there is no workingman's club, there is no common playground for the people and their children."

"Pullman and Its Lessons," 203; Roy Rosenzweig, *Eight Hours for What We Will* (Cambridge, Mass., 1983), 138–39, 147; testimony of Thomas Heathcoate, *Strike Report*, 430.

15. Testimony of Thomas Heathcoate, *Strike Report*, 425; testimony of Charles Corkery, ibid., 507.

16. Testimony of George Pullman, *Strike Report*, 529, 531, 562–63.

17. Carwardine, *The Pullman Strike*, 23; Richard Ely also noted the lack of architectural diversity and the monotony of the same colored brick throughout the town cried for "some bold break in the general design." Ely, "Pullman, A Social Study," 458.

18. Ely, "Pullman, A Social Study," *Harper's New Monthly Magazine* (Feb. 1885):463; Eaton, "Pullman and Paternalism," gives an argument for the absence of paternalism at Pullman; Thomas Burke Grant argues that Pullman was a survival of feudalism, in "Pullman and Its Lessons," 198.

19. Buder, *Pullman*, 18; Carwardine, *The Pullman Strike*, 19; William Adelman, *Touring Pullman: A Study in Company Paternalism* (Chicago, 1977), 26–27; Grant, "Pullman and Its Lessons," 201.

20. Pullman Company, *The Story of Pullman*, quoted in Stead, *Chicago To-day*, 120; of the 12,000 inhabitants of Pullman in 1890, 6,324 were operatives; Oggel quote in Carwardine, *The Pullman Strike*, 21.

21. Testimony of George Pullman, *Strike Report*, 582; Stead, *Chicago To-day*, 124.

22. Stead, *Chicago To-day*, 122, 183; Grant, "Pullman and Its Lessons," 202; Testimony of Merritt Brown, *Strike Report*, 441–44; Carwardine, *The Pullman Strike*, 49, 51; testimony of George Pullman, *Strike Report*, 532; data on boarders, *Strike Report*, 463, 468.

23. *Strike Report*, xxiii.

24. Testimony of Carwardine, *Strike Report*, 445.

25. Stead, *Chicago To-day*, 223; Eaton, "Pullman and Paternalism," 573.

26. "Were Pullman's Wage Reductions Protectionist Spite?" *American Industries* 3 (Aug. 1894):3.

27. "Were Pullman's Wage Reductions Protectionist Spite?" 4; Grant, "Pullman and Its Lessons," 193–194.

28. Testimony of Thomas Heathcoate, *Strike Report*, 425; testimony of William Carwardine, ibid., 453; testimony of Rev. Morris Wickman, ibid., 462; testimony of Alex Lundgren, ibid., 480; testimony of Edward Bryant, ibid., 509; Carwardine, *The Pullman Strike*, 118.

29. Eaton, "Pullman and Paternalism," 573; Stead, *Chicago To-day*, 31.

30. Massachusetts Bureau of Statistics of Labor, *Sixteenth Annual Report* (Boston, 1885), 1, 17–18, 23–25.

31. Ibid., 19, 23–24.

32. Grant, "Pullman and Its Lessons," 198, 202–04.

33. Ely, "Pullman: A Social Study," 461.

34. Ely, "Pullman: A Social Study," 460–62, 464–65; E.L.C. Morse, "Pullman and Its Inhabitants," *The Nation* 59 (July 26, 1894):61–62; Buder, *Pullman*, 229; Alan Trachtenberg, *The Incorporation of America: Culture and Society in the Gilded Age* (New York, 1982), 223–24.

35. Ely, "Pullman: A Social Study," 462; Frykman and Lofgren, *Culture Builders*, 150, 219–20, 262–63. Likewise, as the working class adopted values of public and personal hygiene, their internalized self-control made them more conscious of their own

inadequacies. But it also gave them the tools for self-respect. "[The worker] sees poverty . . . as depriving men of the capacity to act rationally, to exercise self-control. A poor man, therefore, has to want upward mobility in order to establish dignity in his own life, and dignity means, specifically, moving toward a position in which he deals with the world in some controlled, emotionally restrained way." Sennet and Cobb, *The Hidden Injuries of Class*, 22, quoted in Frykman and Lofgren, *Culture Builders*, 219.

36. Testimony of Thomas Heathcoate, *Strike Report*, 422; see also testimony of Morris Wickman, ibid., 463.

37. T. J. Jackson Lears, "Power, Culture, and Memory," *Journal of American History* 75 (June 1988):140.

38. *Strike Report*, 88, 89; Stead, *Chicago To-day*, 182; see also Craig J. Calhoun, "The Radicalism of Tradition: Community Strength or Venerable Disguise and Borrowed Language?" *American Journal of Sociology* 88 (March 1983):886–914; *Strike Report*, 88–89; Rhodie quote, *Strike Report*, 438.

39. Testimony of Thomas Heathcoate, *Strike Report*, 424; William Carwardine was also of Heathcoate's opinion, see his testimony, ibid., 446.

40. Samuel Gompers in Nelson A. Miles, et al., "Lesson of the Recent Strikes," *North American Review* 159 (Aug. 1894):202–3; Buder, *Pullman*, 218.

41. *Strike Report*, xxviii.

42. Yellen, *American Labor Struggles*, 109; *Strike Report*, xxxi, xxiii; Philip S. Foner, *History of the Labor Movement in the United States*, vol. 2, 261; William M. Burke, *History and Functions of Central Labor Unions* (New York, 1899); Lindsey, *The Pullman Strike*, 114–18.

43. Harvey Wish, "The Pullman Strike: A Study in Industrial Warfare," *Journal of the Illinois State Historical Society* 32 (Sept. 1939):293; Lindsey, *The Pullman Strike*, 126–27; Foner, *History of the Labor Movement*, 269; O. D. Boyle, *History of Railroad Strikes* (Washington, D.C., 1935), 56; see Lindsey's discussion of newspaper opinion in *The Pullman Strike*, 135.

44. Grover Cleveland, *The Government in the Chicago Strike of 1894* (Princeton, 1913), 48; *Strike Report*, xxxiii; W. F. Burns, *The Pullman Boycott* (St. Paul, 1894), 234; testimony of Eugene Debs, *Strike Report*, 129; Jerry Cooper, "The Army as Strike-breaker: The Railroad Strikes of 1877 and 1894," *Labor History* 18 (1977):179–96.

45. Stead, *Chicago To-day*, 250–57.

46. Cleveland, *The Government in the Chicago Strike*, 37; Lindsey, *The Pullman Strike*, 142–48.

47. Testimony of Thomas Wickes, *Strike Report*, 581, 583, 604.

48. Testimony of George Pullman, ibid., 554.

49. Even with reduced wages, the plant did not profit on work contracted after the spring of 1894; testimony of George Pullman, ibid., 557, 567, 579.

50. Testimony of Thomas Wickes, *Strike Report*, 573, 609, 592; testimony of George Pullman, ibid., 557; testimony of John Egan, ibid., 280.

51. *Strike Report*, xxxv; testimony of George Pullman, ibid., 566–67.

52. Testimony of Thomas Wickes, ibid., 594.

53. *Strike Report*, xxxvi.

54. Testimony of George Pullman, ibid., 564, 579.

55. Testimony of Thomas Wickes, ibid., 583, 590; testimony of George Pullman, ibid., 552; testimony of George Pullman, ibid., 553, 556; testimony of Everett St. John, ibid., 252–54.

56. Testimony of Thomas Wickes, *Strike Report*, 585; Stead, *Chicago To-day*, 193.

57. Testimony of George Pullman, *Strike Report*, 562; testimony of Thomas Wickes, ibid., 583.

58. Testimony of John P. Hopkins, ibid., 350.

59. Ibid.

60. Testimony of John Egan, ibid., 271.

61. Buder, *Pullman*, 87, 196, quoted in Yellen, *American Labor Struggles*, 114; testimony of Albert W. Sullivan, *Strike Report*, 326; Burns, *The Pullman Boycott*, 145.

62. Testimony of Eugene Debs, *Strike Report*, 176; Burns, *The Pullman Boycott*, 85, 235; Colston E. Warne, *The Pullman Boycott of 1894: The Problem of Federal Intervention* (Boston, 1955).

63. Testimony of John Egan, *Strike Report*, 271; testimony of Thomas Wickes, ibid., 621; journalists recounted the railroads' "resolve to exterminate organized labor." See Henry J. Fletcher, "The Railway War," *Atlantic Monthly* 74 (Oct. 1894):537.

64. Testimony of Thomas Heathcoate, *Strike Report*, 422.

65. Testimony of George Pullman, ibid., 563.

66. Testimony of Thomas Wickes, ibid., 621–22.

67. Testimony of Everett St. John, ibid., 256.

68. Testimony of John Egan, ibid., 281; testimony of Everett St. John, ibid., 258.

69. Testimony of Thomas Wickes, ibid., 581–84; testimony of Albert Sullivan, ibid., 330; Stead, *Chicago To-day*, 242.

70. Testimony of Albert W. Sullivan, *Strike Report*, 332; see also Gustavus Myers, *History of the Great American Fortunes* (Chicago, 1911), vol. 1, for an account of Pullman's attempt during the strike to discredit strikers as lawless; testimony of George Pullman, *Strike Report*, 622; testimony of S. C. Wade, ibid., 291.

71. Testimony of John McLean, *Strike Report*, 486; testimony of John Egan, ibid., 279.

72. Testimony of George Pullman, ibid., 563, 582; testimony of John Egan, ibid., 278; Miles, et al., "The Lesson of the Recent Strikes," 194–95.

73. Testimony of Albert W. Sullivan, *Strike Report*, 331, 334, 336.

74. Testimony of Albert Sullivan, *Strike Report*, 331, 333; testimony of Thomas Wickes, ibid., 582; see Carroll D. Wright, "The Chicago Strike," *Publications of the American Economic Association* 9 (Oct. and Dec. 1894):505–22.

75. Testimony of Thomas Wickes, *Strike Report*, 580–81; Stead, *Chicago To-day*, 214.

76. Stead, *Chicago To-day*, 179, 195.

77. Stead, *Chicago To-day*, 240; *The Nation* 59 (July 12, 1894):19; ibid., 59 (July 19, 1894):32; ibid., 59 (July 26, 1894):55; "The Boycott of the Pullman Co.," *Harper's Weekly* (July 7, 1894):627; "Suppress the Rebellion" ibid., (July 14, 1894):635; "Some Lessons of the Great Strike," ibid., (July 21, 1894):674; "A Word to the Working Men," ibid.:698; see also "The Real Issue in the Strike," *The Outlook* 50 (July 7, 1894):89; "Legal Aspects of the Disorder at Chicago," ibid., 50 (July 14, 1894):54; untitled editorial, ibid., 50 (July 21, 1894):85–89; "The Strike: Suggestions of Remedy," ibid.:89–90.

78. Burns, *The Pullman Boycott*, 145, 243, 244, 317.

79. Buder, *Pullman*, 185; Gerald Eggert, *Railroad Labor Disputes: The Beginnings of Federal Strike Policy* (Ann Arbor, 1967), 189; Foner, *History of the Labor Movement*, 269; Stead, *Chicago To-day*, 86, 237, 240, 242, 243, 263.

80. Quoted in Burns, *The Pullman Boycott*, 70, 77.

81. *"Revolutionary Statesmanship," Harper's Weekly* (Nov. 24, 1894):43; Thomas M. Cooley, "The Lessons of the Recent Civil Disorders," *The Forum* 18 (Sept. 1894):1; Fletcher, "The Railway War," 534–36; "The Nation and the New Slavery," *The Nation* (July 12, 1894):19; ibid., (July 19, 1894):32; Edgar Bancroft, *The Chicago Strike of 1894* (Chicago, 1895), 39; see also Dr. Joseph Nimmo, "The Insurrection of June and July 1894 Growing Out of the Pullman Strike," an address delivered before the National Statistical Association, Washington, D.C., Oct. 9, 1894, and pub. (Washington, D.C.: 1894), 30; W. J. Ashley, "The Railroad Strike of 1894," *The Church Social Union* series B, no. 1 (April 1895):9; Carroll D. Wright, "The Chicago Strike," 35; George McDermott, "The Pullman Strike Commission," *Catholic World* 9 (Feb. 1895):631.

82. Burton Bledstein, *The Culture of Professionalism: The Middle Class and the Development of Higher Education in America* (New York, 1976), 80–81, 101–04, 282–83; Robert Wiebe, *The Search for Order, 1877–1920* (New York, 1967), 120; Charles W. Eliot, "Some Reasons Why the American Republic May Endure," *The Forum* 18 (Oct. 1894):138.

83. Grant, "Pullman and Its Lessons"; "The Real Issues in the Strike," *The Outlook* (July 7, 1894):8–9; H. von Holst, "Are We Awakened?" *The Journal of Political Economy* 2 (Sept. 1894):485–516; W. H. Caniff, "The Relation of the Railway to Its Employees," *The Engineering Magazine* 8 (March 1895):977–984; T. L. Greene, "The Law of Strikes," *The Nation* 59 (Oct. 18, 1894):281–82.

84. Bancroft, *The Chicago Strike of 1894*, 41; Nimmo, "The Insurrection of June and July 1894," 24, 29; David McG. Means, "The Principles Involved in the Recent Strike," *The Forum* 17 (Aug. 1894):634, 643; Miles, et al., "The Lesson of the Recent Strikes," 186; Albert Shaw, "The Pullman Strike," *The Review of Reviews* 10 (Aug. 1894):135; Fletcher, "The Railway War," 534, 538–40; "Revolutionary Statesmanship," *Harper's Weekly* (Nov. 24, 1894):43; A.H.P. Leuf, "An Open Letter to the U.S. Strike Commission," *To-Day* 1 (Oct. 1894):429; McDermott, "The Pullman Strike Commission," 635.

85. Eliot, "Some Reasons Why the American Republic May Endure," 140–45.

86. Shaw, "The Pullman Strike," 134; Wright, "The Chicago Strike," 35, 40; "law and order" quote from "Revolutionary Statesmanship," *Harper's Weekly* (Nov. 24, 1894):43.

87. Fletcher, "The Railway War," 536.

88. Wright, "The Chicago Strike," 34; "May a Man Conduct His Business as He Please?" *The Forum* 18 (Dec. 1894):428–30; "Steps Toward Government Control of Railroads," ibid., 18 (Feb. 1895):709.

89. *Strike Report*, xxi; Grant, "Pullman and Its Lessons," 190–204; McDermott, "The Pullman Strike Commission," 629.

90. Wright, "The Chicago Strike," 704–05; Leuf, "An Open Letter to the U.S. Strike Commission," 432; Fletcher, "The Railway War," 534, 538–39; Shaw, "The Pullman Strike," 134.

91. Bancroft, "The Chicago Strike of 1894," 44–73; Nimmo, "The Insurrection of June and July 1894," 14, 19; Means, "Principles Involved in the Recent Strike," 640.

92. Martin Sklar, *The Corporate Reconstruction of American Capitalism 1890–1916: The Market, the Law, and Politics* (New York, 1988), 184.

93. Ibid., 34–38; Wright, "Steps Toward Government Control of Railroads," *The Forum* 18 (Feb. 1895):709; Fletcher, "The Railway War," 534; Gompers, in Miles, et

al., "The Lesson of the Recent Strike," 202; see also Leuf, "An Open Letter to the U.S. Strike Commission," 433; "The New Theories of Wages," *The Nation* 59 (July 26, 1894):59; Means, "Principles Involved in the Recent Strikes," 643; Nimmo, "The Insurrection of June and July 1894," 28; Henry Holt, "Punishment of Anarchists and Others," *The Forum* 17 (Aug. 1894):667; Miles et al., "The Lessons of the Recent Strike," 194.

94. "Comment," *The Yale Review* 3 (Aug. 1894):113; von Holst, "Are We Awakened?" 487; "The Boycott of the Pullman Company," *Harper's Weekly* (July 7, 1894):627; Holt, "Punishment of Anarchists and Others," 651–58; Fletcher, "The Railway War," 537; "Some Lessons of the Great Strike," *Harper's Weekly* (July 21, 1894):674; *The Nation* 59 (July 12, 1894):20; Miles et al., "The Lesson of the Recent Strikes," 184; Cooley, "The Lesson of the Recent Civil Disorders," 7; Shaw, "The Pullman Strike," 134; Nimmo, "The Insurrection of June and July 1894," 28.

95. Harry P. Robinson, "The Humiliating Report of the Strike Commission," *The Forum* 18 (Dec. 1894):523; "The Nation and the New Slavery," *The Nation* 59 (July 12, 1894):22; Means, "The Principles Involved in the Recent Strikes," 638; Cooley, "The Lessons of the Recent Civil Disorders," 12–13; Robinson, "The Humiliating Report of the Strike Commission," 524; Theodore Roosevelt, "True American Ideals," *The Forum* 18 (Dec. 1894):746; "This Latest and Greatest Strike," *Bradstreet's* 22 (July 7, 1894):355.

96. Harry P. Robinson in Miles et al., "The Lesson of the Recent Strikes," 198, 201.

97. Roosevelt, "True American Ideals," 747; Ashley, "The Railroad Strike of 1894," 12; "The Boycott of the Pullman Company," *Harper's Weekly* (July 7, 1894):627.

98. Roosevelt, "True American Ideas," 743–50; "The Solidarity of Society," *The Outlook* 50 (Aug. 4, 1894):169; Eliot, "Some Reasons Why the Republic May Endure," 143; Robinson, "The Humiliating Report of the Strike Commission," 525; Caniff, "The Relation of the Railway to Its Employees," 977; Cy Warman, "The Relations of the Employee to the Railroad," *The Engineering Magazine* 8 (Mar. 1895):988.

99. Wright, "Steps Toward Government Control of Railroads," 705, 710; Roosevelt, "True American Ideals," 745, 750; Sklar, *The Corporate Reconstruction of American Capitalism*, 34–38; James Weinstein, *The Corporate Ideal in the Liberal State, 1900–1918* (Boston, 1968), x–xv, "The Solidarity of Society," *The Outlook* 50 (Aug. 4, 1894):169–70.

100. Miles, "The Lesson of the Recent Strikes," 187; see also Robinson, "The Humiliating Report of the Strike Commission," 530.

101. Montgomery, *Workers' Control in America* (New York, 1979), 18–20, 25; Montgomery, *The Fall of the House of Labor: The Workplace, the State, and American Labor Activism, 1865–1925* (New York, 1987), 265.

102. Warne, *The Pullman Boycott of 1894*, 39; Grant, "Pullman and Its Lessons," 196.

103. Testimony of Charles Naylor, *Strike Report*, 113; testimony of Charles Lovejoy, ibid., 76; testimony of George Howard, ibid., 37, 44.

104. Testimony of Eugene Debs, ibid., 129, 169; Nick Salvatore, *Eugene Debs: Citizen and Socialist* (Urbana, 1982), 138–39.

105. Debs quoted in Cleveland, *The Government in the Chicago Strike*, 38; Debs quoted in Salvatore, *Eugene Debs: Citizen and Socialist*, 147.

106. T. J. Jackson Lears, "The Concept of Cultural Hegemony: Problems and Possibilities," *American Historical Review* 90 (June 1985):567–93.

107. Testimony of Eugene Debs, *Strike Report*, 169.

108. See Gareth Stedman Jones, *Languages of Class: Studies in English Working Class History, 1832–1982* (Cambridge, England, 1983), 10, 11, 19, 21.

109. Salvatore, *Eugene Debs*, 345; James Weinstein, *The Decline of Socialism in America 1912–1925* (New York, 1967), 11.

Chapter 3

Modern Management: "The Progressive Relation Between Efficiency and Consent"

Chairman: I think you said, Mr. Taylor, that scientific management was
    to a great extent a state of mind.

Taylor: Without a certain state of mind scientific management cannot exist.
    . . . the idea of peace must replace the old idea of war on both sides.

Hearings Before the Special Committee
of the House of Representatives
to Investigate the Taylor and Other Systems
of Shop Management

The days of compulsion, the days of service without consent are over.

Robert G. Valentine
Scientific Management Consultant[1]

The transformed work routines effected by modern management provided the organizational basis for a hegemonic power structure inside the factory. However, the factory remained a "contested terrain," a site of continual struggle of will, strength, knowledge, and authority between owners and workers. Conquest of that terrain defined the language and ideas governing workers and work. To modern managers, the traditional authority structure of nineteenth-century factories had both created the reasons for, and allowed too much latitude in, the interpretation of the language of work. Near the turn of the century, a new group of engineer-managers refined management techniques to provide scientific and humanistic power relations that would therefore be less class-based and more workable. Basing modern management's authority on science, progress, efficient organization, and the individual's own desire for advancement, managers sought to limit the contestable area of interpretation inside the factory.

Modern managers attempted to impose their own definitions of a fair day's work, right methods, interests, intelligence, free will, mutual obligation, moral economy, and, ultimately, who workers were and what constituted the ultimate purpose of work. Modern managers sought to replace workers' traditional definitions with their own and thus transform the underlying ethos of work. The employer's logic of work relations prescribed a new role for workers in industrial society. No longer did managers define workers in republican-era terms as self-directed property owning producers exercising free will in a virtuous civic society. Instead, workers in the early twentieth century were to be salaried employees who took advantage of an equal-opportunity marketplace and who could be integrated into progressive society. Modern managers' definitions of work and workers were less about personal integrity, self-esteem, accumulated knowledge, or craft solidarity and more about efficiency, job stability, and individual fulfillment within a corporate-led social whole.

The ideal type of factory worker, according to modern scientific managers, was loyal, diligent, and compliant, which, they thought, would contribute to efficiency and stability in factory operation. Managers deemed these traits natural products of human social and economic evolution based on their ''irrefutable'' technological and scientific validity and therefore their undeniable necessity. Through a systematic application of ''economic law,'' they posed natural attributes such as desire for advancement and gain, which prescribed workers' rightful place in efficient production and delegated to them the responsibility to maintain peace within the corporate capitalist order. Scientific managers argued that labor should accommodate to, and actively support rather than hinder, the evolution of national social progress. Conversely, modern managers penalized, ridiculed, or suppressed undesirable traits, however ''natural,'' that subverted efficient production. Whatever management theorists decided constituted workers' optimal nature or behavior became what they needed to be for and within a socially engineered workplace.

Modern managers enforced these new definitions by integrating them into the very organization of work routines on the shop floor, a process that branded workers' control and union defiance as inefficient and thus socially undesirable. How managers treated workers in the modern, scientifically managed workplace and how workers were expected to respond constituted a learning process for owners, managers, and workers, one that injected behavioral norms and a social definition of labor into factory production. The cumulative result was to make the factory an institution of social control and to spread through society the market relations and attitudes necessary for the success of a consumer economy. ''Scientific management was as important an element in the transformation of American ideology,'' David Montgomery found, ''as it was in the reshaping of industry.''[2]

The rationalization of industrial production after 1890 transformed U.S. manufacturing, including its financial organization, consolidation, and the incorporation of most of the nation's largest firms. The growing scale, complexity, and capital requirements of production, coupled with devastating competition, drove manufacturers to seek predictability and accountability in production, prices, and markets. These goals, in turn, compelled them to extend control over material and human variables, creating a "veritable mania for efficiency, organization, and standardization" in factory production.[3] By the first quarter of the twentieth century, the general principles of modern "scientific" management together with technological changes in production had become incorporated in the thinking of owners, managers, and engineers in the factories of advanced capitalist countries.[4] Scrutinizing every aspect of plant activity, engineers and managers redesigned and systematized machinery and tools and reorganized work tasks, flow patterns, and routines to create an integrated system of production. The quest to reduce labor's autonomy and cost and extract its maximum efficiency spurred managers to develop more routinized work.

Modern management practices arose after 1890 from a new breed of college-trained professional engineers who provided a direct link between the technocratic advances of the age and its social development. Engineers were the first to employ the scientific method systematically in the control of production and to attack the "labor problem." The American Society of Mechanical Engineers preferred the term "labor saving management" for modern management because it promised to provide the same efficiency as labor saving machinery.[5] Engineer-managers sought to minimize workers' input into production decisions and defeat their resistance to new forms of industrial discipline. As engineers sought to direct the social elements of production in a scientific manner, they replaced the skills of craftsmen with machinery and predetermined work routines. Human elements of production were synchronized with preset machine speeds and cuts and paced by conveyers and management-devised task assignments. With these changes, engineer-managers injected management's authority into work, a process termed the "transfer of skill," and viewed workers as cogs in the machinery of production.[6] "Work is ever more specialized," observed Robert Valentine, a scientific management consultant, "the steady tendency is to need . . . the thinking, judging human being less and less, so that the mechanically and easily trained human being more and more is used, and . . . tends in his turn to give way to inanimate machinery."[7]

As they scientifically restructured the workplace, engineer-managers generated a scientific vocabulary of labor definition and a set of expectations for labor behavior that redefined workers and their characteristics. In figuring out who workers "were" and what they "needed" to be, managers imposed their own definitions and assumptions—or those of their capitalist bosses—upon work and workers. From these efforts emerged a new labor terminology that specified the worker's role and responsibility in the scientifically managed workplace.

Scientific management, the earliest form of modern management, offered a set of assumptions about human character, morals, values, and normal behavior based on workers' recognizing their own stake in efficient production. Its notions of employing, defining, and disciplining labor were permeated with capital-labor antagonism. Frederick Taylor's immediate goal of securing greater profits for his employers and his long-range plan to curb industrial warfare could be realized, he maintained, through a "mental revolution" achieved by coercive appeals to deterministic notions of workers' "interests."

Near the end of the century competitive capitalism gave way to corporate-led national liberalism that viewed labor as both an interrelating and competing interest among big and small business, professionals, intellectuals, Populists, and progressives.[8] By World War I, more progressive management theorists such as Frank and Lillian Gilbreth and H. L. Gantt retreated from Taylor's extreme anti-labor position toward a more "humanist" approach that drew from psychology and social science to develop ideas about managing workers. As the "labor problem" gradually gave over to the professionalized science of managing human social organization, later management theorists and practitioners of the 1920s, following behaviorists such as Hugo Munsterberg and Elton Mayo, developed a more sophisticated definition of labor that utilized psychology and broader interpretations of the social dimensions of workers' lives.[9]

The material, organizational, and social changes introduced under modern management techniques emerged from corporate capital's interest in developing both efficient factories and a smoothly run society. Along with other professionalized penal, civic, educational, and bureaucratic instruments of control developed and refined in the late nineteenth century, modern management sought to create a new type of worker-citizen-consumer who fit the mechanistic order of rationalized mass production. Modern management's prescriptions for rational behavior formed part of a broad and complex cultural movement near the turn of the century that sought to reorganize American society around the social necessities of liberal corporate capitalism, the belief in progress and efficiency, and the acceptance of the mores of a machine- and production-oriented society.[10]

THE LABOR IDEAS OF SCIENTIFIC MANAGEMENT

Modern management's view of labor begins with the scientific management school that included Frederick Taylor and other early practitioners, Frank and Lillian Gilbreth, H. L. Gantt, and Sanford E. Thompson, Hollis Godfrey, Carl Barth, and, after World War I, Harlow S. Person and Morris Cooke. The major achievement of scientific management was to gain control of production and to systematize organization in the factories where it was used. This was achieved by transferring labor skills and knowledge to management for analysis and returning them to workers in pieces, with the result that management retained the "brains" of production and workers performed the handwork.[11] Scientific management brought newer and higher standards of centralization, organization, and labor utilization to industry, norms that guaranteed higher productivity, better discipline, and more management control, and that continue to represent the ethos of modern industrial organization.

Taylor and an army of practitioners began to spread their ideas of efficiency and control through industry after 1903, gaining avid converts among manufacturers, engineers, and managers. In 1911 Harlow Person became dean of Dartmouth's Amos Tuck School of Administration and Finance and sponsored a nationwide conference on scientific management. That same year fifty companies formed the Employment Management Association in Boston. By the outbreak of World War I more than thirty major factories had officially adopted some version of scientific management, among them Bethlehem Steel, the Link Belt Engineering Company of Philadelphia and Chicago, the Franklin Automobile Company of Syracuse, New York, Brighton Mills at Passaic, New Jersey, the Yale and Towne Manufacturing Company of Stamford, Connecticut, the Tabor Manufacturing Company of Philadelphia, and, in some cases, entire local industries such as the clay and brick trades of St. Louis. By 1922, Harvard, Dartmouth, Rochester, Columbia, and Princeton offered courses to train the new management professionals.[12]

In 1912 a subcommittee of the American Society of Mechanical Engineers (ASME) issued a report that assessed the past twenty-five years of change in industrial management. The "loosely applied term scientific management," the report noted, best characterized the new ideas and techniques of modern management: careful investigation of production methods, shaping new practice on exact knowledge, time and motion study, planning departments, wage schemes that stimulated cooperation, and a new emphasis on workers' human dimensions. The ASME report cited the sixteen most important articles on scientific management published in the society's *Transactions*. Of these, ten were authored by Taylor, Gantt, Barth, James M. Dodge, or Henry Towne, all scientific management engineers, consultants, or owners of Taylorized plants. Even in 1912 Taylor's 1903 paper, "Shop Management," still represented to the ASME, the "only comprehensive outline of industrial management."[13]

Few industrial managers cooperated with the subcommittee's request that they report their use of scientific management techniques to it. Managers seemed to be in "a secretive stage" prompted by their wish to protect technological and managerial trade secrets, their fear of the adverse reflection cast on plants that employed outside experts, and, perhaps above all, their wariness of union resistance. The ASME concluded that modern manufacturers avoided using the name "scientific management" but had "quite generally applied" its principles. Like many managers in the ASME poll, Henry Ford claimed that Ford managers developed their own techniques in the Sociology Department at the Highland Park plant between 1911 and 1914. Ford denied using Taylorism or scientific management as the basis of his new methods of production, but, in effect, his most recent historian, Stephen Meyer found, "Ford managers and engineers Taylorized work tasks and routines." Even by the end of the 1920s N. I. Stone, a New York management consultant, cited as evidence for continuing management opposition "the fact that many plants which have been revolutionized by scientific management refuse to acknowledge the source of the revolutionary influence."[14]

World War I, however, spurred even greater interest in national organization and efficient production. By the decade after the war an overwhelming majority of U.S. industries had adopted modified versions of scientific management, including incentive pay, standardization of tasks, cost accounting, central planning, and integration of all factory operations under the rational control of scientifically trained managers. By 1935 economist John R. Commons reported that the essential ideas of scientific management enjoyed such wide acceptance that they had become "commonplaces of American industrial practice."[15]

The early development of scientific management reveals the process by which modern views of labor emerged from attempts to bring efficiency to machine shop work. Taylor's paper, "A Piece-Rate System," read before the American Society of Mechanical Engineers in 1895, prescribed in its subtitle, "A Step Toward Partial Solution to the Labor Problem." Conceived in the union-busting atmosphere at the turn of the century, Taylorism offered employers a promise of breaking craft unions' power in their plants and redirecting workers' energies to increasing production. Taylor was one of the first engineers to pay attention to human relations, and the literature of scientific management considered industrial relations as important as technological change. While his understanding of worker motivation appears crude when compared to later management psychology, it nonetheless established precedents in the field of industrial relations after 1903. While Taylor's system operated on the premise that workers should adapt to the technological and administrative changes required by scientifically managed production, he and some of his followers, such as Robert Valentine, introduced the idea of obtaining workers' consent and participation.[16] Catering to workers' desires for advancement, Taylor discovered, could make them willing participants in efficient plant management.

Taylor's system purchased worker cooperation through increased wages and personal advancement or exacted compliance through driving shop foremen and wage penalties. Since Taylor had no training in the human sciences, he saw workers as simpleminded automatons who responded to psychologically mechanistic, carrot-and-stick rewards and punishments. Imbued with the social philosophy of frontier individualism and self-reliance, Taylor thought it sufficient to select workers appropriate for a job, train them, and offer them wage incentives based on what he assumed was a worker's desire to make money. This view of human nature denied communitarian or socialist values, republican notions of work, and the idea that job satisfaction might have to do with exercising craft skills, maintaining control of work, or sustaining community solidarity. How did Taylor develop these ideas?

To Taylor, as with most first generation professional manager-engineers, productivity depended on the control employers exercised over work in their plants, a real question in his day since technological knowledge most often rested in the hands of floor bosses and skilled workers. Appropriating workers' knowledge and skill involved not just governing the material aspects of production but addressing the issue of workers' control of work. This led Taylor to examine a previously ignored element in the manufacturing process, the complex relationship between ideas, technology, and material objects, and to recognize that a material reorganization of production could produce changes in workers' thinking and behavior. Manufacturers could take control of work, he surmised, by exploiting the flow of information between factory organization, fabrication technology, and workers' consciousness. Since ideas about production and the social relations of production were learned at the same time as the skills, Taylor felt, the workplace furnished the primary site where workers defined themselves and their relations to capital. It was at work, he surmised, that employers might seize control of those definitions by imposing new social relations and terminology.

In the late nineteenth century, craft unions' strength lay in their ability to enforce series of informal rules enforced at the shop level by individual workmen and committees of union locals. These craft standards effectively reduced employers' control and offered a measure of autonomy to skilled workers.[17] Taylor reasoned that craft unions' power could be broken if craftsmen's skills and standards could be broken down, quantified, transferred to machines, and taught to semi-skilled operatives. National manufacturers' trade associations had already begun to attack collective enforcement of craft union rules in the 1890s, negotiating with skilled workers on an individual basis over wage rates, job classifications, daily output, spoilage, and grievances. Taylor's system carried this struggle to a new plane with technological and organizational changes designed to (a) reorganize work to transfer labor's control to management; (b) replace union collectivity with individualized achievement-oriented work incentives that generated loyalty to the "common interests" of capital and labor, and (c) tie worker self-image and self-definition to employer-determined criteria, to rise and fall with the individual's degree of fulfillment of daily task assignments.

While this need to appropriate the technology of skilled work furnished scientific management's rationale, the social authority and prestige of science provided a more legitimate framework for attacking craft union standards. Described by its practitioners as one of the laws of nature, scientific management asserted the absolute impartiality and objectivity of science data and, by extension, of Taylor's own methods. His insistence on the "one best method" of performing each task presupposed the existence of a numerically verifiable, exact formula for executing it. "Under Scientific Management," Taylor explained, "every single subject, large and small, becomes the question for scientific investigation," for reduction to "clearly defined laws, rules and principles."[18] He defended the "one best way" in the same manner that scientists of his day upheld the seemingly undeniable certainty of physical or mathematical laws. This defense was made easier, Samuel Haber wrote, "for Science had a lustre all its own [in] a generation in which most people believed that progress was written into the laws of the universe."[19] Taylorites linked scientific knowledge with the progressive value of industrialization and the promise of the machine, justifying the centralization of employer power over workers and creating a new orientation toward modern scientific authority. Scientific management claimed to replace the arbitrary and divisive authority of skilled workers and floor bosses that replicated in miniature the labor-capital conflict with the clinical and proven authority of science that, claimed one Taylorite, "plays no favorites." By this logic, scientific management redefined and abstracted manufacturers' efficiency goals into socially beneficial, classless, natural principles.[20] To define work and workers, then, within the framework of scientific progress was to make them instruments of progress that was dependent upon their cooperation and subverted by their "rule-of-thumb" standards.

The idea of social perfection through adherence to scientific law informed the grand impulses of the Progressive Era. An age enamored of material efficiency in machine output eagerly embraced the possibility of achieving social control through replicating machine efficiency in human behavior. Couched in the language of individualism and the work ethic, Taylor's prescription for a mental revolution fit progressive reformers' diagnosis of the social problems of industrial society. Both assumed that work discipline helped eliminate disobedience or unproductive behavior and secure an orderly social whole. "When men spend the greater part of their active working hours in regulating their every movement in accordance with clear-cut formulated laws," Taylor believed, they "form habits which inevitably affect and in many cases control them in their family life, and in all of their acts outside working hours. With almost certainty they begin to guide the rest of their lives according to the principles and laws, and to try to insist upon those around them doing the same."[21] Scientific management's "mental revolution," observed the J. C. Penney Foundation's secretary on industrial relations, "must be carried beyond the individual plant, beyond the total industrial organization, until it embraces the mind of the entire community." Scientific management theorists promised a social transformation as workers' scientifically managed behavior infiltrated "common law and public opinion" and permeated "all social activities" in homes, farms, churches, philanthropic institutions, universities, and government.[22] Rationalized behavior promised to increase production, decrease costs, reduce consumer prices, raise wages and profits, improve the material standard of living, remove the sources of social tension in industry, guarantee individual workers success, and promote civilization and progress.

Taylor developed the fundamentals of his system during his on-the-job experience between 1878 and 1890 as gang boss, engineer, and shop foreman at the Midvale Steel Company of Philadelphia. Experiments in machine shop efficiency led him to analyze the entire structure of men, materials, authority, and work patterns within the traditional factory. He identified two crucial problems that prevented employers' control of work: bosses' tyranny and workers' autonomy. As factories grew larger and more complex and the individual discretionary power of floor bosses, enhanced by their distance from any central management, increased at every level, so did their use of arbitrary power. At Midvale it was understood that each foreman used this power to force the greatest amount of work from those under his supervision, assigning jobs, supervising work, hiring and firing at will. Workers' autonomy represented the other side of the coin. The deliberate restriction of work output, or soldiering, which Taylor found "almost universal in industrial establishments," constituted the "greatest evil with which the working-people of both England and America are now afflicted."[23]

Soldiering was possible only because work was performed according to traditional or "rule-of-thumb" methods, "the principal asset of every tradesman," which remained largely unknown to employers not privy to the transfer of knowledge from craftsman to apprentice. Employers, Taylor noted, derive their understanding of exactly how much work can be done from either their own experience, "frequently grown hazy with age," or from "casual and unsystematic observation" or at best from records showing the fastest time each job was accomplished. Most employers felt that work could be speeded up but "rarely care to take the drastic measures necessary to force men to do it in the quickest time." Thus, it "becomes for each man's interest . . . to see that no job is done faster than it has been in the past."[24] By controlling the rate and manner of production, Taylor surmised, skilled craftsmen kept employers ignorant of the actual amount of time or effort a job required. This technological expertise and relative autonomy along with high pay, leadership, and community standing earned skilled workers a tangible degree of authority, which had to be broken, Taylor thought, if owners were to control work.

The traditional piece rate system of wage payment spurred workers to develop soldiering to a fine art. Employers allocated piece payment according to the maximum amount that "should" be paid for each piece of work. When it became clear that workers could produce more, employers "speeded-up" work without correspondingly raising pay. As newcomers, goaded by the promise of increasing their earnings, inevitably speeded up piece production, employers reduced rates proportionally. Thus, Taylor reasoned, after a worker experienced pay reductions in retaliation for increased output, "he is likely to lose sight of his employer's side of the case and become imbued with a grim determination to have no more cuts if soldiering can prevent it."[25]

Soldiering pitted workers against manufacturers in a struggle for control of productivity. Workers' "deliberate attempt to mislead and deceive" employers caused them to view the employer as "an antagonist, if not an enemy."[26] Apprentices were taught to serve their own interests by subverting those of employers. Taylor sought to interrupt this transfer of information down through the labor hierarchy and replace it with employers' labor ideas. As he analyzed shop floor practices in terms of a contest of power, authority, and knowledge between owners and workers, the latter's skill and authority appeared in scientific management literature as "the problem" to be addressed by an assault on its source, the rule-of-thumb technological expertise of skilled craft workers.[27]

For these reasons, Taylor characterized scientific management as a solution to the management problems *inherent* in traditional factory production in his era. To eliminate the built-in logic for soldiering, Taylor's methods standardized and systematized every detail in the use of labor, materials, tools, space, and time. This shifted technological expertise and decision making from workers to managers and destroyed skilled craftsmen's exclusive knowledge and control. "All of the planning which under the old system was done by the workmen," Taylor wrote, "as a result of his personal experience, must of necessity under the new system be done by the management in accordance with the laws of science; because even if the workman was well suited to the development and use of scientific data, it would be physically impossible for him to work at his machine and at a desk at the same time."[28]

In the machine tool industry, the shift of technological control to planners was made possible by rapid advances in technology that, to managers at least, mandated a more efficient use of time. During his investigation of machine speeds for metal cutting at Midvale Street, for example, Taylor invented a special, high-speed steel for cutting tools and drills, which, because it retained a cutting edge at high temperatures, tripled the speed of metal cutting and finishing. As Midvale's skilled machine operators' productivity tripled, the flow of materials to and from their machines had to increase correspondingly, forcing a speed-up of the entire production process and requiring a more cost-effective use of machinists' time. Scientific task management sought to organize work so that humans produced at a speed approaching machine capacity, a goal craft-controlled work rules would not have countenanced.[29]

Scientific management required a dramatic intensification of the division of labor, further subdividing the individual elements of each machine shop task. For example, Taylor turned a single job, lathe work on steel locomotive wheels, into a series of twenty-two less complicated, more repetitive operations, each with seven separate specifications. The cumulative effect of the small savings in each work step dramatically lowered production costs per unit. The largest saving in the subdivision of labor resulted from forcing skilled workers to perform only skilled work. Traditionally, machinists performed other tasks than their primary assignment, procuring uncut stock or machine tools from the stockroom, cleaning up work areas, or repairing plant machinery. Taylor's subdivision of tasks delegated these unskilled portions of a machinist's job to ordinary laborers and limited skilled workers to more highly paid, more productive, "important" work. In the metal-working industries, Taylor's revolutionary job refinement eliminated many skilled machinists' jobs by reducing them to simplified tasks for less skilled and costly machine tenders. Prefabricated jigs, repetitive, simplified job segments, and increased supervision were used to turn untrained laborers into specialized machine operatives who became the most numerous group of workers. Taken together, the decline in skilled workers' relative numbers, the assumption of their supervisory duties by management personnel, and the reduction of their social interaction with other workers greatly diminished the craftsmen's role as the source of work rules and definitions.[30]

The mystification of the scientific rationale underlying Taylor's reorganized work process further eroded craftsmen's authority. As managers substituted "scientific law'' for workers' knowledge and control, they purposely made it so complicated, specialized, and esoteric that ordinary workmen presumably could not understand it without the help of college-trained experts. Even for skilled mechanics, Taylor insisted, who were "more capable of generalization" and "more likely" to choose scientific methods, the scientific laws governing skilled jobs "are so intricate that the high priced mechanic needs (even more than the cheap laborer) the cooperation of men better educated than himself in finding the laws."[31] Transferring technological expertise and legitimacy from skilled workers to the planning department helped demean craftsmen's traditional work control and portray rule-of-thumb know-how as the antithesis of efficiency.

Taylor often boasted that he had reduced work operations to the point where automatons or gorillas could perform them. In the Taylorized machine shop at Bethlehem Steel, "handymen trained up from laborers" constituted almost 95 percent of the men running the roughing machines and about 25 percent of those on finishing machines. "Craftsmanship in the old sense of the term is doomed," claimed Robert Valentine.[32] Some jobs such as lathe operation could not be reduced to a series of simple tasks and had to be left in the care of skilled workmen. Even these, however, were fitted into the whole plant dynamic and circumscribed by managerial control as they were planned in advance, described in written instructions, speeded up by reducing "unnecessary" motion, governed by a new standardized time rate, observed by scientific managers, and rewarded or punished according to employer-determined norms.

Once scientific managers had subdivided, classified, and standardized tasks, they calculated the number of minutes the task should take to perform. At this point the individual worker's willingness to speed up performances became the focal point of change. Taylor addressed this problem by inventing the differential piece rate, a system of wage bonuses and penalties designed to spur faster work. Traditional piece work or day wage systems "made the mistake" of paying all workmen the same rate or wage regardless of efficiency. The differential piece rate scale wages to individual performance and paid bonuses of 30 to 60 percent when workers' output exceeded what Taylor defined as a "fair day's work." It also imposed penalties for failure to achieve minimum output and for spoiled work. In both cases, the worker forfeited the bonus and suffered the "direct loss of the piece price for each piece by which he falls short." This carrot-and-stick incentive "not only pulls the man up from the top but pushed him equally hard from the bottom."[33] Scientific managers governed every aspect of bonus allocation, choosing the "right" worker for the job, determining the nature of the tasks, doling out pay incentives, and timing and charting all elements of the task that affected speed.

To break worker imposed rates in Midvale's machine shop, Taylor removed skilled workers from the top of the shop's labor hierarchy and replaced them with operatives working under new lines of management authority that ran vertically from management "brains" down to operatives. Taylor's incentive pay was most often introduced in non-union shops or as part of union-busting tactics so that workers could be initiated into the system on an individual basis. The integration of technological changes with management-generated incentive pay schemes, Taylor advertised, spurred workers to work faster and harder, curbed the means to limit output, and produced obedience to managers who controlled the bonus system.[34]

Taylor intended the cumulative effect of these changes to achieve a "unity of interests" between workmen and employers that would shift workers' loyalty from each other to that of their employers. He remained convinced that the "true interests" of labor and capital were "one and the same" and that workers' self-interested behavior could be transformed into allegiance to employer interest in greater output. He often admitted, however, the crudeness of this position. Almost alone among management theorists before World War I, Taylor acknowledged the rational basis for workers' hostility. Given "generations of bitter experiences," workers behaved in a reasonable manner, entirely consistent with their perceived personal and class interests. When Midvale's workers asked Taylor whether "for their own best interest" they should turn out more work, he admitted that, were he in their place, he would "fight against turning out any more work, just as they were doing . . . because under the piece work system they would be allowed to earn no more wages than they had been earning, and yet they would be made to work harder." By this, Taylor acknowledged the futility of the speed-up and the rationality of workers' assessments of their own situation.

The task of managers, then, was to induce each worker to give to employers "his best endeavors, his hardest work, all his traditional knowledge, his skill, his ingenuity, and his good-will—in a word, his 'initiative.' " In short, the worker must somehow drive himself.[35] Since rational workers could not be enticed to drive themselves in their employers' interest, they must serve these interests *without realizing it*. Taylor's system provided this roundabout route by identifying employees' interests not with capital's but with a "higher," scientifically determined, common goal. In place of a clash of interests, his system redirected the initiative and self-interest of both labor and capital to a new "unity of interests"—that of scientifically increased productivity. Rather than deny the existence of surplus profit as did many manufacturers of his day, Taylor used the notion of profit sharing to "take their eyes off the division of the surplus as the important matter, and together turn their attention toward increasing the size of the surplus."[36] Taylorism spoke to workers in terms of these higher interests, affixing individual initiative and interest to personal achievement and gain within an integrated system, and giving the worker a stake in the efficient working of the entire factory. Workers who believed they were working for personal rewards need not be coerced but welcomed any method that increased individual productivity. Taylor was convinced that most immigrants had come to America seeking opportunity, and he reduced the problem of human relations to fulfilling this promise. In his management theory, successful labor relations rested entirely upon mobilizing joint labor-management efforts to increase productivity.[37]

Offering bonuses as an incentive aimed at *individual* effort, Taylorism made personal desire and ability constitute the difference between success and failure and placed the responsibility for failure upon the worker alone. To share in the bonus, workers had to outwardly conform to Taylor's definitions of success in wages, work output, quality of work, and acceptable shop floor behavior. Best of all for Midvale's engineers, however, the immediate bribery of the bonus persuaded many workers to strive for individual self-advancement. We "set [workers] up in business for themselves and [they] must give their best, both for their own interest and that of the organization," explained George D. Babcock, production manager at the Franklin Automobile Company's Taylorized plant. Workers simultaneously serving their own and their employers' interests represented a "shift in loyalty" that Taylor claimed, constituted a revolutionary transformation of worker consciousness, "a complete mental revolution on the part of these men as to their duties toward their work, toward their fellow man, and toward their employers."[38]

In this manner, scientific management attempted to capitalize on the ideological aspects of the material changes it fostered in production; what Alvin Gouldner termed the "dialectic of ideology and technology; what Marx referred to as "intellectual potencies of the material process of production"; and what Taylor himself recognized as the dependence of the mental revolution upon material lessons. He intended these "lessons," the internal, "obvious," technological "logic" of scientific management, to foster in workers an "orderly, persistent, thorough use of the mind, a sort of sublimated common sense."[39] The shop floor authority of scientific managers, constituted and applied as an integral part of production, appeared less coercive and more rational, one of the "necessary" requisites of efficient production. The material subordination of the worker, Taylor thought, guaranteed his outward obedience to shop rules and his inner psychological dedication to an ethos of efficiency.

Instituted primarily in the metal-working industries, Taylor's incentive pay system may have succeeded in prompting many skilled machinists to greater exertion and focusing their interests upon gaining a higher salary.[40] But it did nothing to alter the arbitrary power of traditional shop managers, a foremost problem in plants undergoing conversion to scientific management. Taylor's system replaced the personal authority of traditional floor bosses with college-trained "functional" engineer-managers, who developed scientific work processes by "classifying, tabulating, and reducing" skilled workers' traditional knowledge into "rules, laws, and formulae."[41] This process removed management's "brainwork," like that of workers, from the shop floor to the planning department. Traditional management was "looked upon as a question of men and conducted in part based on personality and familiarity," Taylor claimed. Functional management required a scientific application of rules; its authority now flowed from new formulae of human interaction, fine-tuned for efficiency, administered by professional engineers from behind glass walls, and legitimated by the irrefutable sovereignty of mathematics. And it implied, of course, that the intelligence and knowledge necessary to direct work came only from the new class of scientifically trained, certified professionals, relegating workers to a less knowledgeable and therefore, within the context of the new system, intellectually inferior status.

While scientific management increased the number of managers relative to the old system, it allowed them less authority, prompting Taylor to insist that his system applied the same principles to management as to workers. "Functional management," involved a similar subdivision of management tasks, Taylor explained, "so dividing the work of management that each man from the assistant superintendent down will have as few functions as possible to perform."[42] Daily task orders from the planning office replaced the personal authority and discretion of semi-autonomous floor and gang bosses. Each functional manager learned to perform a prearranged, carefully described, hierarchically controlled job within an integrated management system, a diffusion and weakening of authority that resulted ultimately in the proletarianization of all but the top level of management. Harlow Person's new system of management classification, for example, integrated "managerial labor" with other types of wage labor in the scientifically managed factory. He specified two types of factory labor: mechanical, including skilled and unskilled labor, and managerial, including all ranks of managers from floor foremen to department heads.[43]

Scientific managers sought to standardize products, materials, and methods of production, keep records, provide written work instructions, and govern the storage and movement of tools and parts. Armed with university gained scientific expertise and distinct in white coats symbolic of their authority and exclusivity, functional managers in Taylorized plants exuded a new demeanor on the shop floor, clinically scientific, anonymous, critical, and superior. Persons of executive and supervisory rank, Hugh Aitken discovered at the Watertown Arsenal, regarded themselves as more important people with greater control over what happened in the plant than before.[44] The physical symbol of managerial authority was the planning office, ideally situated in the center of the factory work area but physically separated from workers by a glass wall. A locus of activity and authority, the planning office was stocked with the visible symbols of management—clipboards, stopwatches, charts, records, desks, route and flow charts— and staffed by timekeepers and planners who engaged in continuous surveillance, itself an increasingly palpable factor in scientifically managed work. The planning office supplied each worker with daily task descriptions printed on instruction cards and enforced by a network of functional managers who singled out and rewarded top achievers and punished slackers. The constant monitoring, which made workers and supervisors more visible to the planners, reinforced the disciplinary and intimidating potential of the more linear flow of authority.[45]

Factory reorganization involved assigning specific space to the tool room, the parts room, planning areas, machine operators' areas, and materials handlers' sectors, a utilitarian process, which as it restructured the traditional use of space, began to dissolve informal shop patterns of authority and social interaction and reinforce the new, "scientifically" arranged human relationships. In the process of minutely accounting for each human action in the work flow, managers attempted to govern all social interaction. Machinists, for example, no longer roamed the shop at will, but worked continuously at their appointed stations. Managers in Taylorized factories put these tactics into operation in a manner that made it difficult for workers to control, argue with, or sabotage the system. An all-encompassing management structure and coordinated plant organization compelled workers to participate fully and correctly in each aspect of the work plan or refuse the system in toto. "Anything short of complete utilization of the whole system," Taylor insisted, "leaves such a large part of the game in the hands of the workmen that it becomes largely a matter of whim or caprice on their part as to whether they will allow you to have any results or not."[46]

Scientific managers so integrated each task into the master work plan of the entire plant that soldiering interrupted the flow of work and immediately pin-pointed the "culprit." Furthermore, the close, daily contact and the integration of workers and managers into one system precluded arguments and compelled a degree of cooperation designed to render independent individualism "entirely impossible." "All day long," Taylor claimed, "every workman's acts are dove-tailed in between corresponding acts of the management. First the workman does something, and then a [manager] does something . . . and under this intimate, close, personal cooperation between the two it becomes practically impossible to have a serious quarrel." To preclude arguments or even an exchange of ideas between management and labor on the shop floor, a manager should take special care to "avoid matching his wits with the workman," Taylor advised, "Make dogmatic statements and let it go at that. Argument is the beginning of mental opposition." Outright disagreement was unacceptable. "The great sin at Midvale," reported the steel company's President Charles J. Harrah, "is insubordination or disobedience. That is not forgiven [and] is punished severely."[47]

In Taylorized plants, then, scientific management dramatically increased the uniformity of action and, by implication, reduced independent decision making, both necessary accompaniments to the subdivision and ritualization of work tasks. Workers became accustomed, Taylor found, to "continually and habitually [working] in accordance with scientific laws which have been developed by someone else." After Taylor's system was implemented at Midvale Steel, President Harrah reported, "the regularity of our men is very much out of common."[48] Scientific management had removed worker discretion, forced 100 percent compliance, and allowed no one to work without manager directives. While Taylor often claimed that his hierarchical structure of management authority increased workers' participation in decision making, there was ample evidence for labor's charges of "speed-up" and driving. Before World War I scientific management practitioners repudiated the National Civic Federation's philosophy of industrial democracy, which advocated labor's participation in management, in favor of what Taylor emphasized as "*enforced* standardization of methods, *enforced* adoption of the best implements and working conditions, and *enforced* cooperation.'' Scientific management, despite its claims to neutrality, was still management and ''could be made as much an instrument of oppression as any other method of handling labor,'' admitted James Mapes Dodge, president of the Link Belt Corporation, a Taylorized company.[49]

Taylorism subdivided, deskilled, and speeded up work, removed brainwork from workers, geared incentive to faster work, increased the ratio of control personnel to workers, deliberately obscured technological information, reduced workers' status, habituated them to repetitive, routinized tasks, and demanded absolute obedience to the authority of planners. The process of analyzing movements, measuring work, and determining the techniques that best suited the efficient performance of each task increased Taylorism's network of domination and correspondingly diminished workers' social cohesiveness and their ability to control conditions of their job or enforce craft rules.

With the deference of both capital and labor to the demands of professional scientific managers, the ideology of the latter assumed a more prominent position in the productive process. Taylor's method prodded workers to accept owners' definitions about human and material aspects of production. The ''scientific'' goal of achieving more efficient production was, in effect, capital's goal. The reconciliation of interests was achieved, at least outwardly, as factories functioned smoothly and more efficiently, but under owners' terms, directed by managers whose allegiance to machine rationality and scientific law at once abstracted, depersonalized, and masked their service to owner interests.[50]

THE SOCIAL IMPLICATIONS OF EARLY SCIENTIFIC MANAGEMENT

In redesigning factory social relations, early scientific managers also redefined workers, their organizations, and their proper role in industrial society. Contemporary assumptions about natural law and human behavior together with the quest for absolute control and efficiency conditioned Taylor's image of the worker. In assessing the ''nature of men,'' scientific management drew many distinctions: first, between working people and everyone else, and, second, within various groups of the working population itself. In a 1909 address to the faculty and students of the Harvard Business School, Taylor explained the difference between workers and the class of men represented in his audience. Designating these groups as ''them'' and ''us,'' he claimed that although the nature of both classes is ''essentially the same,'' environmental forces ''temporarily accentuate and intensify certain qualities,'' creating ''actual differences between the two classes.'' Thus, each class rightly perceived the other as a ''different kind of animal,'' the academic group seeing workers ''slouching along the street on their way back from work, with dirty clothes, chewing tobacco, in many cases hardly looking up as they pass by, stolid and indifferent-looking,'' while workers saw ''in men of our class merely the outward signs of prosperity—

good clothes, and the possession of carriages and automobiles—the careless holiday look, accompanied by short working hours."[51]

Observable differences prompted Taylor to identify the behavioral and mental characteristics of each class. Since working men have "spent their entire lives in obeying other people's orders," while "they see men of our class frequently in our capacity of giving orders," they "occupy the position of apparent inferiority to us." Although workers regarded themselves as "just as good and just as important as you and I," they remained eternally suspicious that "many of us, at least, look upon them as our inferiors." Since pretensions to superiority were "fatal" to scientific management, college-trained managers should attempt to soften or mask coercive authority and class differences, cultivate an unassuming manner, dress plainly, speak to workers "on their own level," and "carefully avoid the slightest semblance of snobbery." Midvale's President Harrah practiced this principle deftly: "at home I am an Episcopalian, at the works I am an Irish Catholic or colored Baptist."[52]

"Scientifically" codifying ideas popular among employers at the turn of the century, Taylor distinguished between men who worked with their brains and those with limited mental capacities who worked with their hands. "In most cases," he explained to his audience, "one type of man is needed to plan ahead and an entirely different type to execute the work." Because of the intricate nature of the scientifically controlled work process, the person "best suited to actually doing the work" was incapable of "fully understanding" it. Conversely, those capable of understanding science should perform brainwork rather than physical labor. Unlike workers, these "intelligent and educated men" acquired the "habit of generalizing and everywhere looking for laws" and therefore assumed the responsibility of "mak[ing] a science out of work."[53] Even if a worker obtained the necessary education, the demands of work would leave neither time nor opportunity for scientific inquiry. This hierarchy of types equated social class with intellectual distinctions, making it obvious to Taylor's audience of managers-to-be why the brainwork of production should be reserved to them.

Within the laboring class, Taylor assigned a degree of desirability proportional to a worker's physical capacity and willingness to fulfill employers' demands. He specified a range of inversely related mental and physical competence, from "first-class" men like machinists down to "very ordinary" shovelers and pig iron handlers. His analogies between human labor and that of horses and oxen recalled images of an unmechanized age that utilized human labor for heavy moving, the difference between "first-class and the poor ones" being "quite as great as between fine dray horses and donkeys." He often pointed out "big powerful men suited to heavy work just as dray horses are suited to the coal wagon." These distinctions, to Taylor, automatically discredited the "absurdity" of the trade union position that all workers on a particular job should be paid the same wage or rate. Equal payment injured the better worker, he argued, and drove everyone's work performance down to the level of the slowest, poorest worker, which was "quite as absurd as limiting the work of a fine dray horse

to that of a donkey." "Men are not born equal," he insisted, "and any attempt
to make them so is contrary to nature's laws and will fail."[54]

In an age when industrial heavy lifting and moving was done by sheer physical
strength, Taylor emphasized the "enormous differences" between the amount
of work willingly performed by first-class men and "work which is actually
done by the average man." Citing the "definite clear-cut law . . . as to what
constitutes a full day's work for a first-class laborer," Taylor attempted to
scientifically extract this optimum amount by "purposely" making a task so
difficult that it could only be accomplished by a first-class man. Taylor admitted
that this amount of work was often four or more times greater than the worker
had performed under ordinary management and that "not more than one out of
five laborers could keep up."[55] Given these extreme demands, scientific managers
selected the strongest and most able workers who were capable of performing
under great strain. In his famous experiments with pig iron handlers in the
Bethlehem Steel yard in the spring of 1899, Taylor, by alternating work and
rest periods, increased the average daily weight of iron each man carried from
12.5 to 47 tons! Only one man in eight selected had the physical capacity to
sustain a "fair day's work" under these loads, but, Taylor claimed, when first-
class men applied themselves to pig iron loading, "none of them were [sic]
overworked." In a similar application of scientific management to ball bearing
inspection in the Symonds Rolling Machine Company, the work of 120 women
was done by only 35 when those "with quick perception" were selected to
replace "those whose perceptions were slow."[56] Thus, Taylor chose from count-
less types of possible workers only those whose special mental or physical
attributes adapted them to rapid and efficient job performance.

In addition to physical qualities, Taylor added compliance to his definition of
first-class, distinguishing between those "willing and able to adopt the new
methods" and the "losers" who refused to work to capacity. Although the
system claimed to guarantee high wages for those who successfully accomplished
work tasks, it also guaranteed that when one failed, "he should be sure that
sooner or later he will be the loser by it" since failure was the individual worker's
responsibility in the moral universe of Taylor's day. Admitting that by his own
logic he might have been asking a donkey to do draft horse work, Taylor blamed
failure to achieve his standards upon workers' personal shortcomings, particularly
laziness. Any worker could become a first-class man if he put forth the effort.
Those who chose not to do so acted according to their own free will, despite
Taylor's notions of innate differences. Taylor insisted, moreover, that the accelerated work pace was not injurious over a long period of time but, on the
contrary, made the worker "stronger, happier and more contented." Thus, "the
only man who does not come under 'first-class' is the man who can work and
won't work." Such men compared to otherwise first-class dray horses who "are
so absolutely lazy that they won't haul a coal wagon. And in the same way . . .
we have some balky workmen . . . who, physically well able to work, are simply

lazy, and who through no amount of teaching . . . or kindly treatment can be brought into the 'first-class.' ''[57]

The social conditions of labor surplus in a period of widespread unemployment also shaped Taylor's image of workers. Factory operatives who "failed to rise to certain standards are discharged," he wrote, "and a fresh supply of carefully selected men are given work in their places." Born in the atmosphere of a buyer's labor market, this principle instructed managers to, in effect, sift through the pack of job seekers until they found healthy physical specimens, thus using the pressure of the labor market to motivate workers. The length of the hiring line outside the factory gate that symbolized the nation's reserve army of unemployed or day laborers, coupled with the skillful exploitation of workers' ever-present fear of being replaced, allowed Taylorites to demand high levels of extreme exertion. Taylor privately acknowledged the extreme pace and exertion his methods required, but he admitted that the odds favored securing a "fresh supply."[58]

Deploring the "mental incapacity" of many workers, Taylor based plans for increased production on the scientific study and application of their varying intellectual qualities. Scientific managers chose workers whose mental abilities "fit" the requirements of each job, assigning skilled mechanics to the best jobs, and "dull men" to "dull jobs." A pig iron handler, for instance, "must be so stupid and phlegmatic that he more nearly resembles in his mental makeup an ox." A man of this type, neither a "rare specimen of humanity" nor "highly prized," was simply "so stupid that he was unfitted to do most kinds of laboring work . . . so stupid that the word 'percentage' has no meaning to him, and he must consequently be trained by a man more intelligent than himself. . . . A man with only the intelligence of an average laborer can be taught to do the most difficult and delicate work if it is repeated enough times; and his lower mental caliber renders him more fit than the mechanic to stand the monotony of repetition."[59]

Taylor's description of workers' mental attributes reinforced the business community's notions of the intellectual inferiority of the working masses. Workers were either "stupid" or "ignorant," perhaps both, although he alternately blamed their "lack of education" or "insufficient mental capacity" for their inability to comprehend the scientific complexities of the modern work process. The degree to which he actually believed this is arguable, since he often praised the technological expertise of skilled metalworkers. But such distinctions underscored the requirements for maximum work and minimum thought inherent in his and subsequent modern management systems. "A belief in the original stupidity of the worker is a necessity for management," as Harry Braverman observed, "otherwise it would have to admit that it is engaged in a wholesale enterprise of prizing and fostering stupidity."[60]

To Taylor, moral as well as physical and intellectual differences separated inferior from better quality workers. Most people by nature were motivated primarily by money and "ordinary" goals of self-advancement and would work hard for a permanent, liberal wage increase. He cautioned against increasing wages over 30 percent, however, for "if overpaid, many will work irregularly and tend to become more or less shiftless, extravagant and dissipated." By this logic all workers, even the first-class were potentially, perhaps fundamentally, lazy and required external incentives and controls.[61] Morally shocked by those he felt failed to perform their best, Taylor distinguished between hardworking and, therefore, moral and lazy, immoral workers. He often emphasized the virtues of "first-class men" who possessed "character and special ability of high order," who were practically all sober (a steady drinker could not keep up the pace), who saved money and, as a consequence, lived better. But the worker who produced less than first-class men did not and ought not live as well. Otherwise, "that would imply that all those in the world were entitled to live equally well whether they worked or whether they were idle, and that is certainly not the case."[62]

While Taylor conceded workers' rational assessment of their personal and class interests, he remained certain that "the broad principles which affect their best interests" eluded them. "The ignorance of man on the subject of his real interests is prodigious," the preface to the first French edition of *Principles of Scientific Management*, read. "Especially is this true in the case of working [men]," largely because "they do not as yet have the smallest knowledge of the economic sciences." A faulty perception of true interests, clouded by that working-class bane, immediate gratification, inevitably led workers to restrict output and choose unions for redress of their grievances. Such perceptions drove workers to "begrudge a fair and even a large profit to their employers," and even worse, to "feel that all the fruits of their labor should belong to them." Workers seldom appeared conspiratorial or evil in Taylor's thinking. He attributed their false assumptions to "ignoran[ce] of the underlying truths of political economy" rather than to "wrong motives."[63]

In the labor ideology of scientific management, unions furnished the most critical area wherein workers needed "correct education." Since craft unions maintained solidarity in the skilled trades, "one of the most . . . difficult problems with the art of management is how to persuade union men to do a full day's work if the union does not wish them to do it." Condemning unions' "serious delusions" and "cant phrases," Taylor castigated their enforcement of craft traditions and "soldiering" that made workers "lazy, demoralized and uncompetitive." Employer recognition of unions precluded individual treatment of workers so necessary in scientific management. Therefore, Taylor cautioned, "all precautions should be taken which prevent the formation of a union. Workmen should . . . never be addressed collectively, either in a meeting or through printed notices, because if they are talked to in a body, or through notices and circulars the logical answer is for them to appoint a committee or a spokesman to represent them, and this is the starting point for a combination or union."[64]

To Taylor, the control of production effectively eliminated the desirability or even the possibility of bargaining over any of its parts. In this light, unions represented a separate, unpredictable power bloc within the factory that undermined managerial authority and in so doing violated scientific laws governing the work process. Scientific management sought to break union solidarity with appeals to each worker's individualism, personal self-esteem, and desire for self-advancement. The offer of individual incentives had a "moral suasion on the workman which is powerful." The differential piece rate drove a wedge between union members willing to enforce a uniform daily rate for all workers and those aspiring to individual advancement. It was not in the interest of highly paid workers, Taylor insisted, to join a union with "cheap men." When Midvale Steel escaped the steel strikes of the 1880s, he announced that the "best men" had recognized that the "success of labor organization meant the lowering of their wages in order that the inferior men might earn more." Again and again he drew the distinction between the "best men," who correctly identified union subversion of their "real" interests in the name of group solidarity, and the "inferior" union men.[65]

Unions represented a disruptive social force that subverted the true "harmony of interests" of workers and owners and the formation of which "is almost invariably followed by strikes and almost open war between the management and the men." Because unions deliberately restricted output, they were subverting efficient production and "robbing the people." "The boycott, the use of force or intimidation, and the oppression of non-union workmen by labor unions are damnable," Taylor charged in his strongest language; "these acts of tyranny are thoroughly un-American and will not be tolerated by the American people." In this vein, the restriction of output was "deliberate robbery of the poor of the fruits of industrial production." "Labor leaders incurred special ire for "scaring up grievances whether they exist or not." Opportunism motivated some union leaders such as the "blatant demagogue," Samuel Gompers, while others "out of ignorance . . . misdirected their followers, teaching them "wrong doctrines."[66]

Taylor saw the shop floor as a contest over knowledge and authority between capital and labor. His definition of workers reflected his worldview derived in part from shop floor conflict. His system depended on narrowly conceived, production-driven categories, such as the scientifically determined "one best way" of performing a job. Workers in Taylorized factories received training in the "right methods of doing work" and the "right habits of doing the right methods," which presupposed a limited range of human response based on class types and made little allowances for individual psychological differences in learning or for outside social influences. Taylor separated mental from manual work and valued mental planning over the actual execution of a job. Workers should be scientifically selected, trained, and placed in jobs for which they were best suited, mentally and physically. Increased output came through a stepped-up work pace and incentives for gain. For Taylor, workers were obstinant, recalcitrant, willful, and stupid—qualities he sought to defeat. Motivated, self-interested, and rational qualities, he sought to encourage. Taylor's management theory defined workers in terms of the very instruments of their motivation. If they balked, they must be driven; if they were lazy, they must be noticed. Thus, driving and enticement became integral parts of management theory and of the notions of what practices worked with workers. With these definitions, Taylor laid the groundwork for modern management's definitions of workers and their role in rationalized production, definitions that would change with the evolution of corporate power and status in the early twentieth century.

THE RESPONSE TO SCIENTIFIC MANAGEMENT

Scientific management, as David Montgomery has shown, was not instituted smoothly or welcomed by most skilled workers in the metal trades, but, as Taylor often admitted, had to be imposed or enforced. Skilled tradesmen initiated a broad range of responses from "submerged and opaque resistance" to outright fights to assert collective union rules and to force employers to modify or abandon aspects of scientific management. Among their complaints was that scientific management ignored the human element. Workers were most successful in resisting stopwatches or the unequal payment schemes, although such resistance did not fundamentally alter the most important factors in scientific management, such as job standardization and plant reorganization. Worker resistance did, however, increase the resolve of management to impose the open shop and bring unions under control. Machinists often held out for straight hourly or piece wages for a given task, but employers still reserved the authority to assign wages and raises to workers on an individual basis according to graduated, non-union standards that reflected skill levels created by modern management. Scientific management's ultimately successful fight against workers' control and union power, Montgomery wrote, "undermined the very foundations of craftsmen's functional autonomy" by disrupting their "styles of work, their union rules and standard rates, and their mutualistic ethic." After the widespread application of scientific management in industry following World War I, "some degree of worker restriction remained, but on a guerilla basis," while overt, craft union directed, work restriction disappeared. The combination of scientific management and welfare activity had by the 1920s "succeeded in excluding unions from most industries and persuading union leaders to oppose their members' restrictive practices in others," Montgomery found. Personnel management since the 1920s has "represented a cooptive and repressive response to workers' initiatives."[67]

The public also took note of the new management techniques. With the Interstate Commerce Commission's hearings on the Eastern Rate Case of 1910 and 1911, the "efficiency craze hit America . . . like a flash flood," Sam Haber wrote. Louis Brandeis' arguments that the nation's railroads could save a million dollars a day using scientific management caused widespread interest in "waste in industry" and linked Taylorism, economic efficiency, and scientific reform in the public mind. Only the railroads and their workers' unions were resistant to scientific management. The very term *scientific management*, reported Edward L. Hunt, "appealed to the imagination of everyone," as plant managers rushed to implement the "panacea." The public, too, "seized upon the term and gave it a generalized application" as broad as that of the term *efficiency*, witnessed by the enormous growth of popular efficiency literature after the case.[68]

The Watertown Arsenal strike of 1911 intensified public scrutiny of scientific management and demonstrated widespread union resistance to the new form of management. The Watertown strike was initiated by foundry moulders in an un-Taylorized portion of the federal arsenal who resisted changes, particularly the introduction of stopwatches, that had been initiated peacefully in 1909 in the machine shop. There scientific management had more than doubled output while increasing product quality and earnings. The men were back at work in ten days and scientific management continued in the arsenal's shops with few modifications. The strike forced a congressional investigation that criticized scientific management for its mechanistic view of labor and its neglect of the "human factor" and inspired a law banning scientific management in government work. The investigation also pointed out Taylor's authoritarian and arbitrary measures, which helped foster a growing opposition among some managers and engineers.[69]

But plant reorganization under scientific management did not always involve the visible introduction of stopwatches or visits from prominent consultants. In the steel industry as well as in structural steel construction, foundries, cotton mills, printing and lithography, machine shops, and paper products, reported James Mapes Dodge in 1911, Taylor's system was established "without protest" where it lowered costs, raised profits and wages, and improved relations with workers.[70] Many such firms reported little difficulty in instituting the system and, moreover, experienced what Dodge termed a "remarkable freedom" from strikes in the postwar labor strife between 1919 and 1921. Scientific management had heralded "industrial peace," H. H. Farquhar, professor of industrial management at Harvard's Graduate School of Business Administration, glowingly if naively exulted at the war's end.[71] Although the results of its application to industry in the prewar years have not been adequately summarized by historians, reports of owners such as Dodge and managers such as George Babcock of the Franklin Automobile Company of Syracuse, New York, as well as studies of labor policies in plants such as the Ford Motor Company, indicate the favorable experiences of some of the thirty large plants that converted to Taylorism before World War I.[72]

In 1911 the Franklin Automobile Company employed Carl Barth, one of Taylor's associates, to institute scientific management in its Syracuse plant, which employed 2,400 non-unionized people in a 200,000 square foot plant producing 100 cars a month. Five years later Barth reported the "radical upheaval" in plant organization had cut production time by 75 percent, brought production costs down by 60 percent, and increased the average wage of plant workers by 60 percent. Barth attributed these gains to the "unbounded enthusiasm and capacity for work" of Franklin's production manager, George Babcock.

Problems Babcock found at the Franklin plant resembled those Taylor had identified at Midvale twenty years before: shop foremen's abusive power, workers'
autonomy, 110 to 200 percent annual turnover, absenteeism, unsatisfactory work,
irregular scheduling, materials shortages, unsuitable tools, a high ratio of prep-
aration to operation time, and a lack of standardization between tools and machines. In the tense atmosphere of the shops, frustrated workers produced a great
deal of "unsatisfactory work," and foremen and workers were constantly at
odds: "opinion was pitted against opinion and a general feeling of indefiniteness
permeated the factory." Nevertheless, Barth declared, compared to others of its
size, the Franklin plant represented a "highly efficient, modern one in every
respect."[73]

Barth and Babcock set out to "achieve manufacturing supremacy" at the
Franklin plant replacing traditional production and management techniques with
a "mechanical procedure" that fulfilled most of Taylor's prescriptions. The
Planning Department "concentrated all discretionary power within the factory
in a "highly efficient" center and established norms that "could be deviated
from only by authorization of the Production Manager." Babcock's "unique
and truly wonderful control boards," as Barth termed them, streamlined plant
operations to achieve an uninterrupted flow of materials and the efficient utilization of human power. Large, upright, boards that anticipated modern flow
charts presented a visible schematic of every human and material factor within
the plant, each individually rerouted as daily operations required. From control
boards in the Dispatch Room, managers issued shop orders, job cards, tool lists,
and routing instructions. The Tool and Operation Department fashioned specialized tools and readied the machinery before each day's work began. These
techniques standardized production so that "every process will be carried out
exactly as planned, and can be repeated as many times as desirable, in exactly
the same manner with exactly the same results," Babcock insisted.[74]

Babcock's claims bespoke what he took to be a smoothly running, profitable
factory at Syracuse. Having attracted a "considerable number of excellent men"
who acted as "pacesetters" and shifted to other industries those who "did not
wish to work" under Taylorism, the production manager announced "freedom
from all labor troubles." The workers' "very human desire to secure a high rate
of pay" rendered them dependent upon scientifically standardized work norms,
and managers made certain that any deviation seemed detrimental to making
money. Statistical evidence suggested that workers received "benefits" in the
form of fewer absences and tardies, reduced turnover, shorter hours, higher
earnings, and better living conditions. Babcock cited the sick leave records from
1911 to 1915 of Franklin's employee-run Mutual Benefit Association as proof
that Taylorism's "so-called 'speeding up' methods" had not caused illness due
to overwork. The Motor Car Division, prior to the application of scientific
management, reported an annual labor turnover of 77 percent, of whom 17
percent were laid off, 47 percent resigned, and 9 percent were discharged. In
January 1916, after four years of Taylorism, the company reported that, of men

employed since January, 1912, 51 percent still worked at the Franklin plant; of those employed since January, 1913, 80 percent were still at the plant; since January, 1914, 86 percent, and of those hired after January, 1915, 90 percent still remained. The company reported that the unadjusted average earnings of its employees rose from 24 cents per hour in 1908 to 43 cents per hour in 1917, although the cost of living had increased 46.8 percent between 1905 and 1916, making hollow the claim of workers' gains. More important from the point of view of the plant's production manager, Taylor's system purportedly created a "spirit of cooperation and mutual respect [which] pervades the shops." Questions of discipline disappeared, workers appeared "contented and energetic," and "capital and labor seem to have buried the hatchet," Babcock observed.[75]

Similar results were obtained after the installation of scientific management in 1905 at the Link-Belt Company's Philadelphia plant. In 1910 a journalist who interviewed shop employees found that Taylor's methods had speeded up work to a "necessarily high pace" but that workers did not object. "I'm doing the work so as to get the most money," one reported, and "the boss's way is the best way I know." Through the differential piece rate, "the incompetent automatically weed themselves out," the interviewer observed, and the ones remaining achieved a "high standard" of output, "probably much above that found in most Philadelphia shops." Along with increased output, the plant superintendent reported an improvement in the quality of work. In response to a question about the increased fatigue caused by high work speeds, one worker said that he was kept so busy all day that he had no time to think of being tired. The interviewer reported that conversations with plant employees indicated that they were content, spurred by their increased output, and proud of their employment at Link-Belt.[76] While it is difficult to take such claims at face value or determine how representative the Franklin or Link-Belt plants were, the universalization of modern management practice in more modern firms after World War I was due in part to its reputation for providing higher productivity and reducing labor problems. Such "proud claims," Montgomery found, "echoed the rhetorical tone of most public discussion of scientific management after 1910."[77]

At the Ford Motor Company, industrial relations and scientific management combined to produce by 1914 one of the nation's most efficient and productive mass production plants. "Management" signified shop floor changes and an onslaught against working class culture carried out through high wages and welfare policies, including sociological investigation, Americanization, the five dollar day, and profit sharing. These techniques wrested control of production from skilled workers and placed most work in the hands of deskilled "specialists," mostly recent immigrants. In the next five years, managers claimed, absenteeism and turnover declined, rates of efficiency and productivity grew to high levels, and workers resisted unionization.[78]

Despite such achievements, continued labor protests and managerial resistance spurred second generation Taylorites to soften its most visible offenses: its crude psychology, high-handed methods, and the tyranny of the stopwatch. Ironically, Montgomery wrote, craftsmen's protests against Taylorism "reached their crescendo at the very time that the operatives who were replacing them in production processes were serving as catalysts for the modification of the teachings of scientific management." After 1910 the work of Frank and Lillian Gilbreth, H. L. Gantt, and Robert Valentine, and other second generation Taylorites began to reflect progressive social consciousness, which had the effect of humanizing what Ohio State's economics professor, Horace Drury, termed Taylorism's "selfish aspects." By 1915 revisionist Taylorites began to reconsider their views of workers and shifted emphasis away from "autocratic control" to gaining workers' consent. The wise manager, observed Robert Valentine in 1916, should "recognize and organize" the "great mass of unorganized forces—the rights, the desires, the opinions, etc., of the workmen," making them "agencies of co-operation in the conduct of his plant." By 1924 Morris L. Cooke heralded the "gradual diminution of the 'commodity' theory" of labor in favor of a "period of 'good will' and 'cooperation,' " as a majority of scientific management practitioners endorsed welfare work, collective bargaining, and industrial democracy. "Control based on power and ownership" gave way to "authority based on knowledge, qualifications, and skill," wrote Edward E. Hunt, member of the Committee on Elimination of Waste in Industry, in 1921.[79]

As its practitioners joined the growing field of personnel management, scientific managers widened their concerns from the profit-maximizing interests of employers to seek "human welfare," the "development of human personality," and obtaining "consent," what Morris Cooke termed "one of the ideals of democracy." Scientific management "has become turned around so that it now promises to serve the ends of a world and a working class set free," Drury argued. By the decade of the 1920s scientific management merged with various forms of paternalistic corporate welfare work, collective bargaining, and professionalized personnel management to surface as the American Plan, a broad set of management-induced corporate liberal reforms. Despite its humanistic tone, labor-capital cooperation under corporate liberalism should not signify the abandonment of factory hierarchy and control, Morris Cooke cautioned. Such cooperation "can only be nourished through good management in an atmosphere of orderliness and system." Most scientific managers would have agreed with H. S. Person in 1919 that "collective bargaining is now a conservative demand." In George Babcock's words, "control must be cooperative, but nevertheless absolute."[80]

The wartime experiences with labor unions of second generation scientific managers like Morris Cooke, Frank Gilbreth, Gantt, Walter D. Scott, and H. K. Hathaway in army agencies such as the Ordnance Department and the Committee on Personnel led to their recognition of the importance of cooperation. As preparedness efforts added patriotic impetus to the quest for national efficiency, a more humanized, welfare-oriented, revisionist scientific management gradually gained acceptance among labor leaders like Samuel Gompers and William Green.

The controversy over scientific management "had provided a forum for the popularization of the Taylorite gospel," Montgomery wrote. As the public became interested, Harlow Person remarked, so did labor. During World War I the AFL's official opposition gave way to public and government demands for higher output, demands which compelled a thorough application of efficiency methods in the nation's industries.[81]

Workers' support was crucial to corporate liberalism. While in the Eastern Rate Case, labor had sided with the railroads in resisting calls for scientific management, it hailed Herbert Hoover's and the American Engineering Council's 1921 "Waste in Industry" report for publicly placing responsibility for eliminating waste on management. After World War I stimulated the patriotic urgency of industrial efficiency, workers gradually began to criticize employers' inefficient planning that, through shortages and stoppages, created "unemployment within employment." Unions began to demand standardized rate setting as a means of eliminating guesswork and providing "stability of conditions, rates and workers' income," Person reported, just as managers began to realize the importance of unions cooperating voluntarily in their drive for corporate stability. Morris Cooke in 1919 praised "the new balance" between employers and employes "which has resulted from the war" that reduced soldiering and caused "workers . . . to feel some measure of responsibility for production." By 1929, the United Textile Workers' and the Loom Fixers' locals of Salem, Massachusetts, initiated the employment of scientific engineers and undertook time study and standardization at the Naumkeag Steam Cotton Company, according to its industrial engineer Francis Goodell.[82]

THE LABOR IDEAS OF MODERN MANAGEMENT

Second generation scientific management theorists found Taylor's approach crude and inadequate in part because of its definition of workers. As Lyndall Urwick observed, Taylor did not appreciate the difference between the human and the material. Nevertheless, Taylor had recognized the need to integrate new social science findings with management: "there is another type of investigation which should receive special attention, namely, the accurate study of the motives which influence men." Other scientific management engineers sensed the importance of psychology. "There is a psychological effect on a worker," Henry P. Kendall, manager of a Taylorized factory, told Dartmouth's National Conference on Scientific Management in 1911, "in having the work divided into definite tasks, each one having its goal in sight and sustaining effort to that end." Some manufacturers who used scientific management, like Richard Feiss, manager of the Clothcroft Shops of the Joseph & Feiss Company of Cleveland in 1916, reported that management was "only beginning to realize the existence of the personal side" and urged the use of psychological placement tests. In 1917 Morris Cooks referred to Hugo Munsterberg's psychological investigations while discussing methods to obtain workers' consent within a hierarchical system.[83] Before 1920 however, scientific management was slow to incorporate the work of important pioneers in applied psychology, such as Lillian Gilbreth, Walter Dill Scott, and Hugo Munsterberg. As modern management practice gradually incorporated human psychology, however, it greatly increased the domain over which modern management sought definition and control.

The new sciences of applied psychology and sociology provided theories about human social behavior and individual motivation that gradually spurred managers to widen their interpretations of "human engineering." Early management psychologists furnished a bridge between the pioneering days and the later, corporate-based, professionalized psychology of personnel management. In their writings, workers undergo a startling redefinition from automation to an individual with complex social and psychological needs. Second generation managers transformed Taylor's "labor problem" into the professionalized science of managing human behavior.

Taylor's wage schemes and those of most early engineer-managers rested on assumptions about human behavior derived from classical economy; namely that rational individuals serving selfish interests benefitted the social whole. They also assumed that economics could be excised from politics and society. The rationally motivated individual naturally sought financial gain, and scientific management based wage incentive schemes on the promise of individual reward. When industrial psychologists loosened these rigid, mechanical categories, behaviorist norms remained, nevertheless, within the context of engineer-determined goals of gearing human behavior to industrial work patterns. This imperative placed industrial psychologists, like engineers, in the service of corporations, despite their claims to scientific neutrality. Industry defined its ends; industrial psychology adopted and presented them in the guise of scientific truth.[84]

Taylor's view of workers remained little affected by modern social science methods due to the limited crossover between university research and industrial application. Managers' belief in their competence to understand workers often rendered them resistant to outside sources of authority, especially that of academics. As late as 1917 Harlow Person, in a presidential address to the Taylor Society, admitted that manufacturers had to reconsider their perception of social scientists as theoretical, impractical, and biased. However, a national climate favorable to scientific application gradually developed as progressive reformers popularized college-trained experts, relied upon investigative government commissions, and finally elected a former academic to the presidency. In the public eye, the new science of psychology promised to master human behavior as an antidote to the dislocations of industrial and urban society. In this context, Taylor's movement helped introduce the study of human work behavior, which in turn "conditioned the industrial climate for the psychologists," Loren Baritz found, "soften[ing] enough of the severity of the industrial atmosphere so that the more esoteric psychologists could take the first steps."[85]

One of the first Taylorites to develop a humanistic approach to worker motivation was Henry L. Gantt, who had become a Taylor protégé in 1887 when he joined the investigations at Midvale. Gantt's approach was less psychological than "humanist," emphasizing a deep concern for workers as individuals, a special sympathy for the underprivileged, and a compulsion to measure democracy by "the opportunity it offered all men."[86] As early as 1901, in a paper read before the American Society of Mechanical Engineers, Gantt called for a policy of teaching rather than driving workers. Financial incentives represented only one of many influences upon employee behavior, he argued. He devised a "task and bonus" wage scheme different from Taylor's in its appreciation of the human factor. Under Gantt's system, if an employee accomplished his standard task, he received a bonus on top of the regular day rate and another if he exceeded the standard. If he failed to reach the standard, he still received the day rate without penalty. Taylor's differential piece rate, by comparison, did not pay guaranteed wages and punished workers for substandard performance. Gantt's plan allowed workers to earn a living while developing skills to increase efficiency, demonstrating a marked departure from Taylor's. In a 1908 paper "Training Workmen in Habits of Industry and Cooperation," read to the American Society of Mechanical Engineers, he introduced the term *psychology of employee relations*, or *industrial relations*. Here, Gantt emphasized management's responsibility to provide training and to organize the shop so that piece workers lost less time. Gantt's system often doubled production, he claimed, demonstrating that concern for worker morale was the most important factor in management.[87]

Other scientific management theorists began to attack earlier features that had generated worker resentment. Morris Cooke declared that "group reactions vitally condition the effectiveness of time study," and he counseled dealing with workers as organized groups, even as unions. By the end of World War I Cooke supported collective bargaining and industrial democracy. With Sidney Hillman of the Amalgamated Clothing Workers, he developed grievance machinery and production standards in that industry. He worked with Gompers to achieve the AFL's formal rapprochement with scientific management in 1919. Through all these efforts, Cooke emphasized the necessity of achieving workers' consent.[88]

While management theorists in the field approached the human problem from the shop floor, academics began to supply a more "scientific" footing. In the 1890s psychologists like Francis Galton in England and Alfred Binet in France studied individual human variations and suggested that applying "mental science" to social problems would reap enormous benefits. By the second decade of the twentieth century a new generation of university-trained applied psychologists and management experts, among them Hugo Munsterberg and Walter Dill Scott, began to alert manufacturers to the profitability of the psychological study of human behavior. Their findings described human behavior as one of the variables in factory production and presented schemes to understand and control it, as they did material factors. In addition to personnel management, their work applied psychology to vocational guidance, advertising, and fatigue studies. By the 1920s industrial psychology appeared as a fully accepted discipline in the university and in industry.[89]

With the discovery of the individual psyche, psychologists expanded Taylor's "economic man" to encompass "psychological man." The prevailing view of man in Western society since the eighteenth century held that universal laws of conscious rationality governed human conduct. Adam Smith had added the notion that rational self-interested decisions became economically productive ones for the social whole. At the end of the nineteenth century, Freud and Darwin inspired academics to develop new ideas that emphasized nonrational instincts motivating individual and social thought and behavior. Prominent psychologists like Harvard's Munsterberg argued that innate mental aptitudes were more important than education, physical strength, rationality, and even morality. Almost all psychologists saw instincts as the key to uncovering the laws of human behavior. Instincts, William McDougall, a Harvard professor of psychology wrote, governed human conduct by making the individual perceive external stimuli in a certain way and, in turn, react or have an impulse to react in a predictable manner. McDougall identified eleven, then fourteen instincts, William James twenty-eight, and Ordway Tead, a popular college lecturer, ten. Managers thought in terms of instincts too. "The worker is a bundle of instincts," wrote A. Lincoln Filene, general manager of the Wm. Filene and Sons Company of Boston; "he wants to create, to possess, to gain power, to have his work and merit properly recognized, to play, to protect himself and his own." Psychological inquiry merely had to determine which instinct governed what behavior and then market these unique findings to manufacturers, advertisers, and educators.[90]

The psychologist Lillian Gilbreth served as one of the first links between social science and early industrial management. She first introduced behavioral concepts into modern management and insisted on the importance of psychological factors in worker productivity. She and her husband, Frank Gilbreth, emphasized human development to its "fullest potential through effective training, work methods, improved environment and tools, and a healthy psychological outlook." Stressing unity of man and environment, they were the first managers to consider the modern corporation as a social entity and the first to attempt to understand production in human terms. The Gilbreths, among Taylor's closest associates, contributed to scientific management theory by developing rules of time and motion economy, to determine which motions done in what order best accomplished a task. In these studies, they considered mental conditions as well as external factors. Using photography in motion study as early as 1892, they systematized the study of hand motions, refining traditional classifications such as "move hand" into seventeen fundamental motions, such as "select" or "grasp." They developed elaborate mnemonic, color-coded schemes for "micromotion engineers" to simultaneously visualize, group, compare, interpret, and interlock individual work motions with wider factory operations. Their work laid the foundation for modern practices of job simplification, work standards, and incentive wage plans. Largely through their efforts, scientific management literature by the middle of the 1920s reflected the influence of modern psychological methods.[91]

The Gilbreth's models for scientifically classifying work elements into an integrated organization named and coded every conceivable industrial element, from finance, purchasing, planning, advertising, distribution, selling, accounting, teaching, and manufacturing, the latter broken into variables of production, equipment, tools, and surroundings, each, in turn, with more detailed subdivisions. Indeed, modern managers quickly recognized that a standardized technological vocabulary was essential to requiring that workers follow predetermined designs and for removing control over traditional terminology from workers. Thus, classifying and integrating human variables assumed central importance in the Gilbreth's theory of industrial control. They expanded Taylor's primitive categories to include anatomy, brawn, contentment, creed, earning power, experience, fatigue, habits, health, mode of living, nutrition, skill, temperament, and training. Their emphasis on the subtle interrelation between the human psyche and industrial variables elevated the human psyche to machine-level importance. "There are not always clear dividing lines between the *operation of devices* and the *mental . . . operations of the human being*," they observed. Nevertheless, they remained confident that their measurement methods yielded records of "many and probably all mental operations."[92]

While the Gilbreths' micromotion studies addressed the issue of Taylor's arbitrary rate setting, Lillian's psychology addressed his mechanistic notions of worker motivation. Along with early management psychologists, she saw workers in terms of previously unrecognized human variables. In *The Psychology of Industrial Management*, subtitled *The Function of the Mind in Determining, Teaching and Installing Methods of Least Waste*, she argued that while the practical value of psychology remained untapped, Munsterberg and other experimental psychologists had produced "instruments of precision," quantified measurement, and investigation of individual variation, thus giving psychology its scientific legitimacy. Psychological investigation used time and motion study, micromotion study, and the chrono-cyclegraph to measure work, output, tools, and units of individual performance accurately.[93] Psychologists had discovered that "the body reflects every shade of psychic operation; that in all mental action there is some physical expression." This discovery enabled the Gilbreths to offer scientifically determined laws that designated human psychological types based on new methods of identifying and naming the emotional traits most necessary for efficient production and amenable to managerial direction.[94]

In devising measurements for determining the amount of work an individual could perform and the amount of rest required during its performances, Taylor laid the groundwork for determining and defining capacity. His notions of capacity, however, arose from physical factors or simple "willingness" and measured results with little consideration for the individual worker's psyche or recognition of traditional craft unions' notions of capacity. Lillian remained limited by Taylor's production and shop floor view of workers. Like Taylor, she measured workers by the method, time-cost, and results of their work, as well as by their capacity to learn. Similarly, her theory of psychology drew upon Taylor's class-based notions of differences in human intellectual capacity. But she rejected Taylor's driving and speed-up methods in favor of using psychology to eliminate worker anxiety and enhance performance. Gilbreth enlarged Taylor's notion of the "right methods" to encompass the "psychologically right methods" of teaching and working, and she added the "workers' psychic satisfaction" to the measurement of results. She based her methods on new appreciations of what constituted individual psychological makeup and argued that individuals possessed a special set of characteristics that deviated from group norms and distinguished one from another.[95] Gilbreth claimed to identify and utilize this individuality to better accommodate workers to work conditions. Rather than crudely forcing workers to adopt new techniques in predetermined mechanical work situations, she studied the relation between the technology, the physical aspects of the shop, and individual workers' emotions, perceptions, and physical capabilities.

Taylor saw the individual worker primarily as a rational economic unit whose emotional state was secondary to the task at hand. His "mental revolution" depended upon workers' discovering their own stake in increased productivity. Elevating psychology to the primary factor in scientific management, Gilbreth expanded Taylor's definition of workers beyond observable economic factors to include "all the idiosyncrasies" that distinguish human behavior and individual personality. Gilbreth emphasized the complexity of psychological cause and response and introduced the notion of conscious versus "unconscious" factors in human behavior. Under the scrutiny of Lillian and her generation, Taylor's rational economic man gave way to one motivated by habits, emotion, impulse, instinct, night work, fatigue, fear, worry, and even temperature. The mental revolution now depended upon workers' consent and cooperation based on managerial attention to their newly discovered and named psychological needs.[96]

Like Taylor, Gilbreth thought that observable individual characteristics like intelligence or physical strength naturally qualified workers for certain jobs, but she expanded the range of "natural talents" to include the senses, attention span, memory capacity, imagination, discrimination, association, judgment, will, and "native reactions," such as ambition, pride, pugnacity, love of racing (speed), love of play, and love of personal recognition. Workers had varying degrees of these faculties, which managers could channel and shape within a scientifically devised learning environment. A naturally qualified person learned practical skills for efficient work that "raise[d] him from the lower plane to the highest mental and manual plane which he is able to fill." This spurred the individual to attain the fullest development within the limitations of his natural ability. Gilbreth deemed "natural" those qualities that most enhanced efficiency and productivity, and her psychological methods selected and ranked workers accordingly. The best "special natural talents" for production planners, for example, included ingeniousness, observation, and constructive imagination. "It is not every man who is fitted by nature to observe closely, hence to plan," she maintained, giving scientific weight to prevailing ideas among managers of the close correspondence between natural intelligence and job capacity. Psychological researchers allowed managers to assign workers to jobs that "fit" their intelligence. "The fact of a known standard intelligence range for each occupation," observed Ordway Tead in 1924, lecturer in personnel administration at Columbia University, citing psychological research and field work by Henry C. Link of the Link-Belt Company, Millicent Pond at the Scovill Manufacturing Company, and Johnson O'Connor at General Electric, "may in light of further study prove to be one valuable index for successful and permanent placement."[97]

Following William James, Edward Thorndike, and other psychologists of her day, Gilbreth believed that physical habit altered brain cells. This finding led them to argue that workers could be taught to respond in a "largely predictable" manner to a repeated stimulus. Under scientific control, habitual, unthinking physical motion "trains hand and muscle," and, in turn, "the education of hand and muscle train [*sic*] the mind," Gilbreth wrote. Thus, habit created action that determined perception. "Good" or desirable physical habits "educated" corresponding mental faculties. As workers performed these "involuntary impulses . . . without intervening thought," work speed inevitably increased. Workers' own perceptions and spontaneous, self-generated actions no longer held value in Gilbreth's scheme. Psychologists selected those qualities that enhanced work, made them the standard of excellence, and developed management techniques to instill them in workers as automatic behavior. Within the context of science-based industry, then, personnel managers and planners, not workers, specified the motions, judgment, standards, and knowledge and instructed workers that these were the best habits to form and the best way to go about work.[98]

Until modern forms of work organization appeared in the early twentieth century, the term *habit* often signified an individual controlled by his behavior who lacked initiative and originality. "For a long time, intelligence and reason were taken as the good in human behavior," wrote C. S. Yoakum in 1927, professor of personnel management at the University of Michigan's School of Business Administration, "and emotions and habits, as well as impulses, were conceived to be things which must always be kept under control." Modern managers, however, created a favorable meaning for *habit*, desiring that "the great majority of workers should form habits of industry . . . which would lead them to be sober and industrious at all times and in all places."[99] Lillian Gilbreth insisted that correct habits conditioned a worker to the imperative of plant control, teaching him to "not think but only perform," lest he disrupt processes of which he presumably had no knowledge. Since rational brainwork should not take place outside the planning office, "it is out of the question to permit the deviations resulting from individual initiative." Ideally, she prescribed, the daily instruction card replaced the worker's memory in the conduct of plant operations. Gilbreth perpetuated Taylor's charges that workers' deficient knowledge invited outside control and that mental and manual work required different abilities. She likewise justified appropriating skilled workers' brainwork by repeating his claim that they were ignorant of the best methods and failed to understand the whole of factory operations. Her admittedly exaggerated example of a West Indian who carried a loaded wheelbarrow on his head, she insisted, illustrated the prevailing inefficient methods of even skilled craftsmen.[100]

In Gilbreth's class-based theory of psychological management, workers ran on the engines of desire for self-advancement within modern industrial society. Like Taylor, she saw workers as eager to compete, willing to defer gratification by sacrificing comfort for gain, and subject to manipulation through rewards and punishments. Managers could employ such direct incentives as promotions, wages, bonuses, and shorter hours as psychological levers to stimulate native reactions, especially ambition, competition, and the desire for personal recognition. Once workers came to believe that employers treated them "squarely" with scientific, individualized job selection, and the promise of promotion, they were free to apply their natural love of speed, play, and pursuit of ambition at work. In order to hold workers' attention and stimulate competitive urges, rewards must be positive, predetermined, assured, and prompt, she advised. They should also fulfill the worker's desire for personal recognition and make the most of his or her individuality.

"The psychology of the prompt reward" dictated that the more prompt the reward, the greater it served as a stimulus to perform. Extra high output must be rewarded quickly, Gilbreth maintained, so that the worker related output to reward "while the fatigue and effort of doing the work is still in his mind." Poor performance garnered immediate punishment, which "served just as surely an incentive to action as is reward" and which included fines, discharge, or assignment to lower paying or less desirable work. Statistical comparisons of workers' efficiency records made public within the factory stimulated self-improvement and competition. In this manner, new standards of personal value and social recognition sprang from scientifically managed work performance.[101]

The task of administering rewards and punishments in management psychology fell to the shop disciplinarian. With university training, the disciplinarian understood and applied the laws of psychology, judging actions within the context of a worker's other acts, learning motives and causes, and investigating the employee's physical condition and social background. The disciplinarian learned as much as possible about each employee's natural and acquired characteristics and kept a cumulative record of each person's "virtues and defects." He must appear more a friend to the worker than to the employer when administering discipline and must consider the employee's "sensitiveness" as well as the necessity for "sharp" or "shaming" discipline. Gilbreth, like Taylor, distinguished the "strong" but presumably "lazy" worker from the one who was merely working the wrong job but she provided attitude measurements for making the distinction.[102]

The standardization of plant activity, part of a national movement toward the simplification of business practices, was central to Gilbreth's management psychology. Herbert Hoover had found "wide voluntary cooperation" in industry for the efforts of the National Bureau of Standards to require commercial specifications that eliminated "unessential differences," imposed uniformity and "impersonal standards of practice," and permitted increased efficiency in large-scale, repetitive operations. Scientific measurement, qualification of job performance variables, and psychological tests made possible the standardization of even the human aspects of plant work, the psychological managers believed. Because traditional management had allowed "too much variation" in individual feeling, behavior, and personal relationships, the Gilbreths sought to standardize workers' social and psychological relations and "control attitudes by eliminating the shifting viewpoint" so that workers' attitude toward their work and their relationships with others at work "remains fixed." "Standards," Harlow S. Person wrote, "provide the Basis of Understanding necessary to Co-operative effort." Through standardization, measurement, and validation of improved output, workers "come to feel that these methods are right and that because of this, his [*sic*] work must be of value."[103]

Thus, standardization criteria provided norms of self-valuation: personal satisfaction, efficient work, higher pay within the scientifically managed factory. Most importantly to the emergent class of psychological managers, the individual received the "inner reward" of self-knowledge gained through striving for maximum output. These valuations, however, defined the individual in terms of a self-referenced, personal universe and thus denied or ignored workers' roles in the power relations of social production and society as a whole. The broad focus on therapeutic self-realization that appeared near the turn of the century, Jackson Lears has argued, had the effect of encouraging political passivity. In this sense, a workplace that encouraged the "fulfillment" of atomized individuals served existing power relations was more hegemonic than one that generated class solidarity.[104]

Naming and standardization mutually reinforced one another in psychological management. Psychologists developed an "accurate and definite terminology" for the elements of industrial activity designed to become part of a worker's reality. "The effect of [standardized terminology] upon the mind is excellent," Gilbreth wrote, "because the use of a word very soon becomes a habit—its association becomes fixed." And the use of a fixed word "leads to definiteness." "Only as we learn to classify," Morris Cooke advised, "and as a result of such classification, to eliminate, to simplify, to standardize, and to codify, does any genuine science of management emerge." Gilbreth rejected traditional management's value-laden definitions, such as "driver," which suggested a "mental and physical contest" between manager and worker. Management psychologists substituted standardized terms such as *first-class man* or *instruction card* for traditional definitions in order to eliminate "any feeling that personal prejudice affects the discipline" and "to conserve the old spirit of cooperation between the master and his apprentices.'' In the course of applying sanctions, Gilbreth renamed ''unfortunate'' terms. *Punishment* translated into *adjustment*, and *disciplinarian* into *peacemaker*.''[105]

In 1920 H. K. Hathaway lamented the slow development of universal classification schemes among scientific managers. Standardized terminology exploded during that decade. Modern managers, as with professionals in almost every field, developed elaborate classification and symbolization schemes that abstracted management nomenclature and removed it from worker control. Morris Cooke, for example, impressed with place value symbolization in the Dewey Decimal System, created a mnemonic job and materials classification system in which it was not necessary for workers to know the meaning of a symbol in order to use it. ''Hundreds of workmen use symbols every day without the slightest idea as to their significance,'' Cooke wrote and, to illustrate his point quoted James Mapes Dodge, ''One does not have to know French to use plaster of Paris.''[106]

Gilbreth's psychology of naming redefined not just individual terms, but whole concepts. Scientific management did not cause a ''speed-up,'' she maintained. It did not drive the worker or create antagonism but provided a ''push-up,'' raising everyone ''as high as he is capable of being raised'' through efficient work, promotions, and self-betterment. Thus, it promoted workers' well-being and individual expression. ''Eliminating wasted motion, trial and error'' enhanced individualism and allowed the exercise of free will, she maintained, offering a startlingly corporate definition of the self-seeking individual. Industrial psychology helped a worker ''develop the possibilities of his best self by using and specially training those talents which are most marked in him.'' Gilbreth equated the ''best self'' with the development of a narrow range of talents designed to make workers more compliant and efficient, thus subsuming individual expression and personal fulfillment within individual task performance, itself part of an integrated, corporate-industrial whole. One exercised one's individuality by performing up to capacity in the factory. Gilbreth's psychology defined ''loyalty'' as an obligation to serve prosperity and the common welfare. She criticized the selfishness of a ''brotherhood'' of unions that only recognized fellow workers and ignored the brotherhood of society at large.[107]

Through renaming and symbolization, Gilbreth added the legitimacy of psychology to scientific management's assault on ''traditional'' craft-based work knowledge. Since it relied upon ideas handed down orally from generation to generation and operated by informal, variable, unquantifiable methods that resulted in ''vagueness and lack of definiteness in knowledge, in process, in results,'' traditional knowledge resulted in the ''inaccurate perpetation of unthinking custom.'' In contrast, scientific management of work replaced traditional experience with professional expertise, which ''must operate according to known, formulated, and applied laws.'' Even armed with ''science,'' the manager's attack on traditional knowledge remained a contested area in factory operations. In 1924 Morris Cooke at once hailed the incorporation of ''routine, time-study, and the machine-tool slide rule'' and condemned the persistence among workers of ''narrowness of view, adherence to the outworn, and absence of any recognizable technique.''[108]

Attention to workers' psychic needs led Gilbreth to claim that management instituted ''welfare work'' in Taylorized factories through its recognition of the deleterious effects of alcohol, smoking, and ''family worries'' as well as its attention to ''food values.'' Her psychology was limited by its paucity of insight into a worker's inner psychological state or social, home, or community life and did not integrate social analysis into management theory. Her definition of *welfare* was limited to efficiency-oriented personal and social development provided at work by scientific management training. For example, she claimed as welfare work the improvement of workers' physical well-being through the elimination of fatigue, their forming good habits through increased regularity, and their mental development through learning better judgment, increased attention, and heightened interest. Gantt claimed workers in Taylorized factories had better color and general appearance, having been encouraged to dress better and become ''of a higher type.'' And they improved morally by developing responsibility, self-control, ''squareness,'' contentment, brotherhood, and the ''will to do.'' Best of all, they were ''inspired with a great desire for activity, after all, the best and finest thing that any system of work can give,'' Gilbreth observed. ''Is there any conceivable satisfaction to life except just that,'' seconded Henry S. Dennison in 1927, president of Dennison Manufacturing in Framingham, Massachusetts, ''having the very best you have in your being drawn out in congenial work?'' Furthermore, the Gilbreths claimed, their new methods allowed the full play of workers' individual self-expression, free will, economic independence, and service to society. Workers developed and preserved these republican values only within a scientifically structured and managed industrial system, as the Gilbreths and modern managers after them insisted.[109]

The behavioral school of modern management emerged from academic advocates of a psychological approach. Harvard's Hugo Munsterberg and Northwestern's Walter Dill Scott placed the individual at the center of any effort to extract work or manage corporations more efficiently. Integrating methods from psychology, sociology, and anthropology, behaviorists analyzed individual interests and motivations and group interactions. Munsterberg was perhaps the best-known psychologist in the United States during a time of great public interest in the new discipline. He almost single-handedly created and formalized the science of industrial psychology, a field that quickly laid claim to individual psychological testing, personnel management, and vocational guidance. He earned a doctorate in psychology at the University of Leipzig in 1885, where he studied in the first laboratory for research on human behavior. At the invitation of President Charles W. Eliot and William James, he came to Harvard in 1892 as professor of experimental psychology and set up America's most important research laboratory. In 1913 he published a nonfiction bestseller, *Psychology and Industrial Efficiency*, which argued for the science of ''psychotechnics,'' the application of psychology to industrial management. He wrote not only for academic audiences, but popularized psychology in often sensationalist articles in papers and magazines, such as *McClure's, Ladies Home Journal*, and *Cosmopolitan*, which helped bring psychology to the attention of managers and manufacturers. His visits to General Electric, Waltham Watch, and International Harvester to study worker motivation firsthand also helped foster popular understanding of applied psychology.[110]

In his popular work, he argued the need for a scientific study of the human psychological factors in management. Using Alfred Binet's testing techniques for measuring individual differences, he placed the psychological experiment "at the service of commerce and industry," determining the mental qualities that best corresponded to a given kind of job. Managers then had only to learn where to apply the "psychological levers" to find the right niche for each individual within the factory system. Munsterberg paid tribute to Taylor as the founder of scientific management and applauded its pioneering "signal successes" in organizing work to eliminate wasted energy and fitting individuals to jobs. He greatly expanded Lillian Gilbreth's efforts to integrate a scientific, behaviorist dimension into scientific management as he developed methods for vocational guidance in industry. Munsterberg, like Gilbreth, deplored Taylor's heavy handed tactics and his assumption that workers had to adjust to the material demands of technology. He echoed Gilbreth's notion that managers must accommodate technology and work organization to psychological variations. Excessive driving no longer had a place in scientific management. Instead, scientific managers must determine workers' psychological traits and correctly place workers so that they would obtain job satisfaction and well-being.[111]

Munsterberg developed many of the earliest testing techniques adopted by industry for vocational positions such as telephone operator, ship's captain, and salesman. These assessed the functions of imagination, memory, attention, intelligence, exactitude, rapidity, volition, space-time sense, suggestibility, and judgment. He argued that investigators must consider the subject's individual psychological rhythm with its "psychological motives and counter-motives," his physical condition, including nourishment, blood circulation, "gland activities," and external factors such as color, noise, clothing, chair height, the hour of the day, the weather, and the seasons. The results of these tests demonstrated individual tolerances to work conditions like fatigue and monotony and helped adapt individuals to jobs that utilized their special aptitudes. Jobs that might prove boring to one person might be stimulating to another. He interviewed a light bulb packer who had wrapped in tissue and boxed 13,000 individual bulbs daily for twelve years at a rate of approximately one every two seconds. The woman "assured" Munsterberg that she found her job "really interesting" because of "continuous variation" and the challenge of filling the requisite number of boxes. "This was the trend I usually found," claimed Munsterberg, when studying monotonous work, never questioning whether the woman was really satisfied wrapping and boxing light bulbs. Boring work was not inherently boring but depended upon the "special disposition of the individual," who could be identified through testing for a high tolerance to monotony and fatigue and placed in "satisfying" work. With this line of reasoning, which admirably served the idea that society progressed with everyone assigned to their proper station, Munsterberg "elevated to the level of a science a self-serving and unexamined myth," his biographer Matthew Hale wrote, that menial workers were satisfied and even happy with boring laborious work.[112] With this reasoning, Munsterberg replaced Taylor's crude joining of dull men to dull jobs with the scentific use of vocational selection to fit the psychological aspects of the work atmosphere to workers' minds. Both tactics achieved the same result.

Through these efforts, Munsterberg and industrial psychologists gave the scientific legitimacy of psychology to notions held by Taylor and turn-of-the-century managers concerning the differential value of mental and manual work. With these arguments, management specialists justified their demeaning of manual work and insisted upon the "profound difference in the psychology of mental and manual workers," in the words of N. I. Stone, general manager in 1919 of the Hickey-Freeman Company of Rochester, a textile manufacturing employing 1,200 workers. "How wrong we are in assuming that the workers suffer from the monotony of their simple repetitive operations," he continued. Manual work once mastered by presumably less intelligent beings, "can be done with almost no mental concentration," allowing the worker to be "unconscious of monotony" and indeed preferring "the rhythm of a repetitive operation" to mental effort. The seldom acknowledged obverse of this, of course, was that engineers, managers, professionals, and owners who were presumably more intelligent beings, could not tolerate monotonous work. "Intellectual work" required "mental concentration," Stone continued, while repetitive work became, to the intellectual at least, "monotonous and therefore irksome." As J. E. Otterson, president of the Winchester Repeating Arms Company explained, engineers were logical, analytical, studious, and exhibited an "investigating turn of mind." Most importantly, they "[do] not submit readily to the routine performance of a given quantity of work." With these distinctions, modern psychology offered the answer to fitting workers intellectually and temperamentally as well as physically to different kinds of work. Most modern managers believed with C. S. Yoakum, who by 1912 was Northwestern's dean of the College of Liberal Arts, that "the fundamental principles of labor standards rest[ed] . . . on the right human adjustment at each job."[113]

Despite claims of studying the total individual and superficial references to "social statistics concerning behavior of the masses," Munsterberg's investigations did little to assess workers in terms of class, ethnicity, gender, community, religion, region, or politics. When he did turn to such categories, his notions were rooted in the popular assumptions of early twentieth-century social typing. Most managers, for example, would agree with William R. Leiserson, chairman of the Labor Adjustment Board of the Rochester Clothier's Exchange, that "different nationalities have different mental processes." As manufacturers

discovered psychology, they began to study each group to discover what Leiserson, quoting psychologists, termed their "apperceptive mass," that "experience in the back of their heads that interprets every word."[114] Ethnic groups did
have observable common characteristics, Munsterberg agreed, but popular stereotypes like those of Leiserson, which he termed "group psychology," seemed
arbitrary and contradictory. In any case, ethnic designations referred to averages
within which individuals varied greatly. Inconsistencies in ethnic typing on the
part of managers, however, could be remedied by professional laboratory analysis. "Only subtle psychological individual analysis can overcome the superficial
prejudices of group psychology," he wrote. Gender, however, was a category
that lent itself to the use of crude stereotypes. Munsterberg furnished one of the
earliest statements from applied psychology that cited differences in women's
and men's mental ability. "Certain mental traits [are] characteristic of women
in general in contrast to men in general," and these relate to "certain fundamental
tendencies of their psychophysical organism." Thus certain jobs "are excellently
adapted to the minds of women," and others "stand in striking antagonism to
them." In cases of employment of large numbers of women, then, "decisions
on the basis of group psychology may be adequate."[115]

In Munsterberg's view of society, an individual's mental and physical ability
determined his or her proper social station. "The central issue for the entire
problem [of social organization]," he declared, "lies in the fact that men are
unequal and that social organization in our complicated times demands inequality
of social functions," and presumably of social rewards, his biographer added.
Psychologists' social responsibility lay in devising tests to determine work capacity in order that individuals could dutifully assume their rightful place in a
harmonious, progressive, but nonetheless hierarchical society. Psychotechnics,
by defining workers and assigning them a place, served the "purposes of economic life, the purposes of commerce and industry, of business and the market
in the widest sense of the word."[116]

Denying the power relations in economic life, Munsterberg claimed that psychologists stood above the social fray of industrial society, that their professional
duty was only to "accept economic tasks from the community" and render
impartial service. This service enabled them to claim that they "advanc[ed] the
purposes of modern society" and the "tasks of civilization." Psychologists did
not select social ends but simply determined the means for fulfilling them. Within
"community," Munsterberg observed, social tension arose between the "reck-
less, capitalistic, profit seeking egotism" that desired efficient work and the
"feeble sentimentality" of social reformers who valued the fullest development
of the individual. Above these social tensions lay the "vigorous healthy nation,"
which was "on the whole in agreement" with the need for efficient labor. It
was this national will that psychotechnics served. While Munsterberg saw no
contradiction between claiming not to serve commercial interests and defining
those very interests as the fulfillment of the nation's economic destiny, he clearly
aimed at defeating social revolution and the masses. Workers happily committed

to satisfying work in the knowledge that they were furthering their own personal development and contributing to the "ideal purpose of civilized mankind, the development of economic civilization" were not candidates for socialism. The "social question will be solved," he insisted, when workers become "inspired by the belief in the ideal value of the work . . . as a necessary contribution to the progress of mankind."[117]

New theories of habit and ordinary consciousness transformed ideas about control of workers under modern management. Like that of Lillian Gilbreth, Munsterberg's work challenged notions of individual psychological autonomy and assaulted republican-era ideas of human equality, individual will, natural rights, and personal self-direction. Habits, for example, figured critically in William James' theory of attention and will. Likewise, in 1905 Edward Thorndike's "law of effect" stipulated that satisfying acts became associated with their specific circumstances and recurred correspondingly as those circumstances recurred. "Concrete habits do all the perceiving, recognizing, imagining, recalling, judging, conceiving, and reasoning that is done," argued John Dewey in 1922. And Munsterberg wrote in 1914, "all training and habit formation in the sphere of our actions shape and stamp the perceptions and memories and thoughts in our mind."[118] Purely technological processes in production also "influence and control" human psychological impulses. Manufacturers could thus enlist technology for work discipline. Workers that Munsterberg observed operating steam hammers, for example, worked slowly when the hammer stood quiet but performed with "astonishing quickness" when the hammer's operation "reinforced the[ir] energy" to a level unattainable through "mere voluntary effort." Likewise, Munsterberg advised managers to rearrange shop floor machinery "so that conversations become more difficult or impossible," rather than impose a "tyrannical demand for silence" that workers would resist. In each case, the goal was to replace worker initiative with the imperatives of habit and the discipline of technology, both in the service of efficiency.[119]

In a further assault on free will, Munsterberg echoed earlier management thought by insisting that the average worker was unable to judge his own capacity or know what vocation suited him. "The ordinary individual knows very little of his own mental functions: on the whole, he knows them as little as he knows the muscles which he uses when he talks or walks." Within a wide range of ability, the upper 20 percent were "exceptionally talented" workers who knew what vocation best suited them, while the lower 80 percent needed scientific testing to discover their own abilities. Seeing workers as unaware and thus manipulable led psychologists to devise management schemes that required authoritative direction for most workers. Regardless of ability, however, all workers required a scientifically efficient management to integrate their qualities into industrial processes.[120]

Reliance on psychological testing and the role of psychological experts expanded modern management's assault on the "common sense" knowledge of traditional managers and workers gained from observation, memory, and ex-

perience. In laboratory experiments, psychologists had demonstrated the falli-
bility of human observation, the unreliability of witnesses, and the inaccuracy
of self-knowledge. Modern psychological management's quantifiable, objecti-
fiable, scientific "intelligence," administered by disinterested experts, strove to
replace everyday, rule-of-thumb, traditional knowledge, which it termed "hit
and miss" or "cut and try" and relegated to the dustbin of "unscientific, hap-
hazard methods" of the past.

Munsterberg did not join behaviorists such as John Watson, who argued that
human subjects could be trained for a wide range of aptitudes. Instead, he
remained tied to mechanistic notions of instinct-driven behavior. Although training had its place in allowing workers to fully use their given capacity, ordinary
individuals could not improve on innate characteristics. Even the scientific management of human ability "cannot deceive us as to the fundamental fact that the
decisive tendencies are inherited and cannot be fundamentally changed." Munsterberg devised a survey of American laborers to determine their "individual
dispositions, associations, and reactions" in order to overcome their "inner
resistances" and reduce the role of individual assertion in the factory. Used in
this manner, an "individualized psychology," Matthew Hale wrote, "was simply
a more efficient means of holding individuals to their functions."[121]

Taken together, the notion that purposeful behavior resulted from learned
reaction, the idea that workers cannot accurately perceive their own consciousness or physical surroundings, and the emphasis on innate qualities, allowed
psychologists to posit the demise of free will. With the theoretical elimination
of individual free will and the power of persons to control events, industrial
psychology added its scientific weight to the technological blow struck against
traditional work knowledge and individual discretion by modern factory organization. Modern psychology no longer saw workers motivated by conscious
reason, as Taylor had conceded, but by irrational and often unconscious emotional factors. Psychotechnics sought to suppress the irrational and channel the
more efficient behavior into socially productive work. "Industrial psychology,"
wrote C. S. Yoakum, "discover[s] the usable and non-usable qualities in each
of us. . . . " Psychologists thought workers, as individuals, were habituable and
trainable. Individuals were now products, not controllers, of their surroundings
and best served themselves and society if they worked at subdivided tasks, the
order and purpose of which they had no role in determining. Although psychologists continued to assert that their programs enhanced individuality, it was
on the most determinist and reduced level. Scientifically selected workers in a
scientifically managed environment enjoyed little space for deviation. Channel
urges toward self-help and ambition, the message read throughout the vocational
movement, into reconciling the individual to his use-value in the industrial social
order. Moral action now involved submitting irrational and inefficient impulses
to planning and reason. Morality, in the logic of psychological management,
had ceased to be the conscious exercise of individual free will and become an
instrument of progress, the internalized demands of corporate society.[122]

IMPLICATIONS OF THE MANAGERIAL REVOLUTION

It was not surprising that the worldview of a German social idealist gained acceptance in the United States as laissez-faire declined and liberal corporate capitalism with its own call for an organic industrial society rose. The rhetoric of liberal developmentalism equated the growth of manufacturing industry and its primary goals, making profit and accumulating capital, with national progressive development. "It is only through heightened production that the dream of the race will be realized," wrote Morris Cooke in 1913. "If you can picture a society in which every unit is using his or her highest faculties to the best advantage, you will see that it approximates the millennium." Likewise, industrial managers like B. Preston Clark, vice-president of the Plymouth Cordage Works of Boston, visualized the new unity in organic, often physiological terms, "not a machine, but an organism, something alive and growing."[123]

Modern managers, such as Hathaway, Person, Cooke, and Robert Valentine, helped provide corporate capital with the rhetoric to widen its own quest for efficiency into a broad-based, national coalition of interests that included small businessmen, the new professional class, and workers. Often adopting these groups' language of criticism and protest, corporate capitalism became, in Martin Sklar's words, a "cross-class ideology" whose legitimacy rested on the improved productivity that would result from the mutual self-help of these groups. The liberal corporate state presented itself as the vehicle for fusing diverse social elements into an organic, progressive whole and provided the organizing framework around which elite authority and knowledge could direct the nation's energies. "We are all workers from the president of the company to the office-boy," Cooke wrote, as *work* and *worker* took on new meanings within the context of community obligation and reward.[124]

The new generation of modern managers began to argue that, in the context of corporate liberalism, labor and capital assumed the obligations and responsibilities of a mutual bargain. Before they could demand a fair day's labor, employers had to be able to provide workers with continuous employment, efficient management, and the hope for betterment. "We realize that our safeguard is the stake of the average man in the present economic order," observed Edward Jones, former professor of economics at the University of Michigan and member of the Federal Board of Vocational Education in 1919. In return, workers were obliged to provide low turnover, loyalty, industrial peace, and willing, efficient labor. Efficiency, which demanded hard work, thrift and will power, offered professionals and the middle class in corporate society the new morality and the means to progress. In short, workers must alter their behavior to fit the new age and its new goals. In fulfilling their respective roles, labor and capital gave one another stability within the integrated whole. "We must constructively contribute to the symphony, by supplying ideals, by devising processes, improving methods, inventing equipment, and training hand, heart and mind, if we would earn that portion of the income called, not wages, but profit," observed

George L. Bell, of the Men's and Boy's Clothing Industry of New York City. The plant must be organized, Bell argued, "to allow each [worker] to see the complete picture of the aims of the plant and his part in the structure as a whole." And Bell quoted Walter Dill Scott, "the executive who develops novices into experts and the company which transforms mere 'handy men' into mechanics are public benefactors because of the service rendered to the country."[125]

Traditional definitions of labor were transformed in the new corporatism. In 1919 Joseph E. Cohen, a Philadelphia labor leader and chairman of the Joint Legislative Committee for Labor Legislation in Pennsylvania wrote that employers believed that "labor, like other commodities, should be bought in the cheapest market and should be expected to render the utmost service for whatever wage was paid." In this world "the individual workman was supposed to offer his power to create wealth entirely apart from his procedure as a human being." After capital and labor both accepted their corporate responsibilities, however, management touted labor as an equal partner in forging an industrial future. "Class lines are being obliterated everywhere," exclaimed Clark, as capital declared the class war over. "Class thinking is of the past. It is for each one of us to choose whether we shall look backward, like those monkeys, to those jungles from whence so long ago we came, or . . . turn our faces forward whither we are bound." The struggle is now not between classes, but between those who "stand for a broad and humane sympathy for constructive democracy" and those "darker hosts who, through ignorance or through malice, would set class against class," Clark wrote.[126]

The industrial cosmology of M. P. Follett, a Boston management practitioner, further illustrates the place of labor in corporate liberal rhetoric. In Follett's view, society was composed of a multitude of diverse elements that included business and labor. He borrowed Alfred North Whiteheads' "interplay of diverse values" to characterize these elements. Effective social management required the "functional relating of these diverse elements for a genuinely coordinated 'business unity,' " Follett wrote in 1927. Managers must conceive business as an organic whole and study the "whole activity" of the "integrated organism" rather than analyzing its parts. Organizing the whole would provide "control through effective unity" and forestall dissention in the organism. "You cannot get control without unity, but once unity is achieved, control is established," Follett explained. And the degree of that control depended on "successfully uniting" the workers' consciousness and ideas, making them a "self-creating, organic unity" that continually reproduced itself within the factory. Thus the *process* of managing and organizing the organism impresses the overwhelming reality of its authority upon all its component parts. "The interaction is the control," Follett explained.[127]

The advertising industry furnished one of the earliest markets for applying the instinct theory of psychology. Walter Dill Scott, a psychologist at Northwestern University from 1901 to 1920 and its president until 1939, furnished an important link between academia and industry through his understanding of consumer behavior. In *The Psychology of Advertising in Theory and Practice* (1908), he identified specific human instincts that advertisers might profitably provoke: hunting, hoarding, acquiring, building, and clothing. In 1915 Scott, like Munsterberg, had begun psychological testing for job placement at American Tobacco, National Lead, Western Electric, Loose-Wiles Biscuit, and the George Batten advertising agency. When psychology was extended to advertising, the same argument emerged: the act of purchasing goods enabled consumers to exercise free will and individual choice.[128]

Through Gilbreth, Gantt, Scott, and Munsterberg's work, industrial psychology became known among managers, industrialists, and the public. It was not adopted widely, however, until the 1920s since before the war most managers still questioned the promise of applied psychology and even the usefulness of social science. The psychologists' discovery of new dimensions of workers' mentality contrasted with the notions of several hundred leading manufacturers polled by Munsterberg in 1912. He asked them what psychological qualities seemed essential for various jobs in their plants and found that the manufacturers remained bound by traditional designations similar to Taylor's like "industrious or lazy, honest or dishonest, skillful or clumsy, peaceful or quarrelsome." Munsterberg surmised that the manufacturers' view reflected the "practical way of ordinary life," which was increasingly insufficient for the demands of modern industrial production and management.[129] Nevertheless, the appeal of industrial psychology spread, as manufacturers realized with Henry Dennison that "to get the whole man, we must get at his mind" and "draw out his mental energies." The Carnegie Institute of Technology established a psychological consulting and testing service for industry in 1915. That same year, the Cheney Brothers Silk Manufacturing Company hired the first full-time psychologist in U.S. industry. A year later, the Economic Psychology Association was founded as a clearinghouse for industry and academe, establishing in 1916 a Bureau of Salesmanship and Research supported by thirty companies. In 1917 the first general textbook in applied psychology appeared, and the *Journal of Applied Psychology* began publication.

The coming of the war and the national quest for "industrial preparedness" gave the greatest impetus to psychological testing and management as the National Research Council established a Committee for Psychology, which oversaw military testing and spurred interest in psychological job aptitude testing. Scott directed the Committee on Classification of Personnel for the U.S. Army during World War I, developing tests that rated army personnel by intelligence, education, and experience and placed them in jobs corresponding to their abilities. He also developed systematic ranking scales that translated qualitative characteristics into quantitative data and generated a numerical statement of comparative worth. Robert M. Yerkes, a Munsterberg protégé, devised the army's famous standardized mental tests. The usefulness of psychology to the war effort detailed in numerous articles in the popular media added to its respectability. By 1923 the American Management Association organized and trained its energies on the human factor in work management.[130]

The cumulative effect of modern science-based management helped create for employers, engineers, and later generations of management practitioners new ways of thinking about the men and women who sold their labor to modern industry. As it instructed the worker in the rationality of industry and in the authority of that rationality, modern management redefined the roles of employer and employee, their relationship to one another, to industrial production, and to society. As a managerial revolution, it promoted the reorganization of work around discipline, obedience, and the cult of the expert. It established the social legitimacy on the shop floor and in society of the profession of scientific engineer-managers, which evolved into a full-scale technocratic bureaucracy. It continued to view workers, even after it discovered their psyches, simply as a source of work unattainable by machines and aimed to make the most efficient use of them.[131]

While modern management claimed to widen the exercise of free will, it claimed to know what workers really wanted and offered its corporate-driven notion of a "good job" and higher productivity as a substitute for workers' own ideas. It equated workers' happiness with their ability to obtain material goods that would flow from higher productivity based on their own efforts. It promoted the "true" unity of capital and labor within the context of a corporate-led social family, and it assumed that workers could willingly be integrated into this and broken from habits of class solidarity. Finally, modern management offered industry techniques to provide new forms of social integration of behavior in the factory.

The labor ideas of modern management reinforced common themes of bourgeois progressivism: social progress managed by professional elites, the elimination of waste, sloth, and inefficiency to guarantee rising productivity, and the demise of laissez-faire capitalism and labor unruliness in favor of public-spirited, nationalist, liberal corporatism. Through scientific legitimacy and social beneficence business developed the myriad forms of its new social authority and its right to command.

NOTES

1. U.S. Congress, House of Representatives, *Hearings Before the Special Committee of the House of Representatives to Investigate the Taylor and Other Systems of Shop Management* 3 vols. (Washington, D.C., 1912), vol. 1, 212; Robert G. Valentine, "The Progressive Relation Between Efficiency and Consent," *Bulletin of the Taylor Society*, hereafter cited as *BTS*, 2 (January 1916): 10.

2. David Montgomery, *The Fall of the House of Labor: The Workplace, the State, and American Labor Activism, 1865–1925* (New York, 1987), 249–50; Martin Sklar, *The Corporate Reconstruction of American Capitalism 1890–1916: The Market, the Law, and Politics* (New York, 1988), 7; David Noble, *America by Design: Science, Technology*

and the Rise of Corporate Capitalism (New York, 1977), 264; Edward E. Hunt, "The Influence of Scientific Management," in The Taylor Society, H. S. Person, ed., *Scientific Management in American Industry* (New York, 1929), 36.

3. Montgomery, *Workers' Control in America* (New York, 1979), 3; Daniel Nelson, *Managers and Workers: Origins of the New Factory in the United States, 1880–1920* (Madison, 1975); Noble, *America by Design*, 33–50, 263.

4. On the evidence for incorporation of scientific management, see Noble, *America by Design*, 257–320; Hugh Aitken, *Taylorism at the Watertown Arsenal: Scientific Management in Action, 1908–1915* (Cambridge, Mass., 1934), 85–134; Peter F. Drucker, *Technology, Management and Society* (New York, 1958), 46–47; Stephen Meyer, *The Five Dollar Day: Labor Management and Social Control in the Ford Motor Company, 1908–1921* (Albany, N.Y., 1981), 19–22; Montgomery, *The Fall of the House of Labor*, 214–56.

5. On the professionalization of engineering, see Noble, *America by Design*, 33–50; Burton Bledstein, *The Culture of Professionalism: The Middle Class and the Development of Higher Education in America* (New York, 1976); Gerald Geison, ed., *Professions and Professional Ideologies in America* (Chapel Hill, 1983), 3–11; Monte Calvert, *The Mechanical Engineer in America: Professional Cultures in Conflict* (Baltimore, 1967).

6. Noble, *America by Design*, 260.

7. Valentine, "The Progressive Relation Between Efficiency and Consent," 8.

8. Sklar, *The Corporate Reconstruction of American Capitalism*, 35.

9. Edward E. Hunt, *Scientific Management Since Taylor* (New York, 1924), 226–37.

10. Sklar, *The Corporate Reconstruction of American Capitalism*; Alan Trachtenberg, *The Incorporation of America: Culture and Society in the Gilded Age* (New York, 1982).

11. Loren Baritz, *Servants of Power: A History of the Use of Social Science in American Industry* (New York, 1960), 29.

12. Horace B. Drury, *Scientific Management: A History and Criticism* (New York, 1922), 39; important works on scientific management include Samuel Haber, *Efficiency and Uplift: Scientific Management in the Progressive Era, 1890–1920* (Chicago, 1964); Aitken, *Taylorism at the Watertown Arsenal*; Milton Nadworny, *Scientific Management and the Unions, 1900–1932* (Cambridge, Mass., 1955); Daniel Nelson, *Frederick Taylor and the Rise of Scientific Management* (Madison, 1980); for a list of companies adopting Taylorism between 1901 and 1917, see Nelson, *Managers and Workers*, 68–78.

13. American Society of Mechanical Engineers, *Transactions of the American Society of Mechanical Engineers*, hereafter cited as ASME, *Transactions*, 34 (1912): 1140–49; see also "Developments in Machine Shop Practice in the Last Decade," ibid., 851–65.

14. Meyer, *The Five Dollar Day*, 19–20; Baritz, *Servants of Power*, 33; ASME, *Transactions*, 34 (1912): 1146; N. I. Stone, "The Response of Workers to Scientific Management: Experience in a Union Shop," in Person, ed., *Scientific Management in American Industry*, 448; Stone was former labor manager for the Hickey–Freeman Company of Rochester and chief statistician for the United States Tariff Board.

15. Frank B. Copley, *Frederick Winslow Taylor: Father of Scientific Management* (New York, 1923), vol. 1, 31; Nelson, *Managers and Workers*, 59, 60; for a discussion of scientific management in Europe and Japan, see Judith Merkle, *Management and Ideology: The Legacy of the International Scientific Management Movement* (Berkeley, 1980).

16. Robert B. Wolf, "Individuality in Industry," *BTS* 1 (Aug. 1915): 2–8; Robert G. Valentine, "Scientific Management and Organized Labor," *BTS* 1 (Jan. 1915): 3–9.

17. On the formation of modern labor control in England during the industrial revolution, see Sidney Pollard, *Genesis of Modern Management* (Cambridge, Mass., 1965), chapter 5 "Adaptation of the Labor Force," 160–208.

18. U.S. Congress, House of Representatives, *Hearings Before the Special Committee of the House of Representatives to Investigate the Taylor and Other Systems of Shop Management*, 3 vols. (Washington, D.C., 1912), vol. 1, 212; Taylor, *Principles of Scientific Management*, 7; for a discussion of Taylor's principles, natural law, and economic determinism, see Henri Le Chatelier, "Preface to the French Edition" of *Principles of Scientific Management* (no date), in Clarence B. Thompson, ed., *Scientific Management: A Collection of the More Significant Articles Describing the Taylor System of Management* (Cambridge, Mass., 1914), 842–59.

19. Haber, *Efficiency and Uplift*, 11.

20. Hollis Godfrey, "The Attitude of Labor Toward Scientific Management," *Annals of the American Academy of Political and Social Science*, hereafter cited as *Annals*, 44 (July 1912): 71; Harry Braverman, *Labor and Monopoly Capital: The Degradation of Work in the Twentieth Century* (New York, 1974), 86.

21. Taylor, "Workmen and Their Management," unpublished manuscript of a lecture given in 1909 at the Harvard Graduate School of Business Administration (after 1922, the Harvard Business School), Carl Barth papers, file T–241a, Ms. Division, Baker Library, Harvard Business School, 5–7.

22. Robert Bruere, "Industrial Relations" in Person, *Scientific Management in American Industry*, 457; Harlow Person in the forward to the 1947 edition of Taylor's major works continued to promote the social benefits of scientific management fitted, he thought, to a post–World War II era: "The very survival of democratic institutions may depend on a lifting of productivity to new degrees of adequacy which will rapidly eliminate starvation, establish a feeling of greater economic security, and destroy impulses to follow false leaders along the paths of violence toward a totalitarian world." Taylor, *Scientific Management: Comprising Shop Management, Principles of Scientific Management, Testimony Before the Special House Committee* (New York, 1947), xvi; for a general discussion of the social and institutional consequences of technological change, see John Rae, "The Application of Science to Industry," in Alexandra Oleson and John Voss, *The Organization of Knowledge in Modern America, 1860–1920* (Baltimore, 1979), 249–68; this essay also recounts the growth of the engineering profession from 7,300 members in 1870 to over 136,000 in 1920; see also Meyer, *The Five Dollar Day*, chapter 3, "The Social Impact of the New Technology," 37–65.

23. Taylor, *Principles of Scientific Management*, 22, 32, 53; Harlow S. Person, "Scientific Management," *BTS* 2 (Oct. 1916): 16–23.

24. Taylor, *Principles of Scientific Management*, 22.

25. Ibid.; at Midvale Steel, Taylor estimated that workers and management "had about equal weight in deciding how fast the work should be done," before he instituted scientific management there; Taylor, *Shop Management* (New York, 1911), 44.

26. Taylor, *Shop Management*, 23, 24.

27. Taylor, *Principles of Scientific Management*, 22, 32.

28. Ibid., 38.

29. Taylor, *Testimony Before the Special House Committee*, 176; *Shop Management*, 18, 44–45, 122; see also Daniel Nelson, "Scientific Management, Systematic Manage-

ment and Labor, 1880–1915,'' *Business History Review* 48 (1974): 479–500; Harlow S. Person, ''Scientific Management: A Brief Statement of its Nature and History,'' in Hunt, *Scientific Management Since Taylor*, 5–13.

30. Taylor, *Shop Management*, 85–86; David Montgomery found that by 1918, specialized machine tenders and not craftsmen formed the largest group of workers in metal industries such as automobile, electrical, machine tool, and farm equipment; in the automobile industry by 1923, only 9 percent of the workforce was skilled, while 47 percent was machine tenders; Montgomery, *Workers' Control*, 117; see also Meyer, *The Five Dollar Day*, 37–8.

31. Taylor, *Principles of Scientific Management*, 97.

32. Taylor, *Shop Management*, 106; quote Valentine, ''The Progressive Relation Between Efficiency and Consent,'' 9.

33. Taylor, *Shop Management*, 20, 76. Although the differential piece rate system of wage payments disappeared, incentive pay, time study, and subdivided task descriptions persist in U.S. industry. Individual incentive remains geared to pay, itself determined by the skill classification of each job. See Daniel Nelson, *Frederick W. Taylor and the Rise of Scientific Management* (Madison, 1980), 141, 200; for a discussion of wage plans, see Drury, *Scientific Management*, 51–87.

34. Taylor, *Testimony Before the Special House Committee*, 83–84; Montgomery, *Workers' Control*, 116; prevailing business ethos admitted that wage theory rested upon subsistence, see the Engineering Magazine, *Science and the Practice of Management* (New York, 1914), chapter ''The Labor Question,'' 397; see also Henry Gantt, *Work, Wages and Profits* (New York, 1919); Braverman, *Labor and Monopoly Capital*, 78, 86, 97.

35. Taylor, *Principles of Scientific Management*, 10, 32, 52; *Shop Management*, 137; Braverman, *Labor and Monopoly Capital*, 99.

36. Copley, *Frederick Taylor*, vol. 2, 404; Taylor, *Testimony Before the Special House Committee*, 36; *Principles of Scientific Management*, 32.

37. Taylor, ''A Piece Rate System, Being a Step Toward Partial Solution to the Labor Problem,'' ASME *Transactions*, 16 (1895): 12; ''Shop Management,'' ASME *Transactions*, 24 (1903): 22, quoted in Person, ''Principles and Practices of Scientific Management,'' International Industrial Relations Association, *World Social Economic Congress* (The Hague, 1931), 18; Drury, *Scientific Management*, 114.

38. George D. Babcock, *The Taylor System in Franklin Management* (1918, reprinted Easton, Pa., 1972), 82.

39. Alvin Gouldner, *The Dialectic of Ideology and Technology: The Origins, Grammar, and Future of Ideology* (New York, 1976), 76, and Karl Marx, *Capital* 3 vols. (Chicago, 1906), vol. 1, 396–97, cited in Montgomery, *Workers' Control*, 34; Taylor, *Shop Management*, 133; *Principles of Scientific Management*, 10; for an outline of the debate among sociologists over technology determining shop floor attitudes, see Frank Bechofer, ''Relationship Between Technology and Shop-Floor Behaviour,'' in J. N. Wolf and D. D. Edge, eds., *Meaning and Control: Essays in the Social Aspects of Science and Technology* (London, 1973), 121–42; for other studies of the role of ideology in engineering, see Noble, *America by Design*, and William Aiken, *Technocracy and the American Dream* (Berkeley, 1977); Michael Buroway, *Manufacturing Consent* (Chicago, 1979), and Richard Pffeffer, *Working for Capitalism* (New York, 1979); for a progressive scientific management approach that considered workers' habits and needs, see Richard

Hartness, *The Human Factor in Works Management* (New York, 1912), and Edward D. Jones, *The Administration of Industrial Enterprises* (New York, 1919), 5.

40. ASME, *Transactions* 34 (1912): 1140.

41. Taylor, *Principles of Scientific Management*, 36; in 1924, the National Industrial Conference Board found 56 percent of factory wage workers on hourly wages, 37 percent on piecework, and 7 percent on bonus plans, Sumner Schlicter, *Union Policies and Industrial Management* (Washington, D.C., 1941), 282, in Montgomery, *Workers' Control*, 38. For a discussion of Taylor's system as a bureaucratic revolution, see Dan Clawson, *Bureaucracy and the Labor Process: The Transformation of U.S. Industry, 1860–1920* (New York, 1980), chapter 6.

42. Taylor, *Shop Management*, 99; Harlow S. Person, *Industrial Education: A System of Training for Men Entering Upon Trade and Commerce* (Boston and New York, 1907), 44.

43. Person, *Industrial Education*, 45.

44. Taylor, *Shop Management*, 109; Aitken, *Taylorism at the Watertown Arsenal*, 120.

45. H. K. Hathaway, "Planning Department, Its Organization and Function –1," *Industrial Engineering* 12 (July 1912): 6–8; for the evolution of these techniques of shop management, see Hathaway, "Control of Shop Operations," in Harlow S. Person, ed., *Scientific Management in American Industry*, 319–74.

46. Quoted in Aitken, *Taylorism at Watertown Arsenal*, 77; Taylor, *Testimony Before the Special House Committee*, 76.

47. Taylor, *Testimony Before the Special House Committee*, 45; Taylor, "Workmen and Their Management," 25; testimony of Charles J. Harrah, *United States Government Industrial Commission Reports on Conditions of Capital and Labor Employed in Manufactures and General Business* 10 vols. (Washington, D.C., 1901), vol. 7, 352.

48. Taylor, *Principles of Scientific Management*, 63; Harrah testimony, *U.S. Government Industrial Commission Reports*, vol. 7, 352. Harrah praised the low turnover and regularity of men in showing up for work, although admitting that "a wedding with us means sometimes 15 days before it can be considered consummated; and then again we have to bury an Irishman, and that takes about a week."

49. Taylor, *Principles of Scientific Management*, 83; Taylor's italics; Dodge cited in Nadworny, *Scientific Management and the Unions*, 94.

50. Noble, *America by Design*, 261–75.

51. Taylor, "Workmen and Their Management," 14.

52. Taylor, "Workmen and Their Management," 15–18; testimony of Charles J. Harrah, *United States Government Industrial Commission Reports*, vol. 7, 353.

53. Taylor, *Principles of Scientific Management*, 38, 25; *Testimony Before the Special House Committee*, 96.

54. Taylor, *Shop Management*, 189–90.

55. Taylor, *Principles of Scientific Management*, 55–56; *Shop Management*, 24, 54–55, 64.

56. Taylor, *Principles of Scientific Management*, 61; *Testimony Before the Special House Committee*, 64.

57. Taylor, *Shop Management*, 64; *Testimony Before the Special House Committee*, 123, 176.

58. Taylor, *Principles of Scientific Management*, 23; Noble, *America by Design*, 264.

59. Taylor, *Principles of Scientific Management*, 59, 62; *Shop Management*, 28.

60. Taylor, *Principles of Scientific Management*, 25; Braverman, *Labor and Monopoly Capital*, 108.

61. Taylor, *Shop Management*, 27; U.S. Congress, House of Representatives, *Hearings Before the Special House Committee*, vol. 3, 1457, cited in Nadworny, *Scientific Management and the Unions*, 165.

62. Copley, *Frederick Taylor*, vol. 1, 207; Taylor, *Testimony Before the Special House Committee*, 168.

63. Thompson, *Scientific Management*, 847; Taylor, *Shop Management*, 187; Taylor, *Principles of Scientific Management*, 10–11.

64. Taylor, *Shop Management*, 189; Taylor, "Workmen and Their Management," 24; Frank B. Copley, "Taylor and Trade Unions," *BTS* 10 (Aug. 1925): 182–84.

65. Taylor, *Shop Management*, 183; for a discussion of the response of union leaders to scientific management, see Robert Hoxie, *Scientific Management and Labor* (New York, 1915), 120; Copley, Taylor and Trade Unions," 184.

66. Nadworny, *Scientific Management*, 48–49; Taylor, "Workmen and Their Management," 24; Taylor, *Shop Management*, 188; Taylor, *Testimony Before the Special House Committee*, 21.

67. Montgomery, *Workers' Control*, 122–23.

68. Hunt, *Scientific Management Since Taylor*, 11; Haber, *Efficiency and Uplift*, 52–54; Montgomery, *The Fall of the House of Labor*, 246–47; Drury, *Scientific Management*, 38–42.

69. Aitken, *Taylorism at the Watertown Arsenal*; Matthew Hale, Jr., *Human Science and Social Order: Hugo Munsterberg and the Origins of Applied Psychology* (Philadelphia, 1980), 52–55.

70. James Mapes Dodge and Frederick Taylor, "Scientific Management Prevents Strikes," City Club of Philadelphia, *City Club Bulletin* 4 (Jan. 18, 1911): 28; Montgomery, *Workers' Control*, 127–34; H. H. Farquhar, "Positive Contributions of Scientific Management," *BTS* 4 (Oct. 1919): 15–28; see p. 16 for a description of the drop in earnings and output upon the abolition of premium payments at the Watertown arsenal. Brig. General William Crozier, the army's chief of ordinance continued to support Taylorism; see William Crozier, "Scientific Management in Government Establishments," *BTS* 1 (Oct. 1915): 1–8; James Mapes Dodge, "A History of the Introduction of a System of Shop Management," in Clarence B. Thompson, ed., *Scientific Management* (Cambridge, Mass., 1914), 226–31.

71. Quoted in Hunt, *Scientific Management Since Taylor*, 39.

72. Meyer, *The Five Dollar Day*, 11–21; for a summary of Taylorism in shops, see Montgomery, *The Fall of the House of Labor*, 214–44.

73. Babcock, *The Taylor System in Franklin Management*, 3, 4, 13, 25, 80; H. K. Hathaway, "Standards," a paper presented at the annual meeting of the Taylor Society, New York, December 6, 1919, 5.

74. Babcock, *The Taylor System in Franklin Management*, 3, 4, 17, 51, 59.

75. Ibid., 80, 130–33, 147; for a similar report on scientific management at the Acme Wire Company, New Haven, Conn., between 1912 and 1922, see Ernest G. Brown, "The Response of Workers to Scientific Management: Experience in a Non-union Shop," in Person, ed., *Scientific Management in American Industry*, 440–47; for scientific management at the Clothcroft Shops of the Joseph & Feiss Company of Cleveland, see Richard A. Feiss, "Personal Relationships as a Basis of Scientific Management," and "Discus-

sion'' by Henry Kendall, Henry Gantt, Sanford Thompson, Carl Barth, and others, in *BTS*, 1 (Nov. 1915): 5–25; and Richard A. Feiss, ''Scientific Management and Its Relation to the Health of the Worker,'' *BTS* 2 (Nov. 1916): 11–13.

76. ''Scientific Management Viewed from the Workman's Standpoint,'' *Industrial Engineering and the Engineering Digest* (Nov. 1910), 377–80; quote, 378–79.

77. Montgomery, *The Fall of the House of Labor*, 245.

78. Meyer, *The Five Dollar Day*, 11–20, 37–38, 43–46.

79. Montgomery, *The Fall of the House of Labor*, 247; *Workers' Control*, 5, 26, 44, 102, 116; Drury, *Scientific Management*, 112; Morris Cooke, ''Forward: The Problem of the American Manufacturer,'' *Annals* 85 (Sept. 1919), viii; Harlow S. Person, ''The Contributions of Scientific Management to Industrial Problems,'' in Hunt, *Scientific Management Since Taylor*, 32; George, *The History of Management Thought* (Englewood Cliffs, N.J., 1968), 102; Robert Valentine, ''The Progressive Relation Between Efficiency and Consent,'' 7; and Valentine, ''Scientific Management and Organized Labor,'' *BTS* 1 (Jan. 1915): 3–9.

80. Cooke, ''Who is Boss in Your Shop?,'' *Annals* 71 (May 1917), quoted in Drury, 115; Edward E. Hunt, ''The Influence of Scientific Management,'' in Person, ed., *Scientific Management in American Industry*, 37; Drury, *Scientific Management*, 113; Babcock, *The Taylor System in Franklin Management*, 47; H. S. Person, ''The Opportunities and Obligations of Scientific Management,'' *BTS* 4 (Feb. 1919): 1–7, quote, 5; H. S. Person and Robert Wolf, et al., ''Control and Consent,'' *BTS* 3 (March 1917): 5–20.

81. Montgomery, *Fall of the House of Labor*, 247; Baritz, *The Servants of Power*, 29–30; Person, ''The New Attitude Toward Management,'' in Person, ed., *Scientific Management in American Industry*, 23–34; and Stone, ''The Response of Workers to Scientific Management,'' in Person, ed., *Scientific Management in American Industry*, 448; Noble, *America by Design*, 276; Philip Taft, *The A.F. of L. in the Time of Gompers* (New York, 1957), 345–60; George D. Babcock and James Heckman, ''Some Organization Lessons of the War,'' *BTS* 4 (Dec. 1919): 4–12; William Green, ''Labor's Ideals Concerning Management,'' *BTS* 10 (Dec. 1925): 241–53.

82. Harlow S. Person, ''The Contribution of Scientific Management to Industrial Problems,'' in Hunt, *Scientific Management Since Taylor*, 32; Committee on Elimination of Waste in Industry of the Federal American Engineering Societies, *Waste in Industry* (New York, 1921); Herbert Hoover, ''Industrial Waste,'' *BTS* 6 (April 1921): 77–79; Morris Cooke, ''Forward,'' *Annals* 85 (Sept. 1919): vi; Francis Goodell, ''The Technicians Point of View,'' *BTS* 15 (April 1930): 71–79.

83. Taylor, *Principles of Scientific Management*, 119, cited in Lyndall Urwick, ''Management's Debt to Engineers,'' *Advanced Management* 17 (Dec. 1952): 7; Henry P. Kendall, ''Types of Management,'' in Hunt, *Scientific Management Since Taylor*, 14; Richard Feiss, ''Personal Relationship as a Basis of Scientific Management,'' 5, 10; see Wolf, ''Individuality in Industry,'' 4, for an early call for the use of psychology. Wolf was the manager of the Burgess Sulphite Fibre Company of Berlin, New Hampshire, maker of paper products; Morris Cooke, ''Who is Boss in Your Shop?,'' *BTS* 3 (Aug. 1917): 3–10, quote 6.

84. Baritz, *Servants of Power*, 30–31; Noble, *America by Design*, 273–75.

85. Hugo Munsterberg, *Psychology and Industrial Efficiency* (Boston and New York, 1913), 215; Baritz, *Servants of Power*, 2, 28, 31; Harlow S. Person, ''The Manager, the Workman, and the Social Scientist,'' *BTS* 3 (Feb. 1917): 1–7.

86. George, *The History of Management Thought*, 100; Henry L. Gantt, ''Training

Workmen in Habits of Industry and Cooperation,'' ASME *Transactions* 30 (1908): 1037–63; and Gantt, ''A Bonus System for Rewarding Labor,'' ASME *Transactions* 23 (1901): 341–72.

87. George, *The History of Management Thought*, 101; Noble, *America by Design*, 274; H. L. Gantt, ''A Practical Application of Scientific Management,'' *The Engineering Magazine* 41 (April 1911): 1–22.

88. Jean Christie, *Morris Llewellyn Cooke: Progressive Engineer* (New York, 1983), 16.

89. Hale, *Human Science and Social Order*, 107.

90. Munsterberg, *Psychology and Industrial Efficiency*, 52; Baritz, *Servants of Power*, 22; the instinct theory was replaced in the late 1920s by behaviorists' ideas of analyzing each situation to determine specific causes of behavior. See C. S. Yoakum, ''Impulse, Emotion, and Habit in Conduct,'' in Henry C. Metcalf, ed., *The Psychological Foundations of Management* (Chicago, 1927), 36; A. Lincoln Filene, ''The Key to Successful Industrial Management,'' *Annals of the American Academy of Political and Social Science* 85 (Sept. 1919): 9.

91. George, *The History of Management Thought*, 96–99; Frank G. and Lillian M. Gilbreth, ''The Three Position Plan of Promotion,'' *Annals of the American Academy of Political and Social Science* 65 (May 1916), 289–96; and *Applied Motion Study* (New York, 1919); for examples of psychology in the literature of Taylorism, see Frank B. and Lillian M. Gilbreth, ''The Achievements of Motion Psychology,'' *BTS* 9 (Dec. 1924): 259, 283; Ordway Tead, ''Purpose as a Psychological Factor in Management,'' *BTS* 10 (Dec. 1925): 254–67; C. S. Yoakum, ''Experimental Psychology in Personnel Problems,'' *BTS* 10 (June 1925): 154–63; W. V. Bingham, ''What Industrial Psychology Asks of Management,'' *BTS* 9 (Dec. 1924): 243–48.

92. Frank G. and Lillian M. Gilbreth, ''Classifying the Elements of Work,'' *Management and Administration in Manufacturing Industries* 8 (Aug. 1924): 151–54, and part two, 8 (Sept. 1924): 295–97: quote from 151–52.

93. Lillian Gilbreth, *The Psychololgy of Management: The Function of the Mind in Determining, Teaching, and Installing Methods of Lease Waste* (New York, 1914), 23, 90, 251.

94. Gilbreth, *The Psychology of Management*, 160.

95. Ibid., 21, 228; ''The worker has a psychology all his own,'' claimed one scientific manager in 1921. See N. I. Stone, ''Discussion,'' *BTS* 7 (Dec. 1922): 75, quoted in Haber, *Efficiency and Uplift*, 165.

96. Gilbreth, *The Psychology of Industrial Management*, 19.

97. Gilbreth, *The Psychology of Industrial Management*, 77, 228–40; Ordway Tead, ''Personnel Research,'' in Person, ed., *Scientific Management in American Industry*, 97; see also A. W. Kornhauser and F. A. Kingsbury, *Psychological Tests in Business* (Chicago, 1924), and A. J. Snow, *Psychology in Business Relations* (Chicago, 1925); Edward Thorndike emphasized the interrelation of human traits. ''A man's possession of what we call energy . . . seems to be a multiplier for his intellect or skill. A man's loyalty or devotion in any particular job seems to be a multiplier for his other equipment for it. What we call roughly interest in success . . . or ambition, seems to be a multiplier for energy.'' See Edward Thorndike, ''Fundamental Theorems in Judging Men,'' *Journal of Applied Psychology* 2 (1918): 67–76, quote 74.

98. Gilbreth, *The Psychology of Management*, 240, 243–44.

99. C. S. Yoakum, ''The Role of Impulse, Emotions, and Habit in Conduct,'' 35.

100. Gilbreth, *The Psychology of Management*, 148, 171, 176; many scientific managers attempted to substitute daily instructions for traditional knowledge. "Information, which . . . is supposed to be furnished by the knowledge of the workman or gang boss . . . is brought back to the planning room and becomes part of the instruction card." Kendall, "Types of Management," 14.

101. Gilbreth, *The Psychology of Management*, 96, 189, 274–75.

102. Gilbreth, *The Psychology of Management*, 70, 71, 119, 273.

103. H. S. Person, "Principles and Practices of Scientific Management," 18; Gilbreth, *The Psychology of Management*, 138, 179; Herbert Hoover, "Industrial Standardization," in Hunt, *Scientific Management Since Taylor*, 189–96.

104. Richard W. Fox and Jackson Lears, eds., *The Culture of Consumption: Critical Essays in American History, 1880–1980* (New York, 1983), xi, xii, 30–38; and Lears, "The Concept of Cultural Hegemony: Problems and Possibilities," *American Historical Review* 90 (June 1985): 567–93.

105. Gilbreth, *The Psychology of Management*, 7, 10, 72–73; Morris L. Cooke, "Classification and Symbolization," in Person, ed., *Scientific Management in American Industry*, 113–35, quote, 113.

106. Cooke, "Classification and Symbolization, 121; see also H. K. Hathaway, "On the Technique of Manufacturing," *Annals* 85 (Sept. 1919): 231–36, and William O. Lichtner, "Promulgation of Standards by the Taylor Society," *BTS* 5 (Feb. 1920): 12–42.

107. Gilbreth, *The Psychology of Management*, 88, 131–33, 120, 148.

108. Gilbreth, *The Psychology of Management*, 11, 12, 151; Morris Cooke, "Forward," in Hunt, *Scientific Management Since Taylor*, vii.

109. Gilbreth, *The Psychology of Management*, 312, 327–28; Gantt, *Work, Wages and Profits*, 171–72; Henry S. Dennison, "Management and Labor's Interest in the Development of Industrial Psychology," in Henry C. Metcalf, *The Psychological Foundations of Management* (Chicago, 1927), 16.

110. Hale, *Human Science and Social Order*, ix.

111. Munsterberg, *Psychology and Industrial Efficiency*, 214–19; Hale, *Human Science and Social Order*, 152.

112. Munsterberg, *Psychology and Industrial Efficiency*, 195–98; Hale, *Human Science and Social Order*, 153.

113. Stone, "The Response of Workers to Scientific Management: Experience in a Union Shop," 447; J. E. Otterson, "Executive and Administrative Organization," *Annals* 85 (Sept. 1919): 91; C. S. Yoakum, "Labor Standards," in Person, ed., *Scientific Management in American Industry*, 228.

114. William R. Leiserson, "The Worker's Relation to Scientific Management," in Hunt, *Scientific Management Since Taylor*, 222–25, quote, 223.

115. Munsterberg, *Psychology and Industrial Efficiency*, 100–04, 117, 133.

116. Munsterberg, *Brundzuge der Psychotechnik* (Leipzig, 1914), 238, cited in Hale, *Human Science and Social Order*, 125; Munsterberg, *Psychology and Industrial Efficiency*, 3, 15–16, 141.

117. Munsterberg, *Psychology and Industrial Efficiency*, 143, 235; *Psychology and Social Sanity* (New York, 1914), 103, 108, quoted in Hale, *Human Science and Social Order*, 161.

118. Munsterberg, *Psychology: General and Applied*, 136, 143, quoted in Hale, *Human Science and Social Order*, 82.

119. Munsterberg, *Psychology and Industrial Efficiency*, 164, 174–75, 209.

120. Munsterberg, *Psychology and Industrial Efficiency*, 26, 128.

121. Munsterberg, *Business Psychology* (Chicago, 1915), 287, quoted in Hale, *Human Science and Social Order*, 124; Hale, ibid., 159.

122. Hale, *Human Science and Social Order*, 82, 124, 159–60, 186–88; C. S. Yoakum, "Conditions of Research in Industrial Psychology—Changing a Point of View," in Henry Metcalf, *The Psychological Foundations of Management*, 32.

123. Morris L. Cooke, "The Spirit and Social Significance of Scientific Management," *Journal of Political Economy* 21 (June 1913): 481–93, quotes, 485–86; B. Preston Clark, "On the Motives of Industrial Enterprise," *Annals* 85 (Sept. 1919): 37–47.

124. Sklar, *The Corporate Reconstruction of American Capitalism*, 22, 35; Christie, *Morris Llewellyn Cooke*, 16; Cooke, "The Spirit and Social Significance of Scientific Management," 488.

125. George L. Bell, "Production the Goal," *Annals* 85 (Sept. 1919): 1–7, quote, 3, 4; Edward D. Jones, "Publicity as a Policy," *Annals* 85 (Sept. 1919): 314–20, quote, 319.

126. Joseph E. Cohen, "The Drift in Industry," *Annals* 85 (Sept. 1919): 28–36, quotes, 28, 31; Clark, "On the Motives of Industrial Enterprise," (Sept. 1919): 38–40.

127. M. P. Follett, "The Psychology of Control," in Metcalf, ed., *The Psychological Foundations of Management*, 175–77.

128. Walter Dill Scott, *The Psychology of Advertising* (New York, 1908); and Scott, *Influencing Men in Business* (New York, 1911); Baritz, *Servants of Power*, 27; George, *The History of Management Thought*, 121–22.

129. Munsterberg, *Psychology and Industrial Efficiency*, 116–17; C. S. Yoakum, "Labor Standards," in Person, ed., *Scientific Management in American Industry*, 229, 235.

130. "Famous Firsts: Measuring Minds for the Job," *Business Week* (Jan. 29, 1966): 63; Henry S. Dennison, "Management and Labor Interest in the Development of Industrial Psychology," in Metcalf, *The Psychological Foundations of Management*, 15.

131. Baritz, *Servants of Power*, 17; Hale, *Human Science and Social Order*, 162–63; Charles Knoeppel, *Industrial Preparedness* (New York, 1916).

Chapter 4

The National Association of Manufacturers: "Capital's Most Efficient Mouthpiece"

"A propaganda for evil is to be neutralized only by a propaganda for good," President David Parry proclaimed in 1903 as the National Association of Manufacturers (NAM) launched an "open and square fight to the finish with the unions" in the realm of public discourse. "Public opinion is the guiding force in this nation today," Parry declared. "Organized labor owes its present power mainly to the support of public opinion" and therefore business must organize on this front. "We have been intimidated by a handful of anarchists and so-called labor leaders," he warned, "and it is now time to settle this issue once and for all." A large and influential national employers' organization, the NAM served as an important voice in the labor-capital discourse from which emerged reformulated attitudes about work, unions, and strike activity in the industrializing United States. The NAM's clearly articulated emphasis on the social and political aspects of language makes its efforts important to understanding the role of employers' ideas in producing social meaning and shaping cultural values.[1] In response to the dramatic growth of union membership between 1898 and 1905, the NAM led a vigorous, nationwide anti-labor campaign, broadcasting a package of rhetorical arguments that distinguished "good" workers from "bad" and condemned unions, strikes, and labor militancy. Disseminated throughout the nation in educational, religious, civic, media, and legal forums, these ideas made the NAM symbolize the vanguard of extreme anti-unionism in the nation's business rhetoric.

Nationwide employers' organizations first appeared in 1886 as manufacturers formed trade associations to promote industry interests. Around 1900, groups such as the National Metal Trades Association and the National Founders' Association, chambers of commerce, lobbying organizations, and boards of trade represented a self-conscious coalescence of the leadership of medium- and large-scale trade and manufacturing firms. These organizations signified the first appearance of corporate capitalism's organized voice in the national discourse over the role of labor in modern society. Their annual conventions, circulation of trade journals, and discussion of labor represented manufacturers' first attempts to codify and publicize their economic and labor policies on a national scale. Their activities were important to building a national consciousness among manufacturing and corporate elites, to establishing a shared sense of goals and problems, and for creating strategies to deflect their critics.[2] Part of this process, as we have seen, involved justification of their management role, based on efficiency and fair treatment of workers. Another was businessmen's eagerness to engage striking workers in contests of sheer power. And yet another was the ideological assault on the nation's opinion through the efforts of organizations like the National Association of Manufacturers.

Joining a massive counterattack against unions by the nation's trade associations after 1900, the NAM was the first manufacturers' organization to mount a national campaign couched in the language of popular political economy and aimed at "the working masses and the entire body politic."[3] In all its endeavors, this campaign recognized the importance of public opinion in the discussion of labor issues. Through legislation, litigation, and education, the NAM's formidable propaganda organization injected a vehement, pro-capitalist, anti-labor body of ideas into U.S. society. The emotional intensity of its arguments set the rhetorical extremes and thus designated the most conservative, "business end" of the debate over capital and labor. Organized in 1895 among medium-sized manufacturers in Northeastern and North Central industrial states, the NAM quickly became widely influential in business circles partly as a result of its anti-union position. Editors of the financial journal, *Bradstreet's*, deemed the NAM in 1897 "highly representative of the manufacturing interests of the country, more so than most other organizations." Similarly, the *London Board of Trade Journal* in 1898 identified the NAM "throughout the world as an institution which represents the manufacturers themselves." By 1908 its membership represented over $22 billion in invested capital, 1 million stockholders, 6 million employees, and, it estimated, 75 to 80 percent of the total manufacturing output of the United States. Recognizing NAM leaders as the nation's most prominent crusaders against unions, John Keith, in a 1904 *Harper's Weekly* series, considered Parry "one of the most important personages of the day," leading a movement "with more social significance than any other at the present time."[4] The NAM itself professed in 1909 to have assembled "the most powerful body of businessmen ever organized in any land, or in any age." In 1914, Forest Crissey in a series of *Saturday Evening Post* articles identified the NAM as "the largest trade organization in the world."[5]

More recent assessments have downplayed the NAM's influence compared to that of the National Civic Federation, based in part on erroneous NCF assertions. The NCF did claim a large business following between 1900 and 1903 as a cross-class coalition of leading industrialists, financiers, and trade unionists that promoted trade agreements and mediation. Yet, anti-unionism held sway among many large and small manufacturers who resisted recognizing the legitimacy of trade unionism. Even some large manufacturers who supported the NCF's idea of a "harmony of interests" became increasingly anti-union between 1904 and 1910, James Weinstein observed. By 1903 "few manufacturers endorsed the NCF's view," David Montgomery has shown, as NCF efforts to control labor through bilateral contracts "proved less effective than the unilateral exercise of management control, backed by the concerted action of all employers in a given locality." In the years after 1903 the NAM and the NCF had "battled for the minds of the same business constituency, and the Parryites had won." The anti-union influence of the NAM among businessmen is well known. These "tireless and energetic propagandists," Philip Taft wrote, "rallied large numbers of employers to their views, and were undoubtedly a factor in the changed climate of opinion confronting the unions in the first decade of the century."[6]

In 1903 the NAM launched its self-proclaimed "belligerent" offensive in nervous response to the rapid membership gains and "class legislation" of its "chief opponent," the American Federation of Labor, which had grown from less than 360,000 to over 1.5 million between 1899 and 1904. Federation leaders accompanied these gains with the sponsorship of federal eight hour and anti-injunction bills, agitation for closed shop unionism, and strikes to force union recognition. In an exaggerated language of heightened class polarization, the NAM depicted labor activity as a dangerous social movement. Public sympathy with union efforts represented "ominous manifestations" of organized labor power that threatened the nation with social revolution. "Labor was already united," warned a NAM member, "labor was moving as one man; labor in splendid phalanx-like precision was moving like an army." Without unified resistance to such "aggression upon its interests," capital would discover too late that "to be disorganized was to be demoralized, and to be demoralized was to be damned."[7] Alarmed especially by the 1902 anthracite coal strike of the United Mine Workers and the growing power of Chicago's teamsters and taking advantage of a labor surplus in the 1903 recession, owners of large manufacturing firms flocked to the NAM, swelling its membership in the five years after 1903 from 988 to over 4,000 manufacturing firms.[8]

With this call to arms, the nation's self-styled "most efficient mouthpiece of capital" took up the challenge of "moulding public opinion" so that labor's efforts "will be bound down in their infancy [and] not come to so dangerous a head." The NAM sought to "educate the mass of the people to right thinking and doing in all matters industrial and social" in order to "arouse the great middle class to a realization of what trade unionism really means." Association officials recognized the importance of recruiting prominent opinion makers in its public assault against labor. "We know from experience in industry and politics," said one official, "that an organized eight or ten percent of a community can sway a whole community." Perhaps not as easily reached, but important, too, was the individual worker's consciousness. On this crucial ground, NAM members strove in their individual plants to counter labor's social criticism with a "simple and sane" treatment of economic issues designed to instruct workers in "right thinking."[9]

TACTICS AND METHODS

Headquartered in a nineteen story Broadway high rise in New York, the NAM's nationwide communication network promoted its principles through public schools, universities, trade schools, churches, the press, and state and national government agencies. The association directed a constant barrage of information at statesmen, clergymen, editors, and educators by funding government lobbies, disseminating "Circulators of Information," organizing local Citizen's Alliances, sponsoring public speakers, and distributing its official journals: *American Industries* and the *American Trade Index*. Informally and through national umbrella organizations, the NAM coordinated its operations with other industrial and commercial interests: employers' trade associations, bankers' associations, chambers of commerce, and industrial managers' associations. Its nationwide mail campaign sent forth large volumes of free material. In a six month period in 1910 community leaders across the nation received 47,000 pamphlets from NAM headquarters.[10]

National Association of Manufacturers officials' rigorous public speaking schedule complemented the mail campaign. In 1910 alone, Chief Counsel James Emery, later president of the National Metal Trades Association, travelled to twenty-four major cities, addressing boards of trade, chambers of commerce, citizens' industrial associations, farmers' organizations, the National Conservation Congress, and the American Academy of Political and Social Science. In that same year President John Kirby, Jr. delivered speeches in ten major cities where each time local newspapers printed his entire address. In one year NAM leaders claimed to have directly addressed some 250,000 persons, reached another 750,000 through official publications, and ultimately gained an audience of 15 million out of a national population of over 90 million through "revival meetings," press releases, and newspaper articles. "Never before in [its] history," said Kirby, touting the 1910 effort, had the NAM more "widely extended" its influence to spread the "gospel of industrial truth in a way that leaves no room for complaint." Although it is difficult to estimate dollar amounts for the NAM's anti-labor campaign, the AFL estimated that the association spent $500,000 in 1907 on its "campaign of education." This can be compared to the $10,000 the AFL spent publishing the *American Federationist* in 1904 out of that year's budget of $83,000.[11]

The NAM believed education furnished the foundation for building a national consensus that would prefer the progressive management of the nation's resources by enlightened patriot-businessmen to union "selfishness." Focusing on the nation's educational system, the association furnished free copies of its *Principles*, yearbooks, *American Industries*, and material from its Educational Literature Series to leading public and college libraries throughout the nation. National Association of Manufacturers speakers worked the university lecture circuit, popularizing their philosophy of individual liberty, private property, and various methods of labor control. Capitalizing on the popularity of formal debate in higher education and on "great public interest" in the nationwide open shop crusade, the association supplied materials to debate teams defending the open shop. Parry reported that the open shop position had won every debate in the nation's universities in 1904. Throughout the remainder of the decade, numerous requests for debate material received "prompt and liberal" deliveries. In one month the association sent forty-two sets of debate materials to Nebraska schools alone.[12]

Public education was only one area of pedagogy to capture the NAM's attention. After 1900 a highly publicized national controversy arose over employer-sponsored industrial education, a reflection of worker control issues latent in the transfer of craft knowledge to factory managers. With the technological and organizational revolution in production in the second half of the nineteenth century had come the rise of semi-skilled, task oriented jobs that no longer required long apprenticeships. The traditional union controlled apprentice system broke down, and as manufacturers sought substitutes for craft union training, they turned to various forms of privately funded industrial education. Like other national organizations shaping the trade school movement, such as the National Society for the Promotion of Industrial Education (NSPIE) the National Association of Corporation Schools, the National Education Association, and the American Federation of Labor, the NAM saw industrial education as a class issue. Unlike the NSPIE, which sought to reconcile class interests, the NAM and the AFL saw vocationalism in terms of control over entrance into the trades and the very existence of closed shop unionism. The NAM supported trade schools, and the AFL opposed them, both organizations addressing the question on precisely the same critical grounds: Who controlled the supply of skilled labor? Who governed apprentices' ideas? AFL locals monitored the quantity and training of apprentices where they had the power to do so, in part to generate union loyalty. To craft union leaders, employer-operated trade school education would eliminate this loyalty and influence workers to serve as strikebreakers. If mechanics attended technical schools, declared a city trade union secretary to the New York Bureau of Labor Statistics, they "would not know anything about unions" or have "any sympathy with their rules and regulations." To such "scab hatcheries," said U.S. Labor Commissioner Carroll Wright, "labor unions declare themselves totally and unalterably opposed."[13]

In 1905, as rival interests shaped the national debate, the NAM mounted a nationwide campaign against union apprenticeship. "The apprentice is the creature of the union," charged NAM President Van Cleave, "and not of the employer. He must observe union rules and walk out when the union strikes" and as a consequence, "is not as loyal and serviceable to his employer." Manufacturers required a "new education" that would "nip diseased ideas in the bud" and produce skilled, willing, loyal workers immune to the "domination and withering blight of organized labor"[14] Through such arguments, the NAM linked the industrial education movement to its open shop campaign and transformed the trade school issue into a symbol of labor-capital strife.

In order to discredit union apprenticeship rules in an age of perceived loss of individualism and public anxiety over increasing bureaucratic organization and concentrated corporate monopoly, the NAM linked its position to wider cultural norms: the cult of laissez-faire, the "natural" law of supply and demand, and the moral law of the self-seeking, free individual. Against labor's "great moral wrong" of "artificially" limiting the number of apprentices, the NAM claimed that open trade schools with unlimited admissions guaranteed every worker the freedom to learn a trade, a "God given birthright, further vouchsafed to him by the Declaration of Independence and the Constitution." This divine and legal right, argued one official, "should be as free as air and sunlight, and all artificial and abitrary hindrances or barriers from whatever source must sooner or later be removed. This is the law and the gospel as embodied and enunciated in the immutable and everlasting principle of the 'Fatherhood of God and the universal brotherhood of man,'—Samuel Gompers and his cohorts, and a few stray closed shop ministers of the Gospel, with closed shop union cards in their pockets, notwithstanding." Thus, the NAM attacked the unions' apprentice system on what it saw as its most vulnerable point, that of elitism and exclusivity. Against labor's unproductive and un-American restrictions, the NAM claimed that its own practices fulfilled the best republican tradition of each man having the opportunity to pursue happiness through economic betterment. Did not union control of apprentices, the NAM asked, operate in a discriminatory way, excluding outsiders? Must not the door of opportunity be open to all?[15]

In more basic terms, as Bruno Ramierz has pointed out, the NAM's attack on union apprenticeships addressed industry's need to disrupt craft union controls, which employers saw as a barrier to rationalized factory production. As David Parry put it, craft union restriction did not account for "varying degrees of natural aptitude and powers of endurance displayed by individuals and seeks to place all men . . . on the same dead level as respects his daily output and his daily wage." As a result, trade unions placed a premium on "indolence and incompetency and there is a restriction of human effort, reducing the aggregate production and increasing the cost of things produced."[16]

A further argument for the establishment of employers' trade schools centered around protecting the American boy from discrimination by foreigners who allegedly favored immigrants' children in alloting union apprenticeships. In reaction to broad changes in the occupational demographics in manufacturing that saw the replacement of native-born, Anglo-Saxon skilled mechanics with the unskilled, usually immigrant operatives, NAM trade school literature charged that the lack of opportunity for skilled training caused large numbers of American boys to wander the streets unemployed. Whether principled and concerned with the fate of American boys or not, NAM officials nevertheless acknowledged that their efforts were "essentially a business proposition of the first water."[17] Designed to curtail union involvement in apprentice employment, increase the supply of skilled labor, control and standardize the technical content of worker education, and reduce worker dissatisfaction, trade school education had proven commercial value.

While educators and the public had been reluctant to support tax funded job training in the public schools prior to 1890, the idea gained ground toward the end of the century. The manual training movement of the 1880s and early trade schools like the New York Trade School, founded in 1886 by Colonel Richard Auchmuty, had stimulated public interest in vocationalism. Progressives took up the cause of industrial education in 1906 with the formation of the National Society for the Promotion of Industrial Education, which coordinated state level efforts and generated support for federal funding. Confining its efforts to prodding the nation's steady trend toward accepting trade education, the NAM left the actual establishment of schools to manufacturers and, eventually, taxpayers. Given labor's "well-known" objections and public resistance to publicly funded vocational training, NAM employers acknowledged in 1906 that "it is too early at this stage of the game to expect that the mass of the people will accept without a murmur public trade schools supported by public taxation." Nevertheless, "the selling of the idea is paramount," explained the special supervisor of industrial education in Boston, "but once sold, it will encounter no further opposition; we want, and are going to have [trade] schools." Since workers were also voters NAM propagandists tried to sell the idea in the factory. Manufacturers should convince workers that their own self-interest lay in individual advancement through merit in an open and equitable vocational system, not through their unions' closed system riddled with favoritism. To this end, each NAM member campaigned in his own plant to "clear the horizon of discussion from the clouds of smoke which arise from the firing line of the pedagogue and the labor leader," in order to convince employees that trade education "simply relieves them of hardships" and guarantees "social and industrial advancement."[18]

In 1905 the NAM formed the Committee on Industrial Education to promote corporate sponsored trade schools. Serving as a clearinghouse for information, the committee linked similar employer movements throughout the nation, encouraging high schools to work cooperatively with business and employers to endow trade schools and defeat the unions' apprentice system. By 1906 the committee had circulated trade school literature to the superintendent of public education in every U.S. city with a population over 30,000. By 1907, the committee reported, other manufacturers' associations, such as the National Metal Trades Association and the National Tile Association, had begun training workers in schools established in their factories and supporting existing private and public trade schools through gifts of equipment and money. Thus, the National Association of Stove Manufacturers and the National Metal Trades Association financed the construction of a fully equipped foundry at an Indianapolis trade school. In Dayton, the National Cash Register Company sponsored training in a cooperative program with local high schools. In Cincinnati, voters appropriated, against local opposition, $1 million for the establishment of a technical school. The Merchants and Manufacturers Association of Milwaukee established the Milwaukee Trade School. And in Pittsburgh, the Carnegie Technical School neared completion at a cost of $12 million. By 1909 the committee reported four consistent years of "great progress" in the proliferation of trade schools, providing "one of the greatest blessings socially, economically, and industrially, that could ever come to the American people." In 1913 the National Association of Corporation Schools was organized through the invitation of the National Cash Register Company and New York Edison, both NAM members. And by 1916 the superintendent of schools of New York reported that ten high schools had cooperative programs with 63 industries representing 23 occupations. In that same year, with 201 corporation apprenticeship schools in operation nationwide, the U.S. commissioner of labor estimated attendance at 60,000.[19]

Various trade school administrators claimed to have instilled in apprentices a "shop spirit" that created an "industrial mental discipline." "We have been successful," said one school official, in "imprinting upon the plastic minds and lives of these youth that loyalty and honesty and integrity are greater even than a union label." As employer operated and state operated trade schools graduated workers who could be counted on to oppose the closed shop, resist union organizers, and willingly serve as scab labor, the term *industrial education* came to signify easily controlled, non-union labor. By 1908 NAM claimed, "new and immensely larger conquests for the 'open shop' are coming through the growth of industrial education." To guarantee a supply of such labor, the NAM advocated reducing the minimum age for trade school apprentices from fourteen to seven, a more opportune time to "impress upon the boy the things we want him to know." Industrialists placed great store in the power of trade school education to aid the social control of working class society. Had such trade schools appeared fifty years ago, remarked one administrator in 1908, "teaching men to work in harmony with employers and recognize that his [*sic*] interest is theirs, then the labor troubles which have so greatly vexed us since the War would have been largely averted."[20]

An independent, nationwide investigation of corporation schools in 1917 by Albert Beatty of the Carnegie Institute of Technology seconded some of these claims. Overwhelmingly, businessmen hiring graduates of the nation's trade schools reported improved output, decreased labor turnover, reduced waste, and fewer accidents. Most importantly, students supposedly motivated by bonuses and an individualistic "desire for gain" aspired to "duty, industry, right conduct," and "unquestioned and unhesitating obedience." These ideals "seem to be inherent in corporation schools," Beatty continued, generating favorable relations between employer and employee. The report cited the important role of the NAM in promoting the growth of corporation schools.[21]

Despite such gains in open shop education provided by manufactures' trade schools, the NAM abandoned its policy of using privately funded vocationalism as a weapon against the closed shop. The association's attempt to link vocationalism with its open shop campaign gave way within its own organization after the rise in 1908 of a faction of more enlightened and corporate-minded employers who acceded to the necessity of selling industrial education as a cross-class issue. In 1910 the NAM joined a national coalition of educators, manufacturers, and labor to seek federal funding for public vocational schools. Industrial ethics had long been popular with public school officials, and they embraced efforts to integrate industrial training with high school education. As the movement grew, states began to fund and administer vocational schools, beginning with Massachusetts in 1906. By 1910 twenty-seven states had programs. Even then, the relative philosophical weight of the business community bore down on publicly funded schools, and it remained confident that it could exercise indirect control. This confidence was borne out when the AFL denounced privately controlled public education for being ''too soft on the side of the manufacturers'' and fostering a pro-business spirit ''new in evil power.'' Convinced of the inevitability of vocational education, however, and unwilling to allow manufacturers to have exclusive influence in public trade schools, the AFL established its own vocational lobby in 1909 and began to support federal funding in 1910. In an address to the National Society for the Promotion of Industrial Education in 1913, Gompers expressed the eagerness of labor to cooperate in developing industrial education in the public schools.[22]

In less than a decade, the nation's trade school movement had seen the burden and the benefits of worker training shift from craft unions to employer-operated schools and, upon securing federal aid with the passage of the Smith-Hughes Act in 1917, to public supported vocational schools. Yet the final blow to union apprenticeship was struck less by the development of vocationalism than by the transformed work routines and the subdivided and deskilled jobs that require little training in the new factory system. For these reasons, trade unions began to lose interest in the restriction of apprentices as evidenced by the declining number of strikes for that purpose.[23]

The nation's political system offered yet another arena for ideological warfare. The face-to-face lobbying of legislators, NAM officials believed, proved a more practical means of promoting ''our interests in Washington'' than ''often slow and less direct'' attempts to influence worker education or public opinion. Admitting that, ideally, law should reflect public will, the NAM's lobbying policy more often followed U.S. District Judge William H. Speer's advice to the 1908 convention: ''Just as public opinion creates law, so you will find law creates public opinion.''[24]

As with many business interests in the Progressive Era that supported the growing centralization and standardization of business practice, the NAM had from its inception endorsed such legislation as uniformity in freight rates and state incorporation and banking regulations. After 1899, spurred by the AFL's ''aggressive'' legislative program, the NAM stepped up its political activity, endorsing or condemning individual legislators and legislation, funding anti-union congressional campaigns, warring against state and federal pro-labor bills, and influencing national party platforms. Most importantly, it opened a well-staffed and well-financed office of lobbyists in Washington. The NAM's bimonthly newsletter, the *Washington Service Bulletin*, linked the business community with events in the nation's capital. Offering timely information on pending legislation, federal court cases, and activities of administrative commissions and bureaus, the bulletin encouraged members to lobby legislators in person, petition congressional committees, and conduct telegram campaigns as crucial votes approached. Mobilizing the "collective judgement" of influential businessmen on industrial questions, the NAM's lobbyists guaranteed the expression of its opinions in legislative policy.[25]

The NAM's 1902 campaign, for example, met the AFL's legislative program head on. As in the debate over union activity during the Pullman strike, employers' arguments confronted unions in a contest of moral and patriotic virtue, pitting lawfulness against lawlessness and freedom against socialism. Attacking the unions' "vicious class legislation" which "make[s] lawful for one class of citizens to do that which remains unlawful for any other class," the NAM denounced the eight hour bill as an attempt "to repeal the bill of rights guaranteeing the freedom of the individual" and the anti-injunction bill as an act to "legalize strikes and boycotts." Confronting business power in its most sacred bastion—the courts—over its most protected right—property—the anti-injunction battle clearly touched a nerve for the NAM and most of the nation's business and manufacturing interests. To remove the courts' injunction power, explained Kirby, is to remove the employers' only protection against "lawless" unions. With the urgency of this "first contest," the NAM "aggressively" opposed legislation "extremely injurious to the industrial welfare" that represented a "test of strength between individualism and socialism." The eight hour bill incurred NAM condemnation as an unwarranted interference with the conduct of business by manufacturers who held government contracts. Joining the combined voice of many of the nation's businessmen, NAM members flooded congressmen with telegrams and defeated the bill in 1902. Until its passage in 1912, the eight hour bill met vociferous NAM opposition in every session of Congress.[26]

The Washington lobby furnished the NAM with important leverage in national policy making. Since its lobbying efforts were limited to manufacturers but overlapped with those of other commercial and business interests, the NAM created an umbrella alliance of local and national business and trade associations in 1907, the National Council for Industrial Defense (NCID). As a mouthpiece for 133 national, state, and local employer organizations, the council constituted an important source of funding for the NAM to sponsor a fully equipped staff of attorneys in Washington for the "systematic work of scrutinizing legislation." During its first year of work, the legal staff, known to association members as the "Boys on the Firing Line," analyzed 29,000 separate House and Senate bills, identifying "dangerous measures that affect the labor relation" and using these analyses to alert congressmen to labor's quest for "class privileges" or the "destruction of personal property rights." All labor bills during the 1907–

1908 legislative session were "effectively resisted," claimed the council's chief attorney, James W. Emery, as NCID funds flowed into the treasuries of open shop congressmen.[27]

By 1910 the NCID's popularity had swelled its ranks to 225 employers' organizations. Its influence among congressmen stemmed from forceful, smooth, and effective lobbying by its Washington staff, which skillfully used the symbols and manners of education and class. One legislator described Emery as "quick, alert, resourceful, keen as a Damascus blade, endowed with refinement and tact . . . and with a fluency of speech that suggests lineal descent from the great Demosthenes himself." Another termed NCID attorney Daniel Davenport "cool, judicial, calm of speech, a master a logical statement." And yet another congressmen admired Emery's "authoritative knowledge" of industrial law, admitting that were it not for his "properly organized effort," dangerous class legislation would appear on the statute books of the nation.[28]

The business community had generated sufficient pressure by 1909 to defeat the AFL's anti-injunction legislation. In one forty-eight hour period, beginning with a call for action on May 8, 1908, the NCID organizational network sent over 10,000 letters and telegrams against a pending anti-injunction bill to President Theodore Roosevelt and Congress. That same year, numerous NAM members went to Washington to join personally in the fight. Congressional committeemen "received information gladly," the delegate reported, and praised them as "patriotic, dignified men who have left their business to come and act as ex-officio members of their committee." The NAM's lobby of "scholarly and eloquent attorneys and witnesses" instructed House Judiciary Committee members that "neither the law nor patriotic public policy would admit or tolerate" the passage of anti-injunction bills. Senior members of Congress remarked to the NAM delegates that they had never experienced a "more powerful expression of business opinion upon a legislative subject."[29]

The NAM's self-proclaimed "amazing record" in defeating labor legislation greatly reduced the number of labor bills presented in committee after 1907 since, according to Parry, at least, the AFL had come to feel that sending them there was "useless" in the face of NAM resistance. "It has almost required a separate session of Congress to beat these measures back step by step," declared Parry. Eventually NAM officials announced that unions had been "effectually checkmated in their efforts to secure socialistic and semi-socialistic laws." By 1909 Van Cleave reported the defeat in Congress of the Hepburn Bill and anti-injunction "agitation." He also claimed victory when the Supreme Court declared unconstitutional an employers' liability law and ruled the AFL's boycott against the Danbury hatters a conspiracy in restraint of trade. National Association of Manufacturers propaganda interpreted these victories as the failure of union efforts in national politics and a demonstration of the power of the country's conservative business elements. "We defeated them in Washington," announced Van Cleave after the 1909 effort.[30]

The contest of ideas found its way into the struggle over national party plat-

forms. The 1904 Democratic convention declared for the open shop in a plank that
"might have been borrowed from an employers' association platform," in the
description of a *Boston Transcript* editorialist. In an attempt to counter business
influence in the 1908 campaign platforms, the AFL sent delegates to the Chicago
Republican convention to, in the NAM's opinion, "frighten the Republican National Committee into sanctioning their anti-Democratic, anti-Republican, and
anti-American propaganda." James Van Cleave succeeded Parry as NAM president in 1906 and worked to make the association an important voice in the Republican party. Meeting the AFL challenge head on, Van Cleave and other officials
journeyed to Chicago and through great effort convinced the Republican platform
committee to abandon the AFL resolutions, in particular the anti-injunction plank.
In a dramatic response to the longstanding congressional battle over anti-injunction bills and encouraged by the 1908 Supreme Court decisions in the Buck's
Stove and Range and Danbury Hatters cases, the Republican convention passed a
resolution affirming that the courts' "powers shall be preserved inviolate." With
the defeat of the AFL's platform, "the briars and thistles of Gomperism were cut
down," proclaimed Van Cleave, postponing for at least four years labor's presence on the Republican platform. In 1912, the Republicans again created a platform that pleased NAM leaders, this time without a fight with labor. Despite the
NAM's major and seemingly successful efforts at managing party platforms, both
Theodore Roosevelt and William Taft gave it a cool response. These presidents
considered the NAM's anti-union and anti-regulation stance a political liability
within the context of the growth of corporate-liberalism among the nation's progressive business, reform, and organized labor interests.[31]

Nevertheless, the NAM continued to confront unions and claim the maximum
impact from its efforts. As early as 1906 association officials claimed to detect
a shift in public opinion regarding union activity. "Only a few years ago,"
announced President Parry, "trade unionism unrestrained and militant was rapidly forcing the industries of this country to a closed shop basis." Public favor
and press sympathy had made it "almost a crime" to criticize the unions. The
public had condoned strikes, assaults on scabs, union violence, and even murder.
Lawmakers had feared political death unless they supported "semi-socialistic"
legislation. Labor had denounced judges who "sought to uphold the law." But
the tide had turned against public approval for the unions, the NAM insisted.
While achieving certain "reforms" in the years since 1900, it conceded, organized labor power had clearly lost footing. Pointing to its active role in helping
curtail this "dangerous situation," the NAM had "rendered a service to the
nation of the first magnitude." By 1910, bolstered by an increasingly organized
business community, President James Van Cleave claimed that "the Courts, the
newspapers and enlightened public sentiment all over the country dealt 'hard
blows' to the AFL [whose] autocracy has been curbed" and the "arrogance and
ignorance of [whose] leaders are not displayed so freely or so openly as they
were before the law reached out for [them]." Four years of effort, Parry maintained, had widely extended the open shop and supported legislators who resisted

the "organized coercion" of labor bills. Strikes no longer were popular, the press no longer sympathetic toward unions, and the police dutifully tracked down criminals. "What has brought about these changes?" asked the president. "The results achieved are proofs of the power of organization."[32]

Gompers agreed in part. The AFL had clearly lost footing and found itself in what he desired as a "most critical situation" due in part to the Supreme Court decisions in 1908 in the Buck's Stove and Range, Danbury Hatters, and Lowe *v*. Lawlor cases, which had declared AFL boycotts illegal and challenged normal trade union activity. By 1904, the employers' counterattack had slowed the dramatic growth of trade unionism, which actually saw a decrease in 1905 for the first time since 1897. In 1905 labor lost almost 50 percent of strikes, the highest percentage since 1894. In addition, wage cuts, the open shop campaign, and intense jurisdictional disputes reduced the effectiveness of craft unions. Not the least of the factors weakening the labor movement was its growing corporatism, which also shaped workers' definitions of the workplace and themselves. The NAM took full credit for the successful offensive against unions. Certainly other factors than those of an embattled business community were at work in view of the broad changes brought about by the reorganization of work processes in industry.[33]

At best, the NAM could claim to be one among several business voices in a nationwide struggle that curtailed the closed shop, defeated selected labor legislation, increased control over trade education, saw growing public approval of employer-led reforms, and witnessed increasing support from courts for union breaking. All this took place in the context of a national mood that at once accepted progressive reforms and acquiesced in employers' use of yellow dog contracts, Pinkertons, lockouts, and state power to thwart labor's radicalism. The NAM experienced mixed results in its efforts to unify the nation's employer associations. Only in 1916 with the founding of the National Industrial Conference Board (NICB) did effective communication occur between NAM interests and the nation's largest corporations. The heaviest contributors to the NICB, Westinghouse, General Electric, General Motors, and Firestone, joined the NAM's mid-sized manufacturers in continuing open shop propaganda and promoting scientific management.[34]

LABOR DEFINITIONS

The NAM endeavored to "answer" fundamental questions in the national discourse between labor and capital: What is labor? Do unions have the right to exist? If so, under what conditions? Which best serves the interests of society, capital or labor? Association literature pictured a national battlefield where reason, law, liberty, and individualism grappled with anarchy, tyranny, and mob rule. It portrayed organized labor as pathetic, lacking mature leadership, and ignorant of its true interests or its natural leaders. At worst, labor represented violence, evil, and the destruction of society. In his initial call to arms in 1903,

President Parry outlined the NAM's definition of unions: "Organized labor knows but one law and that is the law of physical force—the law of the Huns and Vandals, the law of the savage. It does not place its reliance upon reason and justice, but in strikes, boycotts, and coercion. It is a mob power knowing no master except its own will. Its history is stained with blood and ruin. It extends its tactics of coercion and intimidation over all classes, dictating to the press and to the politicians and strangling independence of thought." With such rhetoric, the NAM set the stage for the public dissemination of the most fevered and biting official language to emerge from corporations during the anti-union crusades of the early twentieth century.[35]

Utilizing a series of red scares that had shaken the nation after 1877, the NAM linked social order with individual moral virtue. Its literature attempted to deny modern workers any moral basis for their activities and thus to separate them from the social stature that republicanism assigned to virtuous labor. Workers had rejected the qualities of the honest, hardworking yeoman and demanded exemption from commonly accepted moral and civil standards in favor of expediency and self-interest. Their values now threatened the social whole. "Labor stands today without a soul," one official charged, "without an ideal, without an ambition, without an incentive, without a motive other than 'self' and the needs of the hour."[36]

Labor's anti-social nature was rooted in its ambivalence toward property, an issue at the heart of the matter to NAM leaders. Encouraging middle class fears of a union-inspired, socialist redistribution of property, the NAM warned that workers both coveted and resented wealth and mistook their employers' prosperity as the source of their own misery. No longer able or really expected to aspire to property ownership in industrial society, workers attacked property on the basest impulses: hate, envy, and jealousy. They "strike out blindly against capital as though it were a public enemy, attempting to destroy that which they themselves are greedy to possess," charged the Reverend Maurice Wilson at the NAM's 1909 convention. Labor leaders' "incendiary speeches" energized workers to "seize by physical force that which their merit cannot obtain for them." Anti-injunction bills aimed to "obliterate the property rights [workers] cannot deny," claimed James Emery. Playing to NAM members' anxiety, the Reverend Wilson warned of workers who "sting themselves into a rage against the educated classes . . . since they could not be educated themselves." Such persons seek to "destroy that which they cannot enjoy themselves rather than see it enjoyed by others." Popular discontent was acceptable, continued Wilson, only when based on a "rational and manly attempt" to bring reform. But when workers' anger reflected "bitterness, envy, and jealousy," it became "manifestly evil and a menace to social growth and betterment."[37]

Through this rationale, the NAM attacked workers' "fundamental misconceptions" about what constituted legitimate property rights. It challenged workers' concepts of the social usage of property not by directly engaging their ideas in meaningful social discourse, but by condemning notions of communal decision making concerning the distribution of wealth. It ridiculed workers' hopes and questioned whether they deserved upward mobility through property ownership, picturing workers' refusal to adhere to capitalist notions of private property as petty selfishness and resentment.

Unions represented a special enemy that drew the most bitter venom. Many employers had regarded early unions such as the Knights of Labor as criminal offenses even before the Supreme Court interpreted unions as combinations in restraint of trade. Summarizing union violations of America's sacred values, the NAM detailed a litany of "just causes" for its accusations. Unions violated law and property, perpetrated violence, intimidated other classes through terrorism, dictated to employers, the press, and politicians, destroyed individual rights, coerced unwilling labor into their ranks, demanded an arbitrary division of wealth, caused depressions by curtailing production, and formed the "grandest trust" of the times, the "muscle trust." True union practices, such as those of nonmilitant and company unions, were perverted by "anarchistic and socialistic tendencies" as labor willfully engineered its own difficulties. While the NAM repeatedly claimed that it did not oppose the principle of organized labor, it branded almost all union activity after the turn of the century as "lawless and socialistic" and condemned union regulations as "contrary to the law and rights of man." The message was clear. Theoretically legitimate, unions deserved the right to exist only when they did not threaten capital. President Kirby urged the 1903 convention to insist "that organized labor be denied recognition everywhere until its past blackened record is blotted out."[38]

Together with the efforts of the National Metal Trades Association, the American Anti-Boycott Association, and other open shop employers, the NAM contributed its energy to what it termed the "mounting fury and success" of the open shop drive. Representing a "fundamental, basic principle of American liberty," individualism, and virility, open shop factories allowed free individuals to demonstrate their superior merit through reliance on their own ability and industry. "As American independence was to our forefathers," declared a member, "so the open shop is to the employer of today." By contrast, closed shop unions invaded the constitutional rights and destroyed the "manhood" of the individual.[39]

While less effective in such sectors as the building trades, the open shop drive effectively stopped the rise of unionism in the steel industry. Thus, the NAM's definition of industrial peace became, at least in the metal trades, that of the open shop. By 1906 Samuel Gompers could remark, "Today the United States Steel Corporation is practically free from any 'inconvenience' from the organized labor movement. Peace in its plant is the sort of peace that the Czar of Russia had when he proclaimed 'peace reigns in Warsaw.' " "Insisting that the open shop victory could not have come without public approval, a U.S. Steel official claimed, "the people of this country are with us."[40] "Pushed so vigorously" by the unions, the closed shop contributed "most largely to the growth of an antagonistic public opinion," argued a *Wall Street Journal* editorialist. When unions "seek an absolute monopoly of labor," they offend the sentiments of "fair play and love of liberty which prevails among . . . the people," he wrote.[41] Throughout the open shop campaign, David Parry was recognized as its national leader.

While deploring almost every form of labor collectivity, the NAM also portrayed individual workers as ignorant followers of demagogues. Citing the social dangers of rampant ignorance, it predicted that a "thoughtless mob full of ignorant men," would eventually spell the downfall of the Republic if uncontrolled by "mind." Unions' mindless use of violence indicated a serious ignorance of economic law. With little attention to "clear and coherent propositions" established by the "fathers of the Republic," workers easily slipped under the "evil influence" of the AFL's "specious theories and meaningless platitudes on the subject of economics," the "exploded theories of Carl Marx [*sic*]" and the "ingenuous sophistries of Samuel Gompers." This fundamental lack of understanding gave workers the mistaken hope of improving their condition by "checking production and making life and property insecure." Ignorant men generate ignorant theories, observed C. W. Post, the cereal manufacturer, such as the misleading idea "that 'labor creates all wealth and therefore all wealth belongs to labor.' This false theory sometimes produces . . . an inference that the workmen created the factory, and why not take it and run it." Workers would never desire such takeovers had they developed a "clean cut knowledge of the facts." And the "facts" indicated that labor indeed was no longer the source of wealth. "Physical labor cannot create," Post reasoned in an address to fellow members, "it can only execute; mind is the only creator and it uses physical and material tools to carry out and express in material, its creations."[42]

Labor leaders drew especial criticism. In July of 1910, for example, NAM Chief Counsel James Emery addressed the American Academy of Political and Social Science following an anti-injunction speech by Samuel Gompers. Ridiculing the labor leader, Emery characterized Gompers' talk as confused because he "half-apprehended" the facts, proved none of his contentions, and violated fundamental principles of justice.[43] To the NAM, the unsuccessful strikes of 1903 severely tested organized labor's "spurious" economic doctrines, handing unions a "valuable lesson in economics and law observance."[44] As manufacturers increasingly won individual labor disputes after 1900, they pointed to the decline of sympathetic strikes, the proliferation of open shops, and broken or negotiated strikes. These events, declared Parry, at once vindicated capital's economic theories and signified the falsity of labor's.

Working people's lack of intelligence created additional problems: they failed to recognize their own interests, ignored "rightful" leaders, their employers, and thus fell prey to the manipulation of demagogues. "Our greatest troubles have been brought upon us," claimed NAM officials, because "we have allowed ourselves to drift away from our men, and permitted the walking delegate . . . to mold the opinions of those who work for us with their hands." Seeking to wrest labor from the hands of its "unnatural leaders," regain paternal control, and harmonize class interests, NAM members in 1910 began to champion accident prevention and worker's compensation in their own plants.[45]

Labor radicalism, the NAM claimed, originated from "criminals and outcasts" from other nations, all the more dangerous because unrestrained by nationalist loyalty, the "spiritual kinsman of persons who, in Russia, Turkey or other semi-civilized communities, throw bombs into churches, public halls or crowded streets and murder innocent people." The anthracite miners struck in 1902 because, Parry explained, "Tens of thousands of [them] are Poles, Hungarians, Slavs, and other foreigners, who can not spell a word of English." Many of these came to America with "anarchistic and socialistic sentiments" that made them easy prey for "agitators."[46]

Unions represented a subversive "conspiracy against both the individual and the state." Exercising a "despotism that is without mercy," the Reverend Maurice Wilson revealed, this conspiracy used "violent and virulent" methods, "defiant of the laws of the land and contemptuous of its courts." Directed at the nation's heart, the conspiracy used the un-American boycott and picket, "methods not of strikers but of highwaymen." Strikes represented criminal conspiracies, boycotts were "crimes," limitation of apprentices was "murder to the nation," the eight hour law constituted "socialism" and anti-injunction activity amounted to "anarchy." The specter of anarchy drew a vehement response from 1908 conventiongoers, as Reverend Wilson gave an eloquent warning. Labor anarchy abounded in the land, constituting a "treason still to be put down." In the United States, the "poisonous doctrines of the red flag [must] receive no quarter in the land of the Stars and Stripes."[47]

To the NAM, the AFL represented an alien entity, disloyal to the United States. "There has grown up in our midst," said Counsel Emery, "imperium in imperio, a state within a state, appealing and nourishing that peculiar thing . . . class consciousness." The AFL "sets the decrees of its leaders above the laws of the land," representing an "absolutism which violates the orders of its courts, denounces its judges, and repudiates the authority of the nation." Even Holy Writ "tells us that a house divided against itself cannot stand." Citing the example of the Five Civilized Tribes as "a government within a government," Emery recounted the abolition of separate Indian nations and their forced merging "into the mass of the citizenship." The U.S. government, he said, should deal with the AFL just as it dealt with the Indian, overpowering leaders and forcing them to adhere to "accepted" legal and social norms. The way to confine irresponsible unions within corporate society was to force them to incorporate, NAM leaders reasoned. Their ideas anticipate corporate liberal notions of social stability and responsibility. Courts should compel incorporated unions to be "legally responsible so that the law can reach them," just as incorporated capital is punishable when it violates its agreements. Unions' disregard of contracts compared with the diligence of employers in fulfilling theirs compelled the law to force "reciprocal and equal" duties and responsibilities on both sides.[48]

In contrast to this picture of labor demagoguery with its anarchy, treason, conspiracy, despotism, amorality, ignorance, evil, and corruption, NAM rhetoric portrayed capital as a civilizing and even divinely inspired force. The very embodiment of the Victorian social ideal, businessmen attempted "upon sound principles and with right motives, and through kindness, courtesy and self-sacrifice [to establish] peaceable and sound relations between master and man." At each annual convention, the membership heard a ministerial exhortation affirming the moral and social beneficence and the divine origin of their efforts. Frequent use of phrases like "the gospel of industrial truth" equated businessmen with "righteous people." God himself, the Reverend S. Edward Young assured the association, was the "Great Manufacturer"; lesser manufacturers carried out his work on earth. "We take thy material in our hands and make it more marketable."[49]

Second only to holiness, appeals to a selective history and carefully controlled patriotic images furnished grounds for discrediting labor's social role. "All history proves that progress is the universal law of nature," the NAM maintained, and the entrepreneur, his causes and principles, furnished its driving force. Capital's social responsibility preserved "Amercianism"—the liberty and property rights that were the "cornerstone of modern civilization." "Business and patriotism go hand in hand," reported President Parry; "industrialism is beneficent, civilizing and uplifting. It is the enemy of war, of despotism, of ignorance and poverty. In truth, its foes are the foes of mankind." Thus, the NAM's claim to interpret "all history" and tradition sought to deny the social role of labor and elevate that of entrepreneurs who built and defended the nation and guaranteed its progress.[50]

Such certainty flowed from the NAM's belief in the universal rightness of natural law and classical economics. To curb labor's "improper theories and unsound principles," it offered "unrepealed and unrepealable" economic theories that "cannot be assailed on any sensible grounds." Labor mistakenly believed that "every question is susceptible of arbitration," that there are "no fundamental verities upon which human life is based," that it would be possible by legislation to "repeal the law of gravity." In contrast, the NAM touted the existence of "elementary theories which cannot be sacrificed." If they were surrendered or compromised, then "all is gone and truth itself becomes a shadow." As James Emery put it, "the principles for which we stand are determined and fixed principles . . . , not your ideas or mine," but rather the "heritage we have received from others, the wisdom of all the past." Established at the very outset in English and American law, these eternal principles were passed on through the "immortal document that announced our freedom," the U.S. Constitution, to rest in "decisions of our courts in modern days." The economic guidelines of the NAM were the "same old principles of American government applied once and forever to the solution of the industrial question." It was merely the "correctness and justness of its position based on historical truths," the NAM insisted, that mandated the right to establish its economic policy in society.[51]

The NAM portrayed industrial interests as representing those of the entire society. "The Association does not exist for political power, for aggression of the rights of others or for the individual profit of its members," President Parry explained. "It stands solely for the common good. Whatever advances American industry advances the material prosperity of the entire American people, and whatever is detrimental to American industry reduces the wages, the profits, and the material comforts of the entire people." Any other viewpoint, especially labor's, was based upon "prejudice, class hatred, misplaced sympathy or visionary ideas." "We ask for no class privileges," said a NAM leader, "and only insist that none be granted to others." The rhetoric of classlessness did not fool radical unionists. So clearly did the NAM articulate its own class interests that the Western Federation of Miners welcomed its "straight out tactics" that "allow[ed] the class struggle full scope." In the view of the editor of the *New York Daily People*, open capital-labor confrontations only hastened the socialist triumph. More conservative union leaders saw less value in open battle, however, in part because, as John Mitchell explained, "pulpit, platform, press and public" had united in condemning union "lawlessness."[52]

In contrast to the disruptive presence of labor, capital appeared in NAM literature as a rational, peaceloving social force. Against union lawlessness, capital offered the power of its efficiency, organization, and influence to "control and quiet the national situation." "It seems repugnant to our ideas of twentieth century civilization to fight out this question in the gladiatorial arena," the association declared. "[We] do not desire strife and labor should not seek it." National Association of Manufacturers officials exhorted unions to employ reason, not force "because those things which are gained by violence are half lost in the gaining," while "those things which are gained by reason are gained forever."[53]

Openly defying labor on its own stated grounds of class warfare and ignoring the contradiction in NAM President George Pope's call for manufacturers to "stand together . . . as a class," the NAM nevertheless argued an ultimate identity of class interests. On the contrary, it was union leaders, demagogic politicians, and the "prejudiced writing" of journalists that stirred up class hatred and fostered socialism. Why else, asked Pope, were the relations of employer and employee so cordial only a few years ago? "A spirit of cooperation, a desire to assist, a willingness to serve one's employer, was the keynote of industrial life." Politicians had disrupted this idyll with laws to improve working conditions, laws which, to Pope, "are the breeder of class consciousness and are . . . compelling the employers . . . to be segregated into a class." National Association of Manufacturers members' emphasis on classlessness came from their focus on rugged individualism and fit with their view of an American society that provided the opportunity and encouragement for exceptional persons to succeed through self-denial and perseverance. David Parry's arguments against socialism centered on its "delegating to one individual or small groups of individuals the management of the interests of many individuals."[54]

The NAM equated its social influence with the forces of democracy and patriotism. Repressing questions about the fundamental working of the system and ignoring new forms of hierarchy in the workplace, it assigned individual blame for failure, at least the economic failure of working class existence. Working people and their collective activity were abstracted into the easily discredited "isms" of the age—socialism, anarchism, radical unionism—a process that helped reduce the "labor problem" to a confrontation between right and wrong. Thus the association prescribed labor docility, the open shop, hard work, and deference in place of strikes, closed shop unionism, and workers' control. By discrediting radical social criticism, the NAM sought to thwart the formation of an anti-capitalist collective will. And it insisted that economics was an independent activity that could not be circumscribed by morality. All these efforts it couched in the language of preserving the nation's moral fiber.

The NAM's inflammatory rhetoric, which earned members the title "hotheads among employers," represented a confrontational style that disappeared after 1913 in the conciliatory tone of paternalism, company unionism, and finally "industrial democracy."[55] The emergence of a generation of progressive NAM leaders after 1908, their desire to improve its image after the 1913 scandal that exposed its Washington lobbying activities, and the accession of seemingly anti-business Democrats to the presidency and control of Congress in 1912 forced the NAM to follow a less extreme policy that promoted "industrial betterment."[56]

Articulating the nation's most extreme position in the first decade of the century, NAM rhetoric lent a bitterness to the labor-capital dialogue that kept employers' efforts at union control in the public mind. But vituperative denunciations and frontal assault became less necessary as organized labor increasingly entered into contract negotiation and unions led in rejecting social violence. "In recent years," Hayes Robbins, editor of *Public Policy*, observed, employers had "change[d] in sentiment," retreating from extreme anti-unionism, confident that labor had "safely modified to a legitimate basis the 'extreme measures' it had employed in the past."[57] "Rarely, indeed, does the modern employer dare to espouse out-and-out autocracy," J. David Houser concluded after taking a nationwide survey of employer attitudes toward employees in the early 1920s. Much of the employers' opinion in this survey was "apparently intended for public consumption" and thus "inevitably bore the marks of an attempt to gain general approbation," as employers adopted some form of welfare work in their factories. If they did so with an eye toward the "social reaction toward such an activity," it was only to link in the public eye the twin motives of social benevolence and business acumen.[58]

Despite its softer tone, the message imparted to the larger society endeavored to proclaim and validate the social status and ideological authority of capital and its representatives. What we are, NAM employers proclaimed, is the antithesis of what labor represents, as they pictured themselves as a benevolent social force that directed the nation's destiny toward national development and progress. In contrast, labor's organizations, methods, and ideas appeared as socially destructive. Through resistance to union controlled apprenticeships that restricted social mobility, the NAM voiced old-fashioned, American values of freedom of choice, individualism, and social virtue. Undesirable labor groups, no matter how strongly they represented the same values, were vilified, their ideas censored, and their organizations condemned. These definitions attempted to polarize the relationship between the social function of capital and labor, juxtaposing capital's rational behavior to labor's violence and anarchy. Capital embodied wisdom and knowledge against labor's willful lack of understanding. Capital represented patriotic efforts toward progressive social betterment while labor indulged in a self-interested expediency. And while capital represented virility, labor, despite its capacity for violence, embodied the opposite, presumably impotence. This analogy between sexual potency and national survival was made easier given links in the national psyche between manly vigor and state assertiveness in an age of triumphant economic and geographic expansionism.

Propagated in a highly emotional pitch, often reflecting hatred and fear of working people, NAM propaganda heightened the class consciousness of its members. As these manufacturers articulated their ideas and created national platforms, they generated among themselves a mood of solidarity and affirmed and rededicated a sense of rightness that warranted, to them, a moral, legal, ethical, and scientific mandate for their actions. Their discourse against labor had widened the borders and shifted the center of the critical public dialogue to encompass their extreme anti-unionism. As the NAM had appropriated patriotism, republicanism, and morality for itself, it claimed to inherit and fulfill the republican tradition. In actuality it had violated fundamental tenets of that credo. Its attack on the labor theory of value, for example, challenged not just Marx, but the foundation of the republican producer ideology. It had, through omission, distortion, and the use of selective information, made this most American of beliefs seem un-American, the product of foreign socialists and anarchists bent on destruction.

The significance of the NAM's ideas lay not merely in their circulation among elites or their expression of some conspiracy to hold down labor. It was, rather, a broadcasting of ideological power through normative definitions into the economic and political debates of the age. And, as Robert Wiebe has pointed out, businessmen's tactical advantages of wealth, vision, and organization gave them a lead in the national debate over economic issues.[59] National Association of Manufacturers arguments should be taken perhaps as statements less about reality than about the mentality of an important and vocal segment of the business community during the period of emergence of a new national bourgeoisie. The educational and political activities of the NAM formed part of capital's efforts to transform the cultural ''images'' of labor and capital in an age when these images constituted an important part of its social power.

In the new mood of liberal-progressivism that arose in the decades before the war and came to fruition with wartime productivity, the emphasis on the social disruptions of industrial growth gave way to a laudation of the material and social promise inherent in productivity. Corporate public relations, informed with more tact and finesse, deemphasized irreconcilable interests in favor of enfolding them in the common tasks of modernization, growth, and upward mobility. After the rise of corporate liberalism with its self-interested, corporate-minded workers, the NAM's union busting became unnecessary. It was no longer important to brand unions as evil; it was enough to accuse them of inefficiency, of not being team players, of being socially undesirable because they restrained progress.

In this context, it became easy for capital to favor conservative unions while nurturing distaste for the more threatening aspects of militant unionism, wildcat strikes, sympathy strikes, boycotts, and violence. The NAM's propaganda activity had joined a corporate-led information campaign that helped keep these distinctions uppermost in the public mind. It had helped embed in U.S. political consciousness a growing national suspicion that militant labor was somehow out to subvert the nation and the idea that the principal social threat came from the Left. Public disapproval of the post–World War I strikes and the identification of labor radicalism with the Russian Revolution and world communism had roots in cultural idioms forged in this period. Thereafter, capital never had to reach very far to find public support for its actions toward unions.

APPENDIX: SELECTED MEMBERSHIP IN NAM, 1909

American Steel Foundry

Bessemer Coke Co.

Boston Bridge Works

Buck's Stove and Range Co.

Carter's Ink Co.

Cary Safe Co.

Chicago Portland Cement

Colorado Iron Works

Diamond Chain & Mfg. Co.

Dodge Mfg. Co.

Doubleday, Page & Co.

H. H. Franklin Mfg. Co.

W. S. Frazier Co.

W. P. Fuller & Co.

R. P. Hanes Knitting Co.

H. J. Heinz Co.

Joseph Campbell Co.

Lackawanna Mills

Link Belt Co.

National Cash Register

Nicholson File Co.

Olympia Brewing Co.

Packard Motor Car Co.

Peace Dale Mfg. Co.

Philip Morris & Co.

Pierce Arrow Motor Car Co.

Pittsburgh Plate Glass

Postum Cereal Co.

Remington Typewriter Co.

Searle Mfg. Co.

Sidney Blumenthal & Co.

Sloss Sheffield Steel & Iron Co.

John B. Stetson Co.

St. Regis Paper Co.

Studebaker Brothers Mfg.

Van Camp Packing Co.

Westinghouse Machine Co.

Yale & Towne Mfg. Co.

Source: American Industries, 10 (December 1909): 12–51.

NOTES

1. National Association of Manufacturers, *Proceedings of the Annual Convention of the National Association of Manufacturers*, hereafter cited as NAM, *Proceedings*, 1906, 15; 1903, 133. Parry was president of the Parry Manufacturing Company of Indianapolis, a carriage maker employing 1,400 in 1895. He later became part owner of the Indianapolis Southern Railroad and president of the Overland Automobile Company. His workers were paid piecework rates and, he claimed, presented no union "problems."

2. In the reading room of the Astor Branch of the New York Public Library, over 7,000 trade journals were available in 1900. The combined monthly circulation of the seven machinery, electric, engineering, and mining journals published by McGraw Hill was 80,952; Michael Hickey, "Commercial Value of the Industrial Press," *American Industries* 10 (Oct. 1909): 25; Clarence Bonnett "The Evolution of Business Groupings," *Annals of the American Academy of Political and Social Science*, hereafter cited as *Annals*, 179 (May 1935): 1–8.

3. Clarence Bonnett, *Employers' Associations in the United States* (New York, 1922), 14; Philip S. Foner, *History of the Labor Movement in the United States*, vol. 3 (New York, 1964), 31–39; C. H. Parker, "The Decline in Trade Union Membership," *Quarterly Journal of Economics* 24 (1909–1910): 564–69. William F. Willoughby, "Employers' Associations for Dealing With Labor in the United States," *Quarterly Journal*

of Economics 20 (1905–1906): 110–50. Through trade agreements with various unions, trade associations attempted to curtail union power. Spurred by the revival of prosperity after 1890 and the need for predictable wage costs, contract negotiations peaked between 1898 and 1902. Soon afterward, many of the nation's largest trade associations blamed unions for subverting trade agreements and eliminated the closed shop or abolished unions within their trades.

4. John Keith, "The New Unions of Employers," *Harpers' Weekly* 48 (Jan. 23, 1904): 131.

5. Albert Steigerwalt, *The National Association of Manufacturers 1895–1914; A Study in Business Leadership* (Grand Rapids, Michigan, 1964), 40, 101; NAM *Proceedings*, 1904, 146; 1909, 68; In 1904, 77 percent of NAM membership fell in New York, Pennsylvania, Ohio, Massachusetts, Illinois, Indiana, Michigan, New Jersey, and Connecticut. A majority of members represented iron, steel, and the machinery trades; other industries included tools and hardware, vehicle manufacture, cement and clay products, paper and printing, textiles, oils, paints and pharmaceuticals, crockery and glassware, food products, leather manufacturer, rubber, lumber and pianos, jewelry, and optical goods. See Appendix A for a list of representative companies from *American Industries* 10 (Dec. 1909): 12–51; Crissey quote from testimony of Mr. James A. Emery, general counsel of the NAM before the Industrial Relations Commission, April 8, 1914, cited in NAM, *Open Shop Encyclopedia for Debaters* (New York, 1921), 20.

6. For discussions of the relative strength within the business community of the National Civic Federation and the NAM, see David Montgomery, *Workers' Control in America* (New York, 1979), 61, 62, 66; the NAM had denounced the NCF for having been captured "body, boots and breeches" by the Gompers-Mitchell elements of the AFL; John Kirby, "The Goal of the Labor Trust," *American Industries* 10 (Feb. 1910): 16; traditional accounts of the NCF include Robert Wiebe, *Businessmen and Reform: A Study of the Progressive Movement* (New York, 1962); Philip Taft, *The A.F. of L. in the Time of Gompers* (New York, 1957); Marguerite Green *The National Civic Federation and the American Labor Movement–1900–1925* (Washington, D.C., 1956); James Weinstein *The Corporate Ideal in the Liberal State, 1900–1918* (Boston, 1968), see 11–12 for anti-union NCF membership.

7. NAM, *Proceedings*, 1903, 13; 1904, 243–44; John Kirby, "The Benefits of Industrial Combinations," *Annals* 42 (July 1912): 119–24.

8. The NAM's new, hostile attitude conformed to the general hardening of attitudes by several major trade associations whose directors were also NAM members and whose experience with broken contracts after 1900 led them to accuse unions of failing to abide by the contracts and to adopt a policy of opposition to unions in general. Thus, the National Metal Trades Association terminated its agreement with the International Association of Machinists in 1901; the National Founders' Association terminated the Iron Moulders' Union beginning in 1904, as did the National Erectors' Association the International Association of Bridge and Structural Iron Workers; and in 1906 the United Typothetae of America eliminated the closed shop of the International Typographical Union; Willoughby, "Employers Associations," 119–23; Bonnett, *Employers' Associations*, 14; Montgomery, *Workers' Control*, 57–58; NAM, *Proceedings*, 1903, 14–17; 1905, 209.

9. NAM, *Proceedings*, 1903, 16–17, 229–30; 1908, 325; 1907, 44, 136; 1906, 13; George D. Blackwood, "Techniques and Sterotypes in the Literature of the National

Association of Manufacturers Concerning Industry and Labor,'' M.A. thesis, University of Chicago, 1947.

10. NAM, *Proceedings*, 1910, 97.

11. Ibid., 1910, 96; 1911, 78; 1909, 95; Harold Livesay, *Samuel Gompers and Organized Labor in America* (Boston, 1978), 171. These expenditures can be compared to the $25,000 spent by the New York Building Trades' Employers' Association alone on detectives whose work led to the conviction of leaders of the city's 1902 building strikes. John Keith, ''The New Unions of Employers,'' 132–33. The AFL estimates on NAM expenditures from *American Federationist* (Oct. 1917), quoted in National Association of Manufacturers, *The Law's Supremacy; Decision of the Supreme Court of the District of Columbia in re Samuel Gompers, John Mitchell, and Frank Morrison* (New York, 1912), 8.

12. The National Association of Manufacturers, *Open Shop Encyclopedia for Debaters* (New York, 1921); see Montgomery, *Workers' Control*, 57–63; NAM, *Proceedings*, 1904, 24.

13. Edward Bemis, ''Relation of Labor Organizations to the American Boy and to Trade Instruction,'' *Annals* 5 (July 1894-June 1895): 233; Wright quote, NAM, *Proceedings*, 1907, 116; see also David Cohen and Marvin Lazerson, ''Education and the Corporate Order,'' *Socialist Revolution* 2 (March-April 1972), 47–72, and Sol Cohen, ''The Industrial Education Movement 1906–1917,'' *American Quarterly* 20 (Spring 1968): 95–110; on attitudes of employers toward trade schools, see United States Commissioner of Labor, *Seventeenth Annual Report: Trade and Technical Education* (Washington, D.C., 1902), 367–95; Melvin Barlow, *History of Industrial Education in the United States* (Peoria, Ill., 1967); Marvin Lazerson and W. Norton Grubb, *American Education and Vocationalism: A Documentary History, 1870–1970* (New York, 1974); for a discussion of middle class, corporate, progressive, and labor interests at work in the industrial education movement, see Elizabeth Fones-Wolf, ''The Politics of Vocationalism: Coalitions and Industrial Education in the Progressive Era,'' *Historian* 46 (Spring 1983): 39–55; Bruno Ramirez, *When Workers Fight: The Politics of Industrial Relations in the Progressive Era* (Westport, Conn. 1978).

14. NAM, *Proceedings*, 1908, 36, 325; 1907, 113, 115; 1905, 144; 1906, 56, 77, 81; on the NAM's efforts against organized labor in the industrial education campaign, see Lawrence Cremin, *The Transformation of the School* (New York, 1965), 37–38.

15. NAM, *Proceedings*, 1907, 112; 1908, 23, 114; Carroll Wright, the U.S. commissioner of labor reported that early on, rank and file members of machinists unions had come to accept trade school instruction, realizing that ''the dominant idea of 'everyone for himself' makes it important that every mechanic should acquire all the knowledge possible.'' United States Commissioner of Labor, *Seventeenth Annual Report*, 420; NAM, *Proceedings*, 1904, 131–32.

16. NAM, *Proceedings*, 1903, 19–20, quoted in Ramirez, *When Workers Fight*, 93.

17. ''Industrial Training in the High School,'' *American Industries* 10 (March 1910): 37; *Proceedings*, 1906, 77; 1908, 20; Stephen Meyer, *The Five Dollar Day: Labor Management and Social Control in the Ford Motor Company, 1908–1921* (Albany, N.Y., 1981), especially chapter 3, ''The Social Impact of the New Technology at the Workplace,'' 37–66.

18. Lazerson and Grubb, *American Education and Vocationalism*, 6; NAM, *Proceedings*, 1906, 154; 1907, 116, 134.

19. Robert Wuest, ''Industrial Betterment Activities of the National Metal Trades

Association,'' *Annals* 44 (July 1912): 75–85; United States Commissioner of Labor, *Seventeenth Annual Report* (1902), 20, in Harold Clark and Harold Sloan, *Classrooms in the Factories: An Account of Educational Activities Conducted by American Industry* (Rutherford, N.J., 1958), 6; NAM, *Proceedings*, 1906, 50–55, 61, 63; 1907, 111, 137; 1909, 18; Albert J. Beatty, *Corporation Schools* (Bloomington, 1918), 44, 140, 147.

20. Thus the period 1900–1917 marked the triumph of the vocational education movement, and most later vocational education issues "can best be understood as a reworking and consolidation of themes and practices established during the earlier period." Lazerson and Grubb, *American Education and Vocationalism*, 2; James Van Cleave, *Industrial Education as an Essential Factor in Our National Prosperity* (New York, 1908), 8; NAM, *Proceedings*, 1906, 81; 1908, 115–16.

21. Beatty, *Corporation Schools*, 76–87, 110–11; firms cited in the report included Swift and Company, the Cadillac Company, Winchester Repeating Arms Company, the Southern Pacific Railroad, Burroughs Adding Machine, and Packard Motor Company, which characterized graduates as having been "Packardized."

22. American Federation of Labor, "Reports of the Committee on Industrial Education" (1910), in Lazerson and Grubb, *American Education and Vocationalism*, 105–06; organized labor supported trade schools "due to the influence of Gompers and the ideals of business unionism which were moving organized labor toward accommodation with large scale industry," and because of "labor's assumption that it was not powerful enough to defeat a coalition of businessmen and educators and would therefore have to concentrate on preventing business domination" of the schools; Lazerson and Grubb, *American Education and Vocationalism*, 21; Beatty, *Corporation Schools*, 9; Fones-Wolf, "Politics of Vocational Education," 46–50; Kenneth Gray "Support for Industrial Education by the National Association of Manufacturers: 1895–1917" unpublished Ph.D. diss., Virginia Polytechnic Institute 1908, 99–101; on the corporate state and educational reform, see Joel Spring, *Education and the Rise of the Corporate State*, (Boston, 1972).

23. Lazerson and Grubb, *American Education and Vocationalism*, 34; Bemis, "Relation of Labor Organizations," 221.

24. James W. Van Cleave, "The Work of Employers' Associations in the Settlement of Labor Disputes," *Annals* 36 (Sept. 1910): 122; NAM, *Proceedings*, 1908, 189; 1909, 114.

25. National Association of Manufacturers, *Washington Service Bulletin* 68 (Feb. 1918): 1.

26. NAM, *Proceedings*, 1903, 15; 1910, 92; 1906, 25–26; business used injunctions in labor disputes, the AFL reasoned, upon the theory that "conducting business is a property right, that business property and that the earning power of property engaged in business is itself property [which] could and ought to be protected by the court's 'equity power'." American Federation of Labor Report of the "Committee on Presidents Report" (1906) cited in NAM, *The Law's Supremacy*, 8.

27. Van Cleave, "Employers' Associations," 122–23; NAM, *Proceedings*, 1908, 107, 285; 1910, 94. National Council for Industrial Defense membership included, in addition to the NAM, the American Anti-Boycott Association (League for Industrial Rights), the American Cotton Manufacturers' Association, the National Erectors' Association, the National Founders' Association, the National Metal Trades Association, the United Typothetae of America, the National Association of Implement and Vehicle Manufacturers, the National Association of Cotton Manufacturers, the American Hardware Manufacturers' Association. Source, *National Industrial Council Bulletin* cited in Albion Taylor,

Labor Policies of the National Association of Manufacturers (Urbana, 1927), 29; Wiebe, *Businessmen and Reform*, 109–10.

28. Steigerwalt, *The National Association of Manufacturers*, 125; NAM, *Proceedings*, 1909, 112.

29. NAM, *Proceedings*, 1906, 90; 1908, 289, 107, 121.

30. Ibid., 1907, 14; 1906, 24; 1908, 108; 1909, 59; Foner, *History of Labor*, 3, 229, 337. The failure of the anti-injunction campaign was demonstrated by the increased use of injunctions from 28 issued in the 1880s, to 122 in the 1890s, 328 in the 1900s, 446 in the 1910s, and 921 in the 1920s. Montgomery, *Workers' Control*, 325.

31. "The Open Shop Issue Settling Itself," *Boston Transcript* editorial, reprinted in Public Policy, *Labor, Capital and the Public: A Discussion of the Relations Between Employees, Employers, and the Public* (Chicago, 1905), 110; NAM, *Proceedings*, 1909, 59; 1910, 81, 92; Foner, *History of Labor*, vol. 3, 305; Wiebe, *Businessmen and Reform*, 110–11.

32. NAM, *Proceedings*, 1906, 15–16; 1909, 60; Foner, *History of Labor*, vol. 3, 55, 59.

33. Fones-Wolf, "The Politics of Vocationalism," 46; Taft, *The A.F. of L. in the Time of Gompers*, 262–71; Taylor, "Labor Policies of the National Association of Manufacturers," 82–86; Parker, "The Decline of Trade Union Membership," 566–67; Martin Sklar, *The Corporate Reconstruction of American Capitalism: The Market, the Law, and Politics, 1890–1916*, (New York, 1988), 224–27, 256; Ramirez, *When Workers Fight*, 97–100; Samuel Gompers, "Free Speech and the Injunction Order," *Annals* 36 (July 1910): 255–64.

34. Wiebe, *Businessmen and Reform*, 30–33.

35. NAM, *Proceedings*, 1903, 18.

36. Ibid., 1906, 78.

37. Ibid., 1909, 263; 1907, 19; 1908, 286.

38. Ibid., 1909, 17; 1904, 73; 1903, 199.

39. In industry, the first declaration for open against closed shop came from the National Metal Trades Association in 1901. For a discussion of the open shop drive in the metal trades, see Montgomery, *Workers' Control*, 57–63, 67; NAM, *Proceedings*, 1907, 237; 1904, 76; 1906, 13; see also Open Shop Department, NAM, *Evidence in the Case for the Open Shop*, (New York, 1923).

40. Samuel Gompers, "Discussion," *Annals* 44 (July 1912): 58; Raynal Bolling, "The United States Steel Corporation and Labor Conditions," *Annals* 36 (July 1912): 353–62; see Montgomery, *Workers' Control*, 57–63.

41. "No Monopoly of Labor," *Wall Street Journal* editorial, n.d., reprinted in Public Policy, *Labor, Capital and the Public*, 96.

42. NAM, *Proceedings*, 1905, 282; 1910, 95.

43. James A. Emery, "Use and Abuse of Injunctions in Trade Disputes," *Annals* 36 (July 1910): 127–36, quote 127.

44. NAM, *Proceedings*, 1910, 95; 1905, 282; 1904, 15.

45. National Association of Manufacturers, *Accident Prevention and Relief* (New York, 1911); Foner, *History of Labor*, vol. 3, 43; Ferdinand Schwedtmann, "The National Association of Manufacturers' Attitude Toward Injured Members of the Industrial Army," *American Industries* 10 (May 1910): 18–22; NAM, *Proceedings*, 1904, 75.

46. NAM, *Proceedings*, 1907, 46; Parry quoted in Wiebe, *Businessmen and Reform*, 191.

47. NAM, *Proceedings*, 1909, 264; 1905, 220.

48. Van Cleave, "Employers' Associations," 121–22; NAM, *Proceedings*, 1909, 67, 212.

49. NAM, *Proceedings*, 1906, 68–69; 1908, 187; 1910, 3.

50. NAM, *Proceedings*, 1910, 50; 1906, 13; recognizing the NAM appeals to selective history in dubbing the Buck's Stove and Range boycott "un-American," the AFL condemned the "scribes and screechers" of the gentry "who invoke the eagle's scream in the effort to drown the voice of labor," and countered: "all students of American History know that the 'Boston Tea Party' was an American boycott against British merchants." *American Federationist* (Oct. 1970), cited in NAM, *The Law's Supremacy*, 13.

51. NAM, *Proceedings*, 1910, 96; 1906, 68.

52. NAM, *Proceedings*, 1906, 11–12; 1905, 87; 1903, 95; 1910, 96; "John Mitchell on Violence," *Chicago Tribune* editorial, reprinted in Public Policy, *Labor, Capital and the Public*, 52.

53. NAM, *Proceedings*, 1904, 16, 75; 1906, 71; 1905, 209.

54. NAM, *Proceedings*, 1914, 4–15; 1907, 84; 1911, 65–90, quoted in Wiebe, *Businessmen and Reform*, 190–91, 193.

55. By 1914, the association had softened its anti-union stance to conform with the current popularity of company unions, shop committees, and industrial councils. Such programs, instituted partly by the Federal War Labor Board were favored by the NAM, itself submitting to demands for collective bargaining initiated by the employer or the federal government and whose legitimacy thus rested on a source other than organized labor. This constituted a recognition by the NAM of the value of promoting reform, NAM, *Proceedings*, 1914, 4–15; Phillip G. Wright, "The Contest in Congress Between Organized Labor and Organized Business," *Quarterly Journal of Economics* 29 (Feb. 1915): 239.

56. An early conciliatory gesture toward labor by the new progressive leadership included joining the AFL in efforts to pass vocational educational legislation, the Page-Wilson Bill in 1912. Herbert Mills, a Harvard graduate, Wisconsin manufacturer, and chair of the NAM's Committee on Industrial Education wrote "It will be a great day . . . when the manufacturers and the labor leaders, instead of standing upon their differences and fighting, find even one vital and great issue on which they can unite, and fight side by side with strength and good will." This bill failed in 1912, but Mills continued with the AFL to press for vocational education until the passage of the Smith-Hughes Act in 1917; Herbert Mills to Carroll Page, March 3, 1912, cited in Gray, "Support for Industrial Education," 155; Van Cleave, "The Work of Employer's Associations in the Settlement of Labor Disputes," 373.

57. Public Policy, *Labor, Capital and the Public*, 34.

58. J. David Houser, *What the Employer thinks: Executives' Attitudes Toward Their Employees* (Cambridge, Mass., 1927), 80, 87; Wiebe, *Businessmen and Reform*, 178, 211–12.

59. Wiebe, *Businessmen and Reform*, 213.

Chapter 5_____

Conclusion

Near the turn of the century in the United States, economic expansion and the growing complexity of industrial society generated in the emergent business sector and among professionals and technocrats a broad and complex movement toward cultural hegemony. At a time when social cohesion became increasingly problematic, the traditional concept of a self-regulating society gave way to a demand for a more centralized, interventionist authority, profoundly changing public attitudes toward public policy and private business practice along the way. No group perceived more clearly the necessity of governing society than the nation's large industrialists, in part because it was more to their advantage to think in terms of hegemony. Manufacturers expected the active promotion in the factory and in society of their opinions about work to aid in the subordination of workers to rationalized industrial work, making them disciplined, productive, deferential to experts, and more motivated to achieve.

Taken together, the rhetoric of the Pullman strike, the National Association of Manufacturers, and modern management indicate that a redefinition of the role of labor in America's liberal democracy was taking place, a redefinition by employers that changed the nature of the class struggle in the twentieth century, undermining or transforming older definitions in favor of new forms that befitted the emerging functionalist, technocratic society. American commercial elites, confronted by social dissent and active worker resistance to modern forms of management, reformulated their thinking around a set of values that lauded science and technology applied by experts and called for the combined efforts of capital and labor to forge a progressive industrial society based on private property. Their labor ideology reaffirmed what they took to be the rewards and punishments of a capitalist value system: the work ethic versus leisure or laziness, the collective interest of society over the self-interest of labor, the desire to rise from wage labor to economic independence, and the lure of personal acquisitiveness over class unity.

Growing cultural norms of regimentation and standardization, of surveillance and of centralized, hierarchical authority guided many institutions' attempts to coerce individual behavior, not just those engaged in production. Efforts of industrialists to define a modern labor ideology converged with other elites' attempts to bring order out of seeming chaos. After 1880, the rise of formal, secular, national managerial and bureaucratic authorities in social science, medicine, law, engineering, and management underscored the centralization of social power in the hands of professional elites. In the form of a new managerial class, manufacturers commanded a body of specialized knowledge that governed the new field of work efficiency, its mechanisms, and its practitioners. As managers and other professionals developed new patterns of authority and standardized formal structures of knowledge and method, they tended to absorb decision making from workers in industry and from ordinary people in society.

The centralization of authority included a redefinition of labor-capital relationships, themselves rooted in a class structure that determined whether one was employing or being employed, bossing or being bossed, having some or having less; in short, holding relatively more or less power in a hierarchical social relationship. The rhetoric of Pullman, the NAM, and early Taylorism sustained and even intensified the antagonistic nature of these relationships. The owners of these businesses tolerated obedient workers but reacted violently to dissent, picturing strikes as criminal, forcing unions out of shops, jailing or blacklisting members, and using Pinkertons or troops. As long as manufacturers pitched their ideas in terms of the labor-capital struggle, they tacitly acknowledged that labor's ideas were worth the effort of a confrontational propaganda fight and even worth calling out the troops. Labor posed a palpable and formidable threat to the social acceptance of industrialists' labor ideology in union organization, shop control, street demonstrations, the workers' press, and overt criticisms of the industrial system. The shrill and vituperative level of the great social debate at once validated the stakes and identified the two antagonistic positions.

As various forms of modern management transformed factory organization and employee relations after the turn of the century, however, manufacturers began to minimize their adversarial role toward labor with important results for twentieth-century labor-capital relations. Through such programs as the American Plan they emphasized a new spirit of reconciliation that repressed open confrontation and relied more on praise, incentive, and teamwork in "handling" working men and women. Industrialists who adopted some form of the American Plan attempted to drive underground discussions of class warfare and deflect the focus of the struggle to new "interests," particularly institutionalized self-interest that enlisted workers' allegiance to progress with promises of participation in bourgeois culture and consumer society. The new rhetoric of conciliation offered a more disguised although more orchestrated form of struggle on the part of industrialists, a form that sometimes subsumed class differences under "common interests" and consensus, and that tolerated "approved" dissent or conflict, most often in the form of contract negotiations, against its network of authority. Scientific managers minimized collectively organized disputes and prescribed in their place elaborate rules for individual grievances, which were often smothered under the weight of bureaucratic procedures and absorbed by the rhetoric of conciliation. The institutionalization of collective bargaining acknowledged group protest, but only when governed by formal rules that required unions to uphold contracts and forswear such actions as sympathy strikes and boycotts. Gaining favor throughout American industry by the 1920s, grievance systems and collective bargaining incorporated protest that previously had been recognized and met head on.

Although early Taylorites fought soldiering through bonuses, later managers, integrating new practices from industrial psychology, encouraged a "creative spirit of service" through welfare programs, job security and disability compensation, factory safety, and profit sharing, all attempts to pacify and integrate workers individually and thus to manage their resistance to industrial life. Out of prewar scientific management practices came modern personnel management. In early Taylorized plants, employee relations were governed by the "Discipline Office," a reflection of Taylor's openly manipulative attitude toward workers. As the tone of management changed after 1910, however, that office became known throughout industry as the Personnel Department. The hostile rhetoric of the NAM and the Pullman strike no longer furnished models to businessmen for dealing with labor, although their anti-union bias and distrust of workers' intentions remained a disguised, if integral, part of new management practices. In factories Taylorized during the war, many workers "learned by experience" that scientific managers represented the vanguard of a movement for "more humane and cooperative" methods that appealed to the "creative spirit and the spirit of service," observed Edward E. Hunt, assistant secretary of commerce and a member of Herbert Hoover's Committee on Elimination of Waste in Industry.[1] Samuel Gompers seemed to confirm this at least in part, although he credited labor with having initiated the new practices. The American Federation of Labor dropped its opposition to Taylorism in the spirit of high wages and wartime sacrifice. Organized labor's early resistance helped "humanize concepts and methods of management," Gompers declared after the war, "until now the human nature of workers is recognized as the fundamental factor in determining policies."[2]

Claiming it their class duty to properly instruct the community and their workers, industrialists recognized that efforts to promote their ideology depended on education. Pullman town was conceived as a means of instructing workers through a rational environment, and similarly, Pullman, the general managers, and the NAM saw the public mind as a crucial factor. These employers consciously attempted to spread the struggle against labor into the social realm of public opinion. Similarly, scientific management sought to establish workers' "right education" as a social function of production. All three groups of manufacturers in this study made skillful use of public propaganda, the political realm of language, public space and resources, and the increasing centralization in the hands of corporate America of the technological apparatus of communication. The apparatus ranged in form from architecture to newspapers and journals, from mail campaigns to the lecture circuits of NAM, and to the pneumatic information-routing tubes and control boards of a Taylorized factory.

Industrialists targeted two audiences for education: the working class and the public. Their labor ideology attempted to persuade both audiences that capital embodied traditional values that society held dear. It pitted class-neutral entities such as "public opinion" or "society," which implied the well-being and survival of the social whole, against labor's conspiratorial subversiveness. Transforming such liberal republican notions as freedom, equal opportunity, and individual rights into their own class arguments, employers utilized a selective historical tradition to rest their claims on the universal moral values and historical experience of the nation, and they held these up against the unpatriotic demands of the workers. Employers' ideology used metaphors of patriotism, public interest, and social beneficence to persuade the public of their own authority and competence and to picture workers as incapable or subversive. Labor appeared as a generalization that reflected businessmen's stereotypes, prejudices, and class anxieties, all of which seemed to derive more from conventions and agreed upon codes of understanding than direct observation of their workers.

Manufacturers defended their economic theory as positive, natural, true, and reasonable, integrating their specific rationales concerning unions, labor, and wage theory into a framework of immutable paradigms taken from national, Protestant, republican, and classical economic norms. Various legitimating symbols were appropriated by industrial elites to certify in the public mind the validity of their institutions and emphasize their claim to be the defenders and heirs of the American patriotic tradition. Often they directly confronted their employees' use of public symbols with their own. During the Pullman strike, for example, Debs asked all strikers, their families, and sympathizers to display a white lapel ribbon in sympathy with the strike. The Chicago Board of Trade countered by handing out American flag lapel pins to Chicago citizens in an attempt to brand strikers and their sympathizers as unpatriotic.[3]

The manufacturers in this study sought to shrink the permissible range of social criticism in their debate with workers, confining it to "humanizing" the industrial system but discrediting or discouraging wider examinations of the nation's political economy. Willing to popularize their ideas, they nevertheless attempted to prevent any examination of them or of the material relationships upon which they rested. They attempted to circumvent the real conflict of interests proffered by militant farmers and labor, and preserve, instead, a willingness to work within existing economic relationships. One method of accomplishing this meant asking workers to drop a class oriented frame of reference and focus attention on themselves, their families, and their homes. Modern management, for instance, constituted workers as individuals with separate interests other than, and often against, class, an appeal made more palatable by the growing cult of individual self-fulfillment promised by both advertising and therapeutic secular Christianity.[4] Managers attempted to redistribute conflict and competition in the factory and redirect workers' attention toward individualized imperatives of the time clock and the rate system, hoping to defeat organized soldiering, which implicitly, overtly, and collectively criticized the entire work system under capitalism. Centralized surveillance and planning forced workers to coordinate their interests with that of management if they expected rewards for compliance with faster paced work. Modern management reinforced and was reinforced by the self-absorbing individualism so essential to participation in consumer society. It held out the hope of individual advancement through time and motion thrift, treating workers as mini-entrepreneurs in search of personal "profits."

Workers and Populists had envisioned a utopia where no distinctions existed between capital and labor, based upon republican visions of everyone producing and thus eliminating distinctions between producers and non-producers. When capitalists argued that no distinctions existed between capital and labor, they based their claim on a different interpretation of a commonality of interests. In capital's view, all worked together for the common good with the same goal of efficient productivity. This utopia translated into prosperity for owners through greater profits and preserved the distinction between owners and workers. In this system, workers' notions of labor as personal property gave over to owners' treatment of labor as a market commodity. The craft unions came both to accept and endorse the logic of capitalist production and the concept of labor as a commodity.

The sum of the hegemonic effort of turn-of-the-century business elites seemingly aided in deflecting what appeared to be the impending formation of a nationwide worker- and farmer-based, anti-capitalist collective will. Along with the defeat of the Populists, the rise of nativism, the adoption of the mantle of progressive science, and the growing corporatism of major unions after 1900, middle-class public opinion solidified against radical working-class ideas and activities. The ideology of individual self-fulfillment was reinforced by the almost triumphant emphasis in American culture on material well-being, participation in the market, and optimistic belief in the rewards of individual effort. Against radical labor's evaluation of labor-capital relations, employers advanced a set of values that promoted the power of a person's will to affect his or her future, an assumption that the cream rose to the top and that society was structured to make sure of it, the conviction that mobility was universally desired, and that everyone was mobile for the same reason.

In this context, the promise of mobility ultimately served to demean the working class since its whole rationale was to rise to middle-class status. This contradiction did not emerge entirely from late nineteenth-century conditions, however, but lay in traditional republicanism, which also saw the working class as something from which to escape. The ultimate goal of work—property own-ership—undermined the republican worker-based value system. Together with the hopes of advancement of first and second-generation immigrants, these ideas served as a favorable psychological context for generating values supportive of the emerging corporate system.

It remains problematic to claim that the business hegemony of the Gilded Age amounted to a solution of the "labor problem," either as it existed among skilled workers in the metal trades, as union power in general, or as the street violence of the angered and unemployed. If the American Plan did profoundly humanize the treatment of factory workers, the utopian social world envisioned by George Pullman and Frederick Taylor had not materialized. Instead, the dissenting voices in America at the turn of the century—labor, farmers, ethnic subcultures, im-migrants, blacks, and women—continued to articulate their own views of how society should be organized and what values should prevail, serving as the nation's conscience, pointing the finger of moral responsibility at the purveyors of materialist culture and reminding them that even in their quietest moments their silence should not be taken for consensus. All of this dissent in one way or another targeted the growing pervasiveness of corporate thinking, from its control of the market, to its power in culture and politics, to its consumer ethos. While these separate protests were never united or perhaps even unitable, their individual voices continued to influence business' response into the decade of the twenties and beyond.

Thus, the cultural hegemony of the business elite remained in continual need of re-creation, never representing an accomplished task but rather a process that, however crude and confrontational in the years between 1880 and 1915, had to be continually refined to incorporate the ideas, sentiments, and values of dissenters within the context of the corporations' own truth claims about the promise of American life. The proprietary-capitalist elements of this incorporation, repre-sented by the polemics of the NAM or the use of armed force, gave way to the scientific and "classless" management of seemingly contented and upwardly mo-bile workers in the manufacturing sector. In the political realm, a managed two-party system kept politics free from any but "mainstream" ideas and practices all through the first third of the century, tempered finally in the 1930s, as in any he-gemonic structure, by a flexibility and sensitivity toward the poor, the old, the unskilled, and the unemployed, but sustaining a state led by a middle-class, cor-porate definition of what America was really about.

The political implications of the nature of this new authority are manifold. Any elite, on coming to power, Lawrence Goodwyn has suggested, seeks to consolidate its authority and preclude further social change. Though the man-ufacturing elite did not shrink from the use of force, it sought an easier way to prevent direct assaults on its authority and found it in mass socialization of the working population through the creation of "mass modes of thought that literally make the need for major additional social change difficult for the mass of the population to imagine.''[5] The new ideology, part of a ''new culture in itself,'' created a seemingly permanent means of ensuring domestic tranquility as it convinced many people to ''define all conceivable political activity within the limits of existing custom.'' Such a society that limits the activity of its dissenting groups can ''genuinely be described as 'stable,' '' Goodwyn explains, and future protest ''will pose no ultimate threat because the protesters will necessarily conceive of their options as being so limited that even should they be successful, the resulting 'reforms' will not alter significantly the inherited modes of power and privilege. Protest under such conditions of cultural narrowness is, therefore, not only permissible in the eyes of those who rule, but is . . . positively desirable because it fortifies the popular understanding that the society is functioning 'democratically.' ''[6] For this reason, the political consequences of mass deference to received culture cannot be overstated, especially in the years after 1920 when the industrial and service workforce had increased to so large a percentage of the population and material consumption had become a national pastime in the triumphant business culture of that decade.

Opposition and criticism furnish necessary ingredients in a viable democratic society; thus, to observers such as Goodwyn, ''individual self-respect and collective self-confidence constitute the culture building blocks of mass democratic politics. Their development permits people to act in self-generated democratic ways—as distinct from passively participating in various hierarchical modes bequeathed by the received culture.''[7] Class consciousness, as E. P. Thompson suggested, forms in the process of historical struggle, making it advantageous to labor movements, or to any politics requiring open public debate, that the lines of this struggle remain clearly defined. If individual consciousness is thwarted by a pervasive ideology, individual action no longer provides social or economic alternatives. It may be that by offering what seemingly amounted to the ''received culture'' of corporate liberalism to a large portion of Americans, corporate-led culture set the stage for the creation of the mass acquiescence that diminished true oppositional politics on the part of labor.

By the 1920s, the dialogue between capital and labor over the last half century had been influenced by the systematic attempts of industrial elites and scientific managers to convince the American public of the place labor was to occupy in the industrial society of the future. The dialogue with labor sometimes represented an equitable, two-way exchange, while at other times it constituted a series of pronouncements and polemics from a powerful business sector with immeasurable resources against the relatively less organized, more poorly funded forces of labor. The outcome of the dialogue did not result in the triumph of the better argument based on fully informed, democratic consensus about how American society should be constituted. It resulted, instead, in the triumph of the ''better argument'' as society came to perceive it—better, not because it provided a greater measure of freedom and justice or a stronger republic, but better merely because it prevailed.

NOTES

1. Edward E. Hunt *Scientific Management Since Taylor* (New York, 1924), 13.
2. Quoted in ibid, xiv.
3. Samuel Yellen, *American Labor Struggles* (New York, 1936), 118.
4. See T. J. Jackson Lears, "The Concept of Cultural Hegemony: Problems and Possibilities," *American Historical Review* 90 (July 1985): 567–93.
5. Lawrence Goodwyn, *The Populist Moment: A Short History of the Agrarian Revolt in America* (New York, 1978), xi.
6. Ibid.
7. Ibid.

Selected Bibliography

GOVERNMENT SOURCES

Massachusetts Bureau of Statistics of Labor, *Sixteenth Annual Report*. Boston: Wright and Potter Printing Company, 1885.

United States Commissioner of Labor, *Seventeenth Annual Report: Trade and Technical Education*. Washington, D.C.: 1902.

United States Congress, House of Representatives, *Hearings Before the Special Committee of the House of Representatives to Investigate the Taylor and Other Systems of Shop Management*, 3 vols. Washington, D.C.: 1912.

United States Government Industrial Commission. *Reports on Conditions of Capital and Labor Employed in Manufacturers and General Business*, 10 vols. Washington, D.C.: 1901.

United States Senate, *Report of the Relations Between Labor and Capital*, 5 vols. Washington, D.C.: 1885.

United States Strike Commission, *Report on the Chicago Strike of June-July 1894*, U.S. Congress Senate Executive Document no. 7, 53rd Congress, 3rd Session. Washington, D.C.: 1895.

PRIMARY SOURCES

Ashley, W. J. "The Railroad Strike of 1894." *The Church Social Union*, series B, no. 1 (April 1895): 5–12.

Babcock, George D. *The Taylor System in Franklin Management*. New York: 1918; reprinted Easton, Pa., 1972.

Babcock, George D., and Heckman, James. "Some Organization Lessons of the War." *Bulletin of the Taylor Society*, hereafter cited as *BTS*, 4 (Dec. 1919): 4–12.

Bancroft, Edgar. *The Chicago Strike of 1894*, Chicago: 1895.

Beatty, Albert J. *Corporation Schools*. Bloomington, 1918.

Bell, George L. "Production the Goal." *Annals of the American Academy of Political and Social Science*, hereafter cited as *Annals* 85 (Sept. 1919): 1–7.

Bemis, Edward. "Relation of Labor Organizations to the American Boy to Trade Instruction." *Annals* 5 (July 1894-June 1895): 209–41.

Bingham, W. V. "What Industrial Psychology Asks of Management." *BTS* 9 (Dec. 1924): 243—48.

Bolling, Raynal. "The United States Steel Corporation and Labor Conditions." *Annals* 36 (July 1912): 353–62.

"The Boycott of the Pullman Company." *Harper's Weekly* (July 7, 1894): 627.

Burke, William M. *History and Functions of Central Labor Unions*. New York: 1899.

Burns, W. F. *The Pullman Boycott*, St. Paul: 1894.

Caniff, W. H. "The Relation of the Railway to Its Employees." *The Engineering Magazine* 8 (March 1895): 977–84.

Carwardine, William H. *The Pullman Strike*. Chicago: 1894.

"Certain Dangerous Tendencies in American Life." *Atlantic Monthly* 42 (Oct. 1878): 402.

Clark, B. Preston. "On the Motives of Industrial Enterprise." *Annals* 85 (Sept. 1919): 37–47.

Cleveland, Grover. *The Government in the Chicago Strike of 1894*. Princeton: 1913.

Cohen, Joseph E. "The Drift in Industry." *Annals* 85 (Sept. 1919): 28–36.

"Comment" *The Yale Review* 3 (Aug. 1894): 113.

Committee on Elimination of Waste in Industry of the Federated American Engineering Societies. *Waste in Industry*. New York: 1921.

Cooke, Morris L. "The Spirit and Social Significance of Scientific Management." *Journal of Political Economy* 21 (June 1913): 481–93.

———. "Scientific Management, Collective and Individual." Address to the Philadelphia School of Commerce and Accounts, October 27, 1913, Carl Barth Papers, Cabinet 1, Drawer 1, Baker Library Manuscript Collection, Harvard University.

———. "Forward: The Problem of the American Manufacturer," *Annals* 85 (Sept. 1919): vi.

Cooley, Thomas M. "The Lessons of the Recent Civil Disorders." *The Forum* 18 (Sept. 1894): 1–19.

Copley, Frank B. *Frederick Winslow Taylor: Father of Scientific Management*, 2 vols. New York: 1923.

———. "Taylor and Trade Unions," *BTS* 10 (Aug. 1925): 182–84.

Crozier, William. "Scientific Management in Government Establishments," *BTS* 1 (Oct. 1915): 1–8.

Dodge, James Mapes, and Taylor, Frederick. "Scientific Management Prevents Strikes." City Club of Philadelphia, *City Club Bulletin* 4 (Jan. 18, 1911): 28–30.

———. "A History of the Introduction of a System of Shop Management." In Clarence B. Thompson, ed., *Scientific Management*. Cambridge, Mass.: 1914, 226–31.

Doty, Duane. *The Story of Pullman*. Chicago: 1894.

Drury, Horace B. *Scientific Management: History and Criticism*. New York: 1922.

Eaton, Charles H. "Pullman and Paternalism." *The American Journal of Politics* 5 (Dec. 1894): 571–79.

"Editorial," *The Outlook* 50 (July 21, 1894): 85–86.

"Editorials," *The Nation* 59 (July 5, 1894): 4–6; 59 (July 12, 1894): 19; 59 (July 19, 1894): 32; 59 (July 26, 1894): 55;

Eliot, Charles W. "Some Reasons Why the American Republic May Endure." *The Forum* 18 (Oct. 1894): 129–45.

Ely, Richard. "Pullman: A Social Study." *Harper's New Monthly Magazine*, 70 (Feb. 1885): 452–66.

Emery, James A. "Use and Abuse of Injunctions in Trade Disputes." *Annals* 36 (July 1910): 127–36.

————. *Party Platforms and Industry*. New York: 1920.

The Engineering Magazine. *Science and the Practice of Management*. New York: 1914.

Farquhar, H. H. "Positive Contributions of Scientific Management." *BTS* 4 (Oct. 1919): 15–28.

Faulkner, Harold U. *American Economic History*. New York: 1924.

Feiss, Richard A. "Personal Relationships as a Basis of Scientific Management." *BTS* 1 (Nov. 1915): 5–25.

————. "Scientific Management and Its Relation to the Health of the Worker." *BTS* 2 (Nov. 1969): 11–13.

Filene, A. Lincoln. "The Key to Successful Industrial Management." *Annals* 85 (Sept. 1919): 8–11.

Fletcher, Henry J. "The Railway War." *Atlantic Monthly* 74 (Oct. 1894): 534–41.

Gantt, Henry L. "A Bonus System for Rewarding Labor." ASME *Transactions* 23 (1901): 341–72.

————. "Training Workmen in Habits of Industry and Cooperation." ASME *Transactions* 30 (1908): 1037–63.

————. "A Practical Application of Scientific Management." *The Engineering Magazine* 41 (April 1911): 1–22.

————. *Work, Wages and Profits*. New York: 1919.

Gilbreth, Frank G. and Lillian M. "The Three Position Plan of Promotion." *Annals* 65 (May 1916): 289–96.

————. *Applied Motion Study*. New York: 1919.

————. "Classifying the Elements of Work." *Management and Administration in Manufacturing Industries* 8 (Aug. 1924): 151–54, and part two, 8 (Sept. 1924): 295–97.

————. "The Achievements of Motion Psychology." *BTS* 9 (Dec. 1924): 259–83.

Gilbreth, Lillian. *The Psychology of Management: The Function of the Mind in Determining, Teaching, and Installing Methods of Lease Waste*. New York: 1914.

Godfrey, Hollis. "The Attitude of Labor Toward Scientific Management." *Annals of the American Academy of Political and Social Science* 44 (July 1912): 59–73.

Gompers, Samuel. "Free Speech and the Injunction Order." *Annals* 36 (July 1910): 225–64.

————. "Discussion." *Annals* 44 (July 1912): 55–59.

Goodell, Francis. "The Technician's Point of View." *BTS* 15 (April 1930): 71–79.

Grant, Thomas Burke. "Pullman and its Lessons." *The American Journal of Politics* 5 (Aug. 1894): 190–204.

Green, William. "Labor's Ideals Concerning Management." *BTS* 10 (Dec. 1925): 241–53.

Greene, T. L. "The Law of Strikes." *The Nation* 59 (Oct. 18, 1894): 281–82.

Hartness, Richard. *The Human Factor in Works Management*. New York: 1912.

Hathaway, H. K. "Control of Shop Operations." In Harlow S. Person, ed., *Scientific Management in American Industry*. New York: 1907, 319–74.

————. "Planning Department, Its Organization and Function –1." *Industrial Engineering* 12 (July 1912): 6–8.

————. "On the Technique of Manufacturing." *Annals* 85 (Sept. 1919): 231–36.

————. "The Mnemonic System of Classification." *Industrial Management* 40 (Sept. 1920): 173–83.

Hickey, Michael. "Commercial Value of the Industrial Press." *American Industries* 10 (Oct. 1909): 25.

Holt, Henry. "Punishment of Anarchists and Others." *The Forum* 17 (Aug. 1894): 644–58.

Hoover, Herbert. "Industrial Standardization." In Edward E. Hunt, *Scientific Management Since Taylor*. New York: 1915, 189–96.

————. "Industrial Waste." *BTS* 6 (April 1921): 77–79.

Hoxie, Robert. *Scientific Management and Labor*. New York: 1915.

Hunt, Edward E. *Scientific Management Since Taylor*. New York: 1924.

————. "The Influence of Scientific Management." In Person, ed., *Scientific Management in American Industry* 35–39.

"Industrial Training in the High School" *American Industries* 10 (March 1910): 37.

International Industrial Relations Association. *World Social Economic Congress*. The Hague, The Netherlands, 1931.

Jones, Edward D. "Publicity as a Policy." *Annals* 85 (Sept. 1919): 314–20.

————. *The Administration of Industrial Enterprises*. New York: 1919.

Keith, John. "The New Unions of Employers." *Harper's Weekly* 48 (Jan. 23, 1904): 131.

Kirby, John. "The Goal of the Labor Trust." *American Industries* 10 (Feb. 1910): 16.

————. "The Benefits of Industrial Combinations." *Annals* 42 (July 1912): 119–24.

Kitson, James. "The Iron and Steel Industries of America." *The Engineering Magazine* 1 (July 1891): 484–87.

Knoeppel, Charles. *Industrial Preparedness*. New York: 1916.

Kornhauser, A. W. and Kingsbury, F. A. *Psychological Tests in Business*. Chicago: 1924.

"Legal Aspects of the Disorder at Chicago." *The Outlook* 50 (July 14, 1894): 54.

Leiserson, William R. "The Worker's Relation to Scientific Management." In Hunt, *Scientific Management Since Taylor*, 222–25.

Leuf, A.H.P. "An Open Letter to the U.S. Strike Commission." *To-Day* 1 (Oct. 1894): 428–35.

Lichtner, William O. "Promulgation of Standards by the Taylor Society." *BTS* 5 (Feb. 1920): 12–42.

Marx, Karl. *Capital*, 3 vols. Chicago: 1906.

"May a Man Conduct His Business as He Please?" *The Forum* 18 (Dec. 1894): 428–30.

McDermott, George. "The Pullman Strike Commission." *Catholic World* 9 (Feb. 1895): 627–35.

Means, David McG. "The Principles Involved in the Recent Strike." *The Forum* 17 (Aug. 1894): 633–43.

Metcalf, Henry C. *The Psychological Foundations of Management*. Chicago: 1927.

Miles, Nelson A.; Hampton, Wade; Robinson, Harry; and Gompers, Samuel. "The Lesson of the Recent Strikes." *North American Review* 159 (Aug. 1894): 180–206.

Morse, E.L.C. "Pullman and Its Inhabitants." *The Nation* 59 (July 26, 1894): 61–62.

Munsterberg, Hugo. *Psychology and Industrial Efficiency*. Boston and New York: 1913.

———. *Psychology and Social Sanity*. New York: 1914.

———. Munsterberg. *Psychology: General and Applied*. New York: 1914.

———. Munsterberg. *Business Psychology*. Chicago: 1915.

Myers, Gustavus. *History of the Great American Fortunes*. vol. 1. Chicago: 1911.

"The Nation and the New Slavery." *The Nation* 59 (July 12, 1894): 22.

National Association of Manufacturers. *Accident Prevention and Relief*. New York: 1911.

———. *The Law's Supremacy: Decision of the Supreme Court of the District of Columbia in re Samuel Gompers, John Mitchell, and Frank Morrison*. New York: 1912.

———. *Open Shop Encyclopedia for Debaters*. New York: 1921.

———. *Proceedings of the Annual Convention of the National Association of Manufacturers*, various years.

Nimmo, Joseph. *The Insurrection of June and July 1894 Growing Out of the Pullman Strike*. Washington, D.C.: 1894.

Ogden, R. "The Report on the Chicago Strike." *The Nation* 59 (Nov. 22, 1894): 376.

Otterson, J. E. "Executive and Administrative Organization." *Annals* 85 (Sept. 1919): 90–99.

Parker, C. H. "The Decline in Trade Union Membership." *Quarterly Journal of Economics* 24 (1909–1910): 564–69.

Perry, Arthur. *Principles of Political Economy*. New York: 1885.

Person, Harlow S. *Industrial Education: A System of Training for Men Entering Upon Trade and Commerce*. Boston and New York: 1907.

———. "Scientific Management." *BTS* 2 (Oct. 1916): 16–23.

———. "The Manager, the Workman, and the Social Scientist." *BTS* 3 (Feb. 1917): 1–7.

———. "The Opportunities and Obligations of Scientific Management." *BTS* 4 (Feb. 1919): 1–7.

———., ed., *Scientific Management in American Industry*. New York: 1929.

Person, Harlow S., and Wolf, Robert, et. al. "Control and Consent." *BTS* 3 (March 1917): 5–20.

Post, Louis. "What Rights Have Laborers?" *The Forum* (May 1886): 298.

"The Present State of the Art of Industrial Management." *American Society of Mechanical Engineers Transactions* 34 (1912): 1131–52.

Public Policy. *Labor, Capital and the Public: A Discussion of the Relations Between Employees, Employers, and the Public*. Chicago: 1905.

"The Real Issue in the Strike." *The Outlook* 50 (July 7, 1894): 89.

"Revolutionary Statesmanship." *Harper's Weekly* (Nov. 24, 1894): 43.

Robinson, Harry P. "The Humiliating Report of the Strike Commission." *The Forum* 18 (Dec. 1894): 523–31.

Roosevelt, Theodore. "True American Ideals." *The Forum* 18 (Dec. 1894): 743–50.

Schwedtmann, Ferdinand. "The National Association of Manufacturers' Attitude Toward Injured Members of the Industrial Army." *American Industries* 10 (May 1910): 18–22.

"Scientific Management Viewed from the Workman's Standpoint." *Industrial Engineering and the Engineering Digest* (Nov. 1910): 377–80.

Scott, Walter Dill. *The Psychology of Advertising*. New York: 1908.

———. *Influencing Men in Business*. New York, 1911.

Shaw, Albert. "The Pullman Strike." *The Review of Reviews* 10 (Aug. 1894): 133–38.

Snow, A. J. *Psychology in Business Relations.* Chicago: 1925.

"The Solidarity of Society." *The Outlook* 50 (Aug. 4, 1894): 169.

"Some Lessons of the Great Strike." *Harper's Weekly* (July 21, 1894): 674.

"Steps Toward Government Control of Railroads," *The Forum* 18 (Feb. 1895): 709.

Stead, W. T. *Chicago To-day: The Labor War in America.* London: 1894.

Stone. N. I. "Discussion." *BTS* 7 (Dec. 1922): 75.

"The Strike: Suggestions of Remedy." *The Outlook* 50 (July 21, 1894): 89–90.

"Suppress the Rebellion." *Harper's Weekly* (July 14, 1894): 635.

Taussig, F. W. *Inventors and Money Makers.* New York: 1915.

Tawney, R. H. *The Acquisitive Society.* New York: 1921.

Taylor, Frederick. "A Piece-Rate System, Being a Step Toward Partial Solution to the Labor Problem." *American Society of Mechanical Engineers Transactions* 16 (1895): 856–903.

———. *Scientific Management: Comprising Shop Management, Principles of Scientific Management, Testimony Before the Special House Committee.* New York: 1947.

———. "Workmen and Their Management." Unpublished manuscript of a lecture given in 1909 at the Harvard Graduate School of Business Administration (after 1922, the Harvard Business School), Carl Barth papers, file T–241a, Ms. Division, Baker Library, Harvard Business School, 1–40.

Tead, Ordway. "Purpose as a Psychological Factor in Management." *BTS* 10 (Dec. 1925): 254–67.

"This Latest and Greatest Strike." *Bradstreet's* 22 (July 7, 1894): 355.

Thompson, Clarence B., ed. *Scientific Management: A Collection of the More Significant Articles Describing the Taylor System of Management.* Cambridge, Mass.: 1914.

Thorndike, Edward. "Fundamental Theorems in Judging Men." *Journal of Applied Psychology* 2 (1918): 67–76.

Tolman, William. *Social Engineering.* New York: 1908.

Valentine, Robert G. "The Progressive Relation Between Efficiency and Consent." *BTS* 2 (Jan. 1916): 7–20.

———. "Scientific Management and Organized Labor." *BTS* 1 (Jan. 1915): 3–9.

Van Cleave, James. *Industrial Education as an Essential Factor in Our National Prosperity.* New York: 1908.

———. "The Work of Employer's Associations in the Settlement of Labor Disputes." *Annals* 36 (Sept. 1910): 373–80.

von Holst, H. "Are We Awakened?" *The Journal of Political Economy* 2 (Sept. 1894): 485–516.

Warman, Cy. "The Relations of the Employee to the Railroad." *The Engineering Magazine* 8 (Mar. 1895): 985–91.

"Were Pullman's Wage Reductions Protectionist Spite?" *American Industries* 3 (Aug. 1894): 3.

"Who is Boss in Your Shop?" *Bulletin of the Taylor Society* 3 (Aug. 1917): 3–10.

Willoughby, William F. "Employers' Associations for Dealing With Labor in the United States." *Quarterly Journal of Economics* 20 (1905–1906): 110–50.

Wolf, Robert B. "Individuality in Industry." *BTS* 1 (Aug. 1915): 2–8.

"A Word to the Working Men." *Harper's Weekly* (July 21, 1894): 698–99.

Wright, Carroll D. "The Chicago Strike." *Publications of the American Economic Association* 9 (Oct. and Dec. 1894): 505–22.

———. "May a Man Conduct His Business as He Please?" *The Forum* 18 (Dec. 1894): 425–32.

———. "Steps Toward Government Control of Railroads." *The Forum* 18 (Feb. 1895): 704–13.

Wright, Phillip G. "The Contest in Congress Between Organized Labor and Organized Business." *Quarterly Journal of Economics* 29 (Feb. 1915): 235–61.

Wuest, Robert. "Industrial Betterment Activities of the National Metal Trades Association." *Annals* 44 (July 1912): 75–85.

Yoakum, C. S. "Experimental Psychology in Personnel Problems." *BTS* 10 (June 1925): 154–63.

———. "Conditions of Research in Industrial Psychology—Changing a Point of View." In Henry C. Metcalf, ed. *The Psychological Foundations of Management*, 18–33.

———. "The Role of Impulse, Emotions, and Habit in Conduct." In Henry C. Metcalf, ed. *The Psychological Foundations of Management*, 34–49.

SECONDARY SOURCES

Abercrombie, Nicholas. *Class, Structure, and Knowledge: Problems in the Sociology of Knowledge*, New York, 1980.

Adelman, William *Touring Pullman: A Study in Company Paternalism*. Chicago, 1977.

Aiken, William. *Technocracy and the American Dream*. Berkeley, 1977.

Aitken, Hugh. *Taylorism at the Watertown Arsenal: Scientific Management in Action, 1908–1915*. Cambridge, Mass., 1960.

Baritz, Loren. *Servants of Power: A History of the Use of Social Science in American Industry*. New York, 1960.

Barlow, Melvin. *History of Industrial Education in the United States*. Peoria, Ill., 1967.

Berger, Peter, and Luckmann, Thomas. *The Social Construction of Reality: A Treatise in the Sociology of Knowledge*. New York, 1966.

Bechofer, Frank. "Relationship Between Technology and Shop-Floor Behaviour." In J. N. Wolf and D. D. Edge, eds. *Meaning and Control: Essays in the Social Aspects of Science and Technology*. London, 1973.

Berthoff, Rowland. "Peasants and Artisans, Puritans and Republicans: Personal Liberty and Communal Equality in American History." *Journal of American History* 69 (Dec. 1982): 589–91.

———. "Writing a History of Things Left Out." *Reviews in American History* 14 (Mar. 1986): 1–16.

Blackwood, George D. "Techniques and Stereotypes in the Literature of the National Association of Manufacturers Concerning Industry and Labor." M.A. thesis, University of Chicago, 1947.

Bledstein, Burton. *The Culture of Professionalism: The Middle Class and the Development of Higher Education in America*. New York, 1976.

Blough, Roger. *The Free Man and the Corporation*. New York, 1959.

Bonnett, Clarence. *Employers' Associations in the United States*. New York, 1922.

———. "The Evolution of Business Groupings." *Annals of the American Academy of Political and Social Science* 179 (May 1935): 1–8.

Bowles, Samuel, and Gintis, Herbert. *Schooling in Capitalist America: Educational Reform and the Contradictions of Economic Life*. New York, 1976.

Boyle, O. D. *History of Railroad Strikes*. Washington, D.C., 1935.

Braverman, Harry. *Labor and Monopoly Capital: The Degradation of Work in the Twentieth Century*. New York, 1974.

Buder, Stanely. *Pullman, An Experiment in Industrial Order and Community Planning, 1880–1930*. New York, 1967.

Buroway, Michael. *Manufacturing Consent*. Chicago, 1979.

Calhoun, Craig J. "The Radicalism of Tradition: Community Strength or Venerable Disguise and Borrowed Language?" *American Journal of Sociology* 88 (5): 886–914.

Calvert, Monte. *The Mechanical Engineer in America: Professional Cultures in Conflict*. Baltimore, 1967.

Cantor, Milton. *American Working Class Culture*. New York, 1979.

Casson, John. *Civilizing the Machine: Technology and Republican Values in America, 1776–1900*. New York, 1976.

Cawelti, John. *Apostles of the Self-Made Man*. Chicago, 1965.

Christie, Jean. *Morris Llewellyn Cooke: Progressive Engineer*. New York, 1983.

Clark, Harold, and Sloan, Harold. *Classrooms in the Factories: An Account of Educational Activities Conducted by American Industry*. Rutherford, N.J., 1958.

Clawson, Dan. *Bureaucracy and the Labor Process: The Transformation of U.S. Industry, 1860–1920*. New York, 1980.

Cochran, Thomas. *Railroad Leaders 1845–1890: The Business Mind in Action*. Cambridge, Mass., 1953.

Cohen, David, and Lazerson, Marvin. "Education and the Corporate Order." *Socialist Revolution* 2 (March-April 1972): 47–72.

Cohen, Sol. "The Industrial Education Movement 1906–1917." *American Quarterly* 20 (Spring 1968): 95–110.

Conkin, Paul K. *Prophets of Prosperity: America's First Political Economists*. Bloomington, 1980.

Cooper, Jerry. "The Army as Strikebreaker: The Railroad Strikes of 1877 and 1894." *Labor History* 18 (1977): 179–96.

Cremin, Lawrence. *The Transformation of the Schools*. New York, 1965.

Davis, David B. "Reflections on Abolitionism and Ideological Hegemony." *American Historical Review* 92 (Oct. 1987): 797–812.

Dawley, Alan. *Class and Community: The Industrial Revolution in Lynn*. Cambridge, Mass., 1976.

Dick, William. *Labor and Socialism in America*. Port Washington, N.Y., 1972.

Dorfman, Joseph. *The Economic Mind in American Civilization* vols. 2 and 3. New York, 1946 and 1949.

Dowd, Douglas. *The Twisted Dream: Capitalist Development in the United States Since 1776*. Cambridge, Mass., 1974.

Drucker, Peter F. *Technology, Management and Society*. New York, 1958.

Dubreuil, Haycinth. *Robots or Men: A French Workman's Experience in American Industry*. New York, 1930.

Eggert, Gerald. *Railroad Labor Disputes: The Beginnings of Federal Strike Policy*. Ann Arbor, 1967.

Ewen, Stuart. *All Consuming Images: The Politics of Style in Contemporary Culture*. New York, 1988.

"Famous Firsts: Measuring Minds for the Job." *Business Week* (Jan. 29, 1966): 60–63.

Femia, Joseph. "Hegemony and Consciousness in the Thought of Antonio Gramsci." *Political Studies* 23 (Mar. 75): 29–48.

Fine, Sidney. *Laissez-Faire and the General Welfare State: A Study of Conflict in American Thought*. Ann Arbor, 1965.

Fink, Leon; Lears, T. J. Jackson; Lipsitz, George; Diggins, John; Buhle, Mary Jo; Buhle, Paul. "A Round Table: Labor, Historical Pessimism, and Hegemony," *Journal of American History* 75 (June 1988): 115–61.

Fink, Leon. "The New Labor History and the Powers of Historical Pessimism: Consensus, Hegemony, and the Case of the Knights of Labor." *The Journal of American History* 75 (June 1988): 115–36.

Foner, Eric. *Free Soil, Free Labor, Free Men: The Ideology of the Republican Party Before the Civil War*. Oxford, 1970.

Foner, Philip. S. *Mark Twain: Social Critic*. New York, 1958.

———. *History of the Labor Movement in the United States*, 4 vols. New York 1947–1964.

Fones-Wolf, Elizabeth. "The Politics of Vocationalism: Coalitions and Industrial Education in the Progressive Era." *Historian* 46 (Spring 1983): 39–55.

Foucault, Michael. *Discipline and Punish*. New York, 1975.

Fox, Richard W., and Lears, T. J. Jackson, eds. *The Culture of Consumption: Critical Essays in American History, 1880–1980*. New York, 1983.

Frykman, Jonas, and Lofgren, Ovar. *Culture Builders: A Historical Anthropology of Middle Class Life*. New Brunswick, N.J., 1987.

Galambos, Louis. *The Public Image of Big Business in America: A Quantitative Study of Social Change*. Baltimore, 1975.

Geison, Gerald L., ed. *Professions and Professional Ideologies in America*. Chapel Hill, 1983.

Genovese, Eugene. *Roll, Jordan, Roll: The World the Slaves Made*. New York, 1974.

Genovese, Eugene, and Genovese, Elizabeth Fox. *The Fruits of Merchant Capital*. New York, 1983.

George, Claude S. *"The History of Management Thought."* Englewood Cliffs, N.J., 1968.

Giddens, Anthony. *Central Problems in Social Theory: Action, Structure and Contradiction in Social Analysis*. Berkeley, 1977.

Gilbert, James. *Designing the Industrial State: The Intellectual Pursuit of Collectivism 1880–1914*. Chicago, 1972.

Goodwyn, Lawrence. *The Populist Moment: A Short History of the Agrarian Revolt in America*. New York, 1978.

Gouldner, Alvin. *The Dialectic of Ideology and Technology: The Origins, Grammar, and Future of Ideology*. New York, 1976.

Gramsci, Antonio. *Selections from the Prison Notebooks* ed. and trans. Quinten Hoare and Geoffrey Smith. New York, 1971.

Gray, Kenneth. "Support for Industrial Education by the National Association of Manufacturers: 1895–1917." Unpublished Ph.D. diss., Virginia Polytechnic Institute, 1980.

Green, Marguerite. *The National Civic Federation and the American Labor Movement, 1900–1925*. Washington, D.C., 1956.

Gutman, Herbert. *Work, Culture and Society in Industrial America*. New York, 1967.

Haber, Samuel. *Efficiency and Uplift: Scientific Management in the Progressive Era, 1890–1920.* Chicago, 1964.

Hale, Matthew, Jr. *Human Science and Social Order: Hugo Munsterberg and the Origins of Applied Psychology.* Philadelphia, 1980.

Hall, Peter D. *The Organization of American Culture 1700–1900: Private Institutions, Elites, and the Origins of American Nationality.* New York, 1982.

Hall, Stuart. "Culture, Media and the Ideological Effect." In James Curran, et al., eds. *Mass Communication and Society.* Beverly Hills, 1979, 315–48.

Haskell, Thomas. *The Emergence of a Professional Social Science: The American Social Science Association and the Nineteenth Century Crisis of Authority.* Urbana, 1977.

Higham, John, and Conkin, Paul, eds. *New Directions in American Intellectual History* Baltimore, 1979.

Hill, Christopher. *The World Turned Upside Down.* New York, 1972.

Hobsbawm, E. J. "Labor History and Ideology." *Journal of Social History* 7 (Summer 1974): 371–81.

Houser, J. David. *What the Employer Thinks: Executives' Attitudes Toward Their Employees.* Cambridge, Mass., 1927.

Howe, Daniel. "American Victorianism as a Culture." *American Quarterly* 27 (1975): 507–32.

Jones, Gareth Stedman. *Languages of Class: Studies in English Working Class History, 1832–1982.* Cambridge, England, 1983.

Kasson, John. *Civilizing the Machine: Technology and Republican Values in America 1776–1900.* New York, 1976.

Kirkland, Edward. *Dream and Thought in the Business Community, 1860–1900.* Ithaca, 1956.

———. *Industry Comes of Age: Business, Labor and Public Policy, 1860–1897.* New York, 1961.

Kuhn, Thomas. *The Structure of Scientific Revolutions.* Chicago, 1970.

Lasch, Christopher. *The World of Nations: Reflections on American History, Politics and Culture.* New York, 1973.

———. *Haven in a Heartless World: The Family Besieged.* New York, 1977.

Layton, Jr., Edwin. *The Revolt of the Engineers: Social Responsibility and the American Engineering Profession.* Baltimore, 1986.

Lazerson, Marvin, and Grubb, W. Norton. *American Education and Vocationalism: A Documentary History, 1870–1970.* New York, 1974.

Lears, T. J. Jackson. *No Place of Grace: Antimodernism and the Transformation of American Culture, 1880–1920.* New York, 1981.

———. "The Concept of Cultural Hegemony: Problems and Possibilities." *American Historical Review* 90 (June 1985): 567–93.

———. "Power, Culture, and Memory." *Journal of American History* 75 (June 1988): 137–40.

Lindsey, Altmont. *The Pullman Strike.* Chicago, 1942.

Lipsitz, George. "The Struggle for Hegemony." *Journal of American History* 75 (June 1988): 146–50.

Livesay, Harold. *Samuel Gompers and Organized Labor in America.* Boston, 1978.

Marchand, Roland. *Advertising the American Dream: Making Way for Modernity, 1920–1940.* Berkeley, 1985.

Marx, Karl. *The German Ideology.* New York, 1947.

Matthaei, Julie. *An Economic History of Women in America: Women's Work, the Sexual Division of Labor, and the Development of Capitalism.* New York, 1982.

Merkle, Judith. *Management and Ideology: The Legacy of the International Scientific Management Movement.* Berkeley, 1980.

Meyer, Stephen. *The Five Dollar Day: Labor Management and Social Control in the Ford Motor Company, 1908–1921.* Albany, N.Y., 1981.

Montgomery, David. *Worker's Control in America.* New York, 1979.

————. *The Fall of the House of Labor: The Workplace, the State, and American Labor Activism, 1865–1925.* New York, 1987.

Morgan, H. Wayne. *Victorian Culture in America.* Itasca, Ill., 1973.

Nadworny, Milton. *Scientific Management and the Unions, 1900–1932.* Cambridge, Mass., 1955.

Nelson, Daniel. "Scientific Management, Systematic Management and Labor, 1880–1915." *Business History Review* 48 (1974): 479–500.

————. *Managers and Workers: Origins of the New Factory System in the United States, 1880–1920.* Madison, 1975.

————. *Frederick W. Taylor and the Rise of Scientific Management.* Madison, 1980.

Noble, David. F. *America by Design: Science, Technology and the Rise of Corporate Capitalism.* New York, 1977.

Oleson, Alexandra, and Voss, John. *The Organization of Knowledge in Modern America, 1860–1920.* Baltimore, 1979.

Pfeffer, Richard. *Working for Capitalism.* New York, 1979.

Polanyi, Karl. *The Great Transformation: The Political and Economic Origins of Our Time.* Boston, 1944.

Pollard, Sidney. *The Genesis of Modern Management.* Cambridge, Mass., 1965.

Radosh, Ronald. "The Corporate Ideology of American Labor Leaders from Gompers to Hillman." In James Weinstein and David Eakins, eds. *For a New America: Essays in History and Politics from Studies on the Left.* New York, 1971.

Rae, John. "The Application of Science to Industry." In Alexandra Oleson and John Voss, *The Organization of Knowledge in Modern America, 1860–1920.* Baltimore, 1979.

Ramirez, Bruno. *When Workers Fight: The Politics of Industrial Relations in the Progressive Era.* Westport, Conn., 1978.

Rodgers, Daniel. *The Work Ethic in Industrial America, 1850–1920.* Chicago, 1974.

————. "Tradition, Modernity and the American Industrial Worker: Reflections and Critique." *Journal of Interdisciplinary History* 7 (Spring 1977): 655–81.

Rosenberg, Nathan. *Technology and American Growth.* New York, 1972.

Rosenzweig, Roy. *Eight Hours for What We Will.* Cambridge, Mass., 1983.

Rothman, David. *The Discovery of the Asylum: Social Order and Disorder in the New Republic.* Boston, 1971.

Said, Edward. *Orientalism.* New York, 1978.

Salvatore, Nick. *Eugene V. Debs: Citizen and Socialist.* Urbana, 1982.

Schiesl, Martin. *The Politics of Efficiency: Municipal Administration and Reform in America 1880–1920.* Berkeley, 1977.

Schiller, Herbert. *Culture, Inc.: The Corporate Takeover of Public Expression.* New York, 1989.

Schlicter, Sumner. *Union Policies and Industrial Management.* Washington, D.C., 1941.

Scott, James C. *Weapons of the Weak: Everyday Forms of Peasant Resistance*. New Haven, Conn., 1985.

Sennet, Richard, and Cobb, Jonathan. *The Hidden Injuries of Class*. New York, 1972.

Sklar, Martin. *The Corporate Reconstruction of American Capitalism 1890–1916: The Market, the Law, and Politics*. New York, 1988.

Smithsonian Institution. *Images of an Era: The American Poster 1945–75*. Cambridge, Mass., 1976.

Sobel, Robert. *The Entrepreneurs: Explorations within the American Business Tradition*. New York, 1974.

Soltow, Lee. *Men and Wealth in the United States 1850–1870*. New Haven, Conn., 1976.

Spring, Joel. *Education and the Rise of the Corporate State*. Boston, 1972.

Taft, Philip. *The A.F. of L. in the Time of Gompers*. New York, 1957.

Taylor, Albion. *Labor Policies of the National Association of Manufacturers*. Urbana, 1927.

Thompson, E. P. "Time, Work Discipline, and Industrial Capitalism." *Past and Present* 38 (Dec. 1967): 56–97.

Trachtenberg, Alan. *The Incorporation of America: Culture and Society in the Gilded Age*. New York, 1982.

Urwick, Lyndall, "Management's Debt to Engineers." *Advanced Management* 17 (Dec. 1952): 5–12.

Warne, Colston E. *The Pullman Boycott of 1894: The Problem of Federal Intervention*. Boston, 1955.

Weinstein, James. *The Decline of Socialism in America*. New York, 1967.

———. *The Corporate Ideal in the Liberal State, 1900–1918*. Boston, 1968.

Wiebe, Robert. *Businessmen and Reform: A Study of the Progressive Movement*. New York, 1962.

———. *The Search for Order 1877–1920*. New York, 1967.

Wilentz, Sean. "On Class and Politics in Jacksonian America." *Reviews in American History* 10 (Dec. 1982): 56.

———. *Chants Democratic: New York City and the Rise of the American Working Class, 1788–1850*. New York, 1984.

Williams, Raymond. "Base and Superstructure in Marxist Cultural Theory." *New Left Review* 82 (1973): 3–16.

———. *The Country and the City*. New York, 1973.

———. *Marxism and Literature*. Oxford, 1977.

Williamson, Judith. *Decoding Advertisements: Ideology and Meaning in Advertising*. New York, 1978.

Wish, Harvey. "The Pullman Strike: A Study in Industrial Warfare." *Journal of the Illinois State Historical Society* 32 (Sept. 1939): 288–312.

Wolff, Kurt, and Moore, Barrington, eds. *The Critical Spirit: Essays in Honor of Herbert Marcuse*. Boston, 1967.

Wylie, Irvin G. *The Self-Made Man in America*. New York, 1954.

Yellen, Samuel. *American Labor Struggles*. New York, 1936.

Index

About the Author

SARAH LYONS WATTS is Assistant Professor of History at Wake Forest University.